THE
RACE
MYTH

ALSO BY JOSEPH L. GRAVES

The Emperor's New Clothes

THE RACE MYTH

Why We Pretend Race Exists in America

Joseph L. Graves, Jr.

DUTTON

DUTTON
Published by the Penguin Group (USA) Inc.
375 Hudson Street, New York, New York 10014, U.S.A.
Penguin Books Ltd, Registered Offices: 80 Strand, London WC2R 0RL, England
Penguin Books Australia Ltd, 250 Camberwell Road, Camberwell, Victoria 3124, Australia
Penguin Books Canada Ltd, 10 Alcorn Avenue, Toronto, Ontario, Canada M4V 3B2
Penguin Books (N.Z.) cnr Airborne and Rosedale Roads, Albany, Auckland 1310, New
Zealand

Published by Dutton, a member of Penguin Group (USA) Inc.

First Printing, June 2004
10 9 8 7 6 5 4 3 2 1

 REGISTERED TRADEMARK—MARCA REGISTRADA

LIBRARY OF CONGRESS CATALOGING-IN-PUBLICATION DATA

Graves, Joseph L., 1955–
    The race myth : why we pretend race exists in America / Joseph L. Graves, Jr.
      p. cm.
    Includes bibliographical references (p.   ) and index.
    ISBN: 0-525-94825-2 (acid-free paper)
    1. United States—Race relations. 2. Racism—United States. 3. Race—Classification.
4. Minorities—United States—Social conditions. I. Title.
E184.A1G823 2004
305.8'00973—dc22   2004003294

Printed in the United States of America
Set in Sabon
Designed by Leonard Telesca

To my family,
in particular my sisters
Alice, Marilyn, and Katherine

Contents

Introduction:
The Problem, Simply Stated

The traditional concept of race as a biological fact is a myth. I am going to show you that nearly everything you think you know about race is a social construct. You don't have to be a racist to be wrong about what race is. That doesn't make the effects of a belief in race any less damaging, or the situation any less perilous. Most Americans still believe in the concept of race the way they believe in the law of gravity—they believe in it without even knowing what it is they believe in.

If you ask the average American college student if biological races exist, most will say *yes*. In my classes, when I asked students to identify their own race, most couldn't be any more specific than a vague catchall like "white." They couldn't say what the criteria are for membership in a racial group, and most believed that black, white, Asian, Hispanic, and American Indian are biological races. Some of them thought that every country has produced its own biological race.

A few students responded that races had existed since the beginning of time. I asked them if they meant 1980, when the universe began for them, or 19 billion years ago, in the big bang? Several had to think about it for a while. Some thought races had existed since the breakup of Pangaea, around 300 million years ago—which would have been tough, since humans didn't evolve until 299,999,999 years later! Some thought that races were formed in antiquity at about the time of the fall of the Tower of Babel, as described in the biblical book of Genesis. (Surprisingly, none related the curse of Ham as a source of modern human races.)

Many also believed that race determined intelligence quotient (IQ) and other personality traits, as well as sexual characteristics, athletic ability, and disease predisposition, following commonly held social stereotypes. When asked about intellect, most cited the superior performance of their Asian classmates in their science courses. When asked about sex, most stated that blacks had higher sexual appetites and larger genitals. When asked about athletic ability they again cited the superior performance of black basketball and football players. Finally, almost all agreed that sickle cell anemia, Tay-Sachs, and cystic fibrosis were all proof positive of the existence of racially defined disease.

These examples clearly show the prevailing ignorance that our society exhibits about the definitions and significance of human biological diversity, and its confusion with socially constructed races. In this book, I'm going to show you in detail how to tell the difference, and why it's so important.

How We Got Here

It was the ultimate missed opportunity, with devastating consequences. The European colonists who founded the United States had a chance to start over with an egalitarian social order, but they blew it: They accepted the idea of racial hierarchy that was prevalent in Europe at the time. It was just too convenient: The socially constructed concept of race was a powerful tool that aided them in the conquest of the continent.

This concept allowed them to build a society in which superficial physical differences would be used to determine an individual's worth. It justified *racism,* the belief that groups were different in their very natures, and that these differences should be used to stratify society.

The colonists did not see themselves as racists, nor did many question their treatment of non-Europeans. They saw what they were doing as good, necessary, and even unavoidable. It is ironic that many of these people were outcasts from Europe, who came to the New World seeking religious freedom. Yet they brutally conquered, then imposed their civilization upon, the native people that they called Indians in the New World.

Because they believed that races were genetically different (although they didn't describe it in those terms), many saw the exploitation of the Indians and Africans as no different from the use of farm animals. For such thinkers, the fact that the Bible had no explicit proscription against slavery justified the importation of millions of slaves from the western shores of Africa to meet the growing needs of agricultural production in the colonies.

Even if we accept conservative estimates of the loss of life that resulted from the slave trade, it is still the greatest sustained act of genocide in the history of our species. Those who survived the passage to the New World were gradually transformed into a new biological and cultural population. They had been gathered from different ethnic groups along the western coast of Africa (Fula, Jolla, Mandinka, Manjago, Wolof, and many others); some were African spiritualists, some Islamic, and many of these groups spoke different languages. In America, they would be both genetically and culturally hybridized amongst themselves and with Europeans and Indians.

The economy of the English colonies, and in turn, that of the new American nation, was wedded to chattel slavery. The African descendents enslaved in America would be denigrated, exploited, tortured, and murdered. They would be culturally and scientifically relegated to the bottom of American society. They would be called a variety of names: nigger, mulatto, Nigra, and Negro.

Later, new groups of immigrants from Europe and Asia would arrive. Irish, Poles, Italians, Chinese, Japanese, and (eventually) virtually every nation of the world would send people, bringing both their genes and culture to America. The early pioneers had been predominantly Protestant; Catholics and Jews would later add to the American tapestry. These people would also be named: Paddies, Polacks, Wops, Chinks, Nips, and so forth.

Anglo-Saxon Europeans did not manage to create a racial state in their own image, although many tried hard to accomplish that goal. One, Madison Grant, would argue that the loss of so many Anglo-Saxon males in the Civil War led the country to allow in too many immigrants from non-Teutonic European countries, who were reproducing faster than the Anglo-Saxons. Another, General Francis Amasa Walker, actually stated that the idea of bringing forth sons and daughters who would have to compete with people who were clearly their inferiors had dulled the desires of Anglo-Saxons to have and rear children!

The anti-immigrationists thought that the great race was being destroyed both from within and without. Their thinking would lead to the formation of a large eugenics movement in the United States. Charles Benedict Davenport would become its chief executive officer, and his Eugenics Record Office would help enact laws that led to the sterilization of tens of thousands of Americans against their will.

Despite the efforts of the likes of Grant and Davenport, the Klan, and the segregationists, European Americans who once had sole dominion over America's social and political life now wake up each day in a nation that has been both biologically and culturally hybridized. The founding fathers would not recognize the racial and social composition of today's America.

Today's Euro-American youth idolize Shaquille O'Neal, look up to the great neurosurgeon Dr. Ben Carson, and read Toni Morrison. Thomas Jefferson would have never thought it possible that we could have both a secretary of state and a national security advisor of African-American ancestry.

However, we have paid dearly for the policies of racism, and are continuing to pay in a currency of despair, unfulfilled dreams, and blood. We paid in King Philip's War, in the middle passage, on the cotton fields, in the master's bedchamber, and along the underground railway. John Brown warned us we would pay further, and we saw the fulfillment of that terrible prophecy on the battlefields of the Civil War. We paid along the Trail of Tears and at Wounded Knee. We paid at Promontory Junction: twelve hundred Chinese rail workers died building the Transcontinental Railway, but not a single person of Chinese descent was allowed to attend the pounding of the Golden Spike. We paid all through Jim Crow. We paid in the Japanese internment camps.

Yet we learned little: We witnessed the atrocities of the Holocaust, but then allowed Nazis into America to help us build rockets. We paid still more with the lives of four little girls in Birmingham, with the assassinations of John F. Kennedy, Malcolm X, and the Reverend Dr. Martin Luther King, and in the rebellions of Watts, Detroit, and Newark. We paid by sending disproportionate numbers of young African-American and Hispanic men and women to die on the battlefields of Vietnam. We damn sure paid again when the world watched Rodney King and Reginald Deny being beaten over and over again on network newscasts.

We are paying now with academic underachievement, the drug epidemic, health disparities, unequal justice, urban malaise, and the ongoing social and political division that still exists between the socially defined races. Every time we pay, we slide closer toward hell on a road paved with our racial misconceptions. We will continue to pay until we reject the notion that there are biological races in the human species, and that race determines an individual's worth.

The Essential Elements of Racist Thought

All of America's racist thinkers have relied on three unchallenged assumptions: that races exist; that each race has its own genetically determined characteristics; and crucially, that social hierarchy results from these differences. Here are the five pillars of racist thought:

- Biological races exist in the human species.
- Races have genetic differences that determine their intelligence.
- Races have genetically determined differences that produce unique diseases and cause them to die at different rates.
- Races have genetically determined sexual appetites and reproductive capacities.
- Races have genetically determined differences in athletic and musical ability.

Although not always stated openly, most or part of these views are widely held by many Americans. Not everyone who believes these ideas is an evil person, of course. Given the history of America's approach to race, many are just like my students: They accept these views because no alternative has ever been clearly presented to them. More dangerous are those who still actively use the social construction of race to advance their own economic, social, and political agendas. These individuals never tire of advancing pseudo-scientific arguments to protect the concept of race, and to argue for its utility in solving the crucial problems in our society.

I hope that this book will be the definitive statement of the difference between the biologically and socially defined concepts of race. We're going to look at each of the five pillars of racist thought in turn: the biological aspects, in both historical and contemporary settings, and the ongoing harm that is inflicted on our society by maintaining these false stereotypes. And I will outline my vision of what our society could look like if we eliminate racist thought and practice.

We must recognize that the underlying biological diversity of the human species cannot be artificially apportioned into races, because races are simply not biologically justified. If we can understand that all allegiance to racism is ideological, not scientific, then we may be able to silence the bigots once and for all. We may be able to construct social systems that allow all of our citizens to actualize their biological potential. If we can live up to our creed of equality for all, then maybe we will have a chance to finally actualize the true spirit of democracy and the American dream.

A Note on Terminology

All discussions of the concept of race in America are mired in confusion by both the definition of the concept and the vocabulary used to describe it. Since race is socially constructed, various terms have come into and out of use concerning specific groups in American or world society. At any given time in our history, the motivation for these changes has come from both those describing the groups and from within the groups. Further adding to the confusion is that the terms have also included both biological and social conceptions of race at the same time. For example, when the Spaniards came to the Western hemisphere they first thought that they had arrived in India, hence the use of the term Indians to describe the people they encountered. The Arawaks and Caribe did not know that they were "Indians." The Spaniards also described the various African ethnicities they encountered as "Negroes," which comes from the Spanish word *negro*, meaning black. The English often used the term "neggars" or niggers as a derogatory form of the term Negro.

These terms were all socially constructed, but also took on some implied biological meaning. Indians were people who had descended from the original inhabitants of the Western hemisphere and Negroes had African ancestry. However, as the populations of the New World began to intermix, new terminology had to be invented to describe them, such as *mulatto, mestizo, Creole, half-breed*, again carrying some biological meaning. *Mulattoes* were the offspring of European slave masters and African slave women; *mestizo* meant offspring of Europeans and the natives of the Western hemisphere; *Creole* meant descended from the French, Spanish, or Portuguese settlers of the Caribbean; a halfbreed could refer to any mixture.

Throughout American history, various groups fought to socially define themselves, in opposition to the ideas of the socially dominant European population. No struggle is more illustrative of the confusion over racial terms than that of the African descendents in the Americas. Most likely, the first African slaves brought to the Americas considered themselves members of their own African ethnic groups, such as Fula, Jolla, or Mandinka. However, their descendents were soon stripped of African cultural identity. They became what the masters named them. The struggle for African-American social and political freedom was thus always associated with the question of how to identify. In various historical periods the terms Africans, Negroes, blacks, Afro-Americans, and African Americans have all been preferred terms. Clearly, these terms are socially constructed, but in this sense by the social movements associated with the struggle for freedom. In this book I utilize material from across the entire experience of African descendents in America and use terms that are historically appropriate for a given time period.

Other groups have faced the same issues of self-identification. Therefore I have attempted to use terms that are culturally sensitive and historically appropriate whenever possible. To redress the social dominance that European-Americans have enjoyed throughout the literature I use the principle of parallelism when comparing groups. So, socially constructed terms such as blacks, browns, reds, whites, and yellows are compared equivalently. Whenever possible I refer to recent geographic origin when referring to genetic ancestry. All anatomically modern humans are descended from ancient African populations, however, human groups did migrate out of Africa at different times and ended up in different localities (Americas, Australia, Asia, Europe, and the Middle East). Finally, I am aware that my descriptions in this work may offend some people, however this is not intentional. I am simply trying to remain intellectually consistent and to be clear about what I am and am not talking about when referring to the thorny concept of race.

THE
RACE
MYTH

CHAPTER 1

How Biology Refutes Our Racial Myths

Sometimes, the scientific investigation of one problem presents solutions to another. In 1986, scientists proposed a major undertaking: to sequence the entire human genome, to draw a map of the 100,000 or so genes that make humans distinct from apes or dolphins or squirrels. We knew that each of those genes could be found in a specific place on one of the twenty-three pairs of human chromosomes, but for the most part, we didn't know exactly where.

Remember those twisting ladders of DNA molecules from high-school biology? The DNA of each gene is made up of letters, which are pairs of molecule combinations. There are three billion letters in the human genome. At the Technology Center of Silicon Valley (now called the Tech Museum for Innovation), scientists built a model of what this looks like. Think of a spiral staircase and each step as a telephone directory. Now, wind a second staircase around the first to make a double spiral. Every phonebook is a gene, and the contents are the letters. If you have 100,000 phonebooks, and the information in them isn't listed alphabetically, and you aren't sure which phonebook goes where along the spirals, you've got a big project on your hands.

Producing all three billion letters of the human genome might be the greatest achievement in the history of biology, possibly of all science. The human genome map could tell us about the origin of human disease, the general function of our bodies, and possibly what it means to be human. A number of theoretical and technical problems had to be solved to sequence the genome, not the least of which was whose genome should be read. The scientists directly involved with the genome project immediately began to wrestle with the problem of human genetic variation and the concept of race.

For Every Discovery, a Controversy

Celera Genomics was the only major private corporation in the quest to map the human genome. In February 2001, Celera's CEO, Craig Venter, touched off a minor firestorm when he commented that "race is not a scientific concept."[1] He knew that it wasn't possible to distinguish people who were ethnically African American, Chinese, Hispanic, or white at the genome level. Celera's sequencing of the human genome showed that the average pair of human beings who are not close relatives differ by 2.1 million genetic letters out of those 3 billion, yet only a few thousand of those differences account for the biological differences between individuals.

Venter argued that we all are essentially identical twins at the level of the genome. Celera used DNA extracted from five volunteers, three women and two men, who were ethnically African American, Chinese American, Hispanic, and Europeon American. Their results showed that at the DNA level you could clearly tell the females from the males (due to the genetic differences in the X and Y chromosomes), but you could not identify the race of the individual from the DNA.

Venter's comment should not have been controversial. The Celera study only confirmed at the molecular level something population geneticists and physical anthropologists had recognized for well over fifty years: the nonexistence of biological races in the human species. Still, some prominent biologists felt compelled to attack Venter and defend the race concept in biology. Among them was James Crow (yes, that is his name), who in early 2002 defended the legitimacy of identifying races in humans. In the publication of the National Academy of Arts and Sciences, *Daedalus*, he commented: "Whenever an institution or society singles out individuals who are exceptional or outstanding in some way, racial differences will become more apparent. That fact may be uncomfortable, but there is no way around it."[2]

In support of this notion, rather than citing scientific evidence, he gave as an example a social phenomenon: the overrepresentation of African Americans in track and field, and their underrepresentation in physics and engineering, relative to Asian Americans. His exact comment was: "A stopwatch is colorblind." It's amazing when geneticists of James Crow's stature demonstrate this blind spot when it comes to human variation and the concept of race. It still happens because the social construction of race is deeply ingrained in the thinking of most American intellectuals, including biologists and medical practitioners.

The bias that biologists have shown when they try to explain the importance of genetic variation in humans has been well established. In this book, we're going to focus on the impact that the belief in biological races has on society. To do that, we first need to make sure we all understand what a biological race is, and why human groups don't qualify as races. The starting point for this is looking at how we came to understand the origin of biological species.

Darwin 101: A Race Isn't a Species

How species developed was the most important problem for biologists of the mid-nineteenth century, the equivalent to the twentieth-century discovery of the structure of DNA, or the publication of the human genome in 2001. To solve this problem, scientists first had to see what was so important about biological varieties (*races, subspecies*—the terms are interchangeable), for reasons that will become apparent. Without knowing it, Charles Darwin provided the basic ideas that were needed for a correct definition of biological races when he asked how new species arose in nature.

In *Origin of Species* Darwin described how people had systematically bred domestic pigeons into numerous varieties. He reasoned that all of the existing pigeon varieties must have been derived from one ancestral stock, one that contained all of the characteristics that breeders selected from as they developed the variations. He argued that such a process in nature could eventually produce varieties that were different enough to no longer be able to breed with each other successfully. If they couldn't do that, they would be new species.

Darwin said that a process called *natural selection* was the chief mechanism responsible for these changes. Natural selection, commonly known as *survival of the fittest,* is what happens when certain traits win out when it's time to reproduce. If an organism has a trait that helps it survive, it's more likely to reproduce more, so more members of its species share the same traits. If enough members end up with the same set of traits, you have a new variety. Keep on specializing, and you have a new species.

Darwin recognized that the formation of biological varieties was an essential step on the way to the formation of new species—an intermediate step. Varieties can still interbreed, but distinct species cannot produce fertile offspring, even if they manage to mate, as in the case of horses and donkeys, which produce mules, which are sterile. Gorillas and chimpanzees are separate species; mountain and forest gorillas are subspecies (or geographical races, because they are separate races that arose through geographic isolation).

Darwin and his contemporaries clearly understood what the theory of evolution meant for human beings. He recognized that all of the human races were really members of the same species, as opposed to being separate species of humans. However, it was also 1859, and he knew that this theory would be received with shock and dismay in Victorian society. Sir Charles Lyell, a geologist and mentor to Darwin, warned him that the idea that the black and white races had common ancestry would not be tolerated, and would lead to the expulsion of any professor having the nerve to teach it.

Almost a century and a half of further research has shown that Darwin's insistence on the importance of natural selection in the origin of new species was correct. Evolutionary biologists have studied how populations acquire genetic differences, looking at it from more angles than even a yoga instructor could achieve. And they have confirmed what Darwin said: that varieties (or races) are intermediate steps to legitimate species.

Darwin was wrong, though, for thinking that the human species had a number of distinct varieties. At the time, no one had the data they would have needed to prove otherwise, nor did they see a need to go looking for it. He and other scientists made the same mistake people are still making today: They let what their eyes can see count for more than what scientific analysis can show.

The fact is that no biological races exist in modern humans. In the next few pages, I'll explain how a race is defined and why there isn't enough variation in humans for our differences to qualify as races.

What Does it Take to Be a Race?

To qualify officially as a biological race (or subspecies or variety), an animal or plant has to meet one of two requirements:

1. It can have its own distinct genetic lineage, meaning that it evolved in enough isolation that it never (or rarely) mated with individuals outside its borders, or
2. the genetic distance between one population and another has to be significantly greater than the genetic variability that exists within the populations themselves.

The first requirement is pretty straightforward, but the second takes some explaining. Think of it as a formula, and we're looking for two percentages to plug into it: one for distance and one for variability. To do that, we have to understand how geneticists measure variety, and we have to define genetic distance and genetic variability as painlessly as possible.

Variety Is the Spice of Genetics

We're all pretty familiar with DNA by now: It's the DNA molecules along our chromosomes that determine what makes us the same as other animals, what makes us different from them, and what makes us different from each other.

Along each chromosome, there are specific parts—somewhere between twenty-five thousand and forty thousand of them—that control our traits. At each of these parts there are two chemical messages that code for a trait, like brown eyes or the ability to roll your tongue. Some messages are dominant over others, so that if you get a message from Mom that says "brown" and a message from Dad that says "blue," your eyes are going to be brown. Many more messages have a mixing effect, producing physical features that fall somewhere in the middle of both parents, so that, say, your nose might be bigger than your mother's but smaller than your father's.

The range of possible combinations of these messages is pretty mind-boggling: One egg cell or one sperm cell can have 8,388,608 possible combinations of chromosomes, so for a couple producing a child, the number of potential chromosome arrangements for that child would be 8,388,608![3] This means that there is a tremendous amount of diversity that can be produced by even one pair of parents, yet on average the physical traits of the offspring still resemble a mixture of both of the parents.

No one's saying that these differences amount to races, of course, otherwise, you'd be a different race from your parents.

The large number of combinations of traits just means that, any way you look at it, human genetics is complex.

Measuring Variation: We're Not All That Different

There are ways to compare the complexity of one group of humans with another, no matter how you want to define *group*. A group could be all the people who were born and raised on Maui, or a number of people who have Down's syndrome. With all the possible variety, where do we start measuring variation?

Let's look again at those messages in our DNA. About 33 percent of the spots on the chromosomes where they live allow a lot of possibilities for a particular trait—people can have brown, blue, green, hazel, or golden eyes, for instance. In the remaining 67 percent of the spots, only one type of message is allowed, so that nearly every human being will have identical messages for a particular trait at that spot (wrong messages in these spots can result in genetic disease). So, about a third of our messages are responsible for all of the variety we see in people worldwide.

That seems like a lot, but it's not all. From studying these messages for traits, scientists now know that two individuals from anywhere in the world can potentially share 86 percent of the traits out of that 33 percent. Doing the math, that leaves only 4.62 percent of our genetic makeup responsible for all our individuality. Put another way: the traits of an Irish businessperson, an African-American lawyer, and the prime minister of India are quite likely to be 95.38 percent identical. Geography does play a part, so that if two people are from the same continent, you can reduce the variability by another 10 percent, and if they're from the same village, you can reduce it by yet another 4 percent. So, variety is measured by looking at the percentage of our DNA that makes us unique. What's genetic distance?

Getting within Shouting Distance

Genetic distance is a statistic calculated by examining different groups of people. It is a measurement of how frequently the genetic messages for traits occur in populations. People who share larger proportions of the same messages across their genome are genetically close, and people who do not share the same messages are genetically more distant. For instance, let's examine the message that causes sickle cell anemia, a disease that people think of as associated with race. This message occurs in large numbers in people who live in tropical areas because, it turns out, if you have one sickle cell message and one normal message, you have a better chance of surviving malaria, a typical disease of the tropics. So, the sickle cell anemia message is in high frequencies in populations in western Africa, the Middle East, the Persian Gulf, the Mediterranean, and India. In the case of this message, someone from Ghana is genetically closer to someone from Syria than to someone from Kenya, because Kenyans (who live at high altitudes where there isn't much malaria) don't have a high frequency of sickle cell messages. This clearly shows that sickle cell anemia cannot be associated with any particular race.

This points to an important fact: Geographical distance does not necessarily equal genetic distance. In fact, assuming that two people are genetically different because they look like they came from different parts of the world can be really dangerous for their health. Why? Because things like people's blood type or their ability to accept transplanted organs are dictated by how genetically close they are, not necessarily by where their ancestors came from geographically.

Because people equate race with external physical characteristics, they assume more often than not that a person is more likely to find an organ donor among the members of their own supposed racial group. This misconception in biomedical research or clinical practice that insists on sticking to these false racial categories causes many errors and lost lives.

Location, Location, Location?

If geographic distance doesn't necessarily equal genetic distance, does that make geographic distance irrelevant? No. There is still a strong correlation between geographic distance and genetic distance. After all, it's geographic isolation that is the biggest factor in the development of new traits. It's just a mistake to assume that one type of distance equals the other.

So, whether we're looking at geographically close or distant populations of humans, the question that really matters is still this: If all the genetic information from two populations that we think of as races is examined, how similar are they? And are their differences big enough to qualify them as separate races?

Size Matters: The Standard for Measuring Genetic Variation

To figure this out, we would have to look at a lot more than a couple of indicators like a sickle cell message or blood types. We'd have to evaluate the genetic information from enough people across a big enough number of separated populations for the statistics to be meaningful. Fortunately for you and me, it's been done for us already.

This analysis has used a number of approaches, examining the big three sources: protein variation, nuclear DNA, and mitochondrial DNA. All of these techniques agree that anatomically modern humans are a young species—too young to have developed any significant genetic distances between populations before mass mobility on a global scale started blurring what few differences there were. The result is that there is no unambiguous way to describe biological races within our species.

It's not for lack of a standard: Biologists have studied genetic variation in a wide variety of organisms other than humans for over fifty years, and have described many geographical races or subspecies. The races we have identified outside of humans usually show about 20 percent total genetic distance between their populations, as is the case in, say, the various species of fruit flies.

We do not see anywhere near that much genetic variation in modern humans. The genetic distances in humans are statistically about ten times lower (2 percent) than the 20 percent average in other organisms, even when comparing the most geographically separated populations within modern humans. There is greater genetic variability found within one tribe of western African chimpanzees than exists in the entire human species! In fact, there has never been any degree of natural selection in modern humans equivalent even to the levels used to create the differences in the breeds of domestic pigeons or dogs. In order to support the existence of biological races in modern humans, you would have to use a very different sort of reasoning than has been applied to all other species of animals—and that would be bad science.

One Requirement Bites the Dust

Okay, now we have the first number to plug into our formula for race: Genetic distance between populations of humans is about 2 percent. We still need the other number, for genetic variation within those populations.

The same types of studies that showed us that human genetic distances average only 2 percent have also shown that there is about 8.6 times more genetic variation within the classically defined racial groups than between them. Why? Because there is about 8.6 times more genetic variation between any given individual on the planet and another individual than there is between the populations they belong to. In other words, the variability that makes one African-American person different from another is greater than the variability between African Americans and Swedes or Tibetans or Amazonian tribes.

Remember we said that modern humans share 86 percent of

their genetic variations, so that less than 5 percent of our genome is responsible for our individuality. Now, it's time to look back at the formula for genetic distance versus genetic variability. For any group of humans to be a race, their genetic distance from another group, around 2 percent, would have to be greater than their unique genetic variability, around 5 percent. Two is not bigger than five.

It's a fact that if you add the 10 percent that accounts for shared variations between populations on the same continent, plus the 4 percent shared by local populations, you end up with about 1 percent genetic variability. Since this is lower than the 2 percent statistic for genetic distance, this would technically meet our definition of a race. There are a couple of problems with that conclusion. For one, we would be accepting percentages of variability in humans that are far below the percentages that are applied to all other organisms on the planet as evidence of race. For another, treating populations with 1 percent variability as distinct races would result in identifying over a 1,000 races of humans. Following the argument to its logical conclusion, since families are even more genetically similar than geographic neighbors, we could say that every individual family is a race, or every cultural group that tries to keep itself separate (such as the Amish) is a race. In other words, the distinction becomes meaningless.

That's really the point. The majority of genetic variation in humans occurs between individuals, without regard to membership in socially constructed race. And none of the unique variations we see approach the minimum levels used to identify races in other species.

Homage to Alex Haley: Our Common Roots

Our formula didn't work, so we know that populations of humans just don't meet the required distance-to-variability ratio for being separate races. Identifying a race by physical characteristics such as skin color or eye shape is as invalid as saying that all people who are tall or who have straight hair or who are pigeon-toed constitute separate races. Let's look now at the other requirement for race identification, genetic lineage.

There is no evidence that any group of humans now in existence—geographically or in socially defined races—has an evolutionary or genetic line of descent that is distinct from other groups.

Every person is descended from two parents, four grandparents, and eight great grandparents. With each generation back into our ancestry, the number of lineal ancestors doubles (if all the ancestors are unrelated). If we go back twenty-four generations into our past, about fifteen hundred years ago, we each would have had 33,554,432 ancestors! At that time, the world population was around 206,000,000 people. That means that if we all really had separate, unrelated ancestors, every single one of us would be descended from about 16 percent of the world's population in the year 502 A.D. Obviously the math doesn't work, which strongly suggests that not all of our ancestors came from independent families and that many individuals must have contributed to many family lineages.

In a place like the United States, where the population has been intermarrying for a long time, and has been engaged in interracial sex and conception outside of marriage, it is fairly easy to show that the socially described races do not exist as separate lines of genetic descent. Still, we can and should ask if there ever was a time when the world's populations were truly independent.

In this sense, an independent lineage would be a population that was isolated from mixing genetically with other humans—one that never mated and bred outside its own group. In the animal kingdom, kangaroos are an example of this: The geographic isolation of Australia and its surrounding islands was so complete that this particular species of marsupial developed there and nowhere else. Since we know that race is an intermediate step toward becoming a species, what we're looking for genetically is the human equivalent of a marsupial on its way to becoming a kangaroo.

The Gene Trail: Better than Breadcrumbs?

Humans have been moving around for centuries, so finding evidence of lineage isn't as easy as, say, going to an isolated location like the Seychelles and testing the population there. Geneticists have worked out various ways to test for the existence of separate lineages in other species, so it's worth looking at those for a minute to see if they work on humans.

One way is to calculate the amount of population subdivision that exists in a particular species. A species that has unique lineages within it is going to be subdivided, and you can find subdivisions by finding uneven distributions of genetic information among groups in that species.

Appendix 1 shows what weak subdivision might look like using pie diagrams. In a species that is weakly subdivided we would expect that all local populations show gene frequency percentages closer to the grand average of all the populations. The percentages of the two different genes in this example are shown by different shades. The circle in the center shows the average of all the local populations, and you can see that each isn't very different in shading from the grand average. Appendix 2 shows what strong subdivision would look like. Here, the gene frequencies of the local populations have very different shading percentages from the grand average of the total population. The subdivision statistic can take on values from 0.00 (no subdivision) to 1.00 (completely subdivided) or we could consider this in percentage terms 0 percent to 100 percent. A species with low subdivision does not have races, whereas a species with high subdivision can be said to have races.

It should be no surprise that global samples of modern humans show very little population subdivision compared to other mammals

(0 percent–16 percent), lower than for Kenyan impala and wilde-beest, or the American bighorn sheep, and much lower than highly subdivided predatory animals like the North American gray wolf (70 percent–85 percent). Recently, some scientists have raised crit-icisms concerning the validity of this statistic for examining pop-ulation subdivision. They point out the calculation of this statistic is dependent on the range of allele frequencies found in popula-tions and particular assumptions made about the nature of the population's history and of the genes being studied. The origina-tor of this method, American geneticist Sewall Wright, assumed that the genes in question had unique origins in the populations studied and that the populations were independent of each other. For this reason, Wright felt that an arbitrary value of about 0.250, or about 25 percent, might be an indication of moderate subdivi-sion and a threshold for identifying genetic races. However, we know that most human genes did not arise independently nor do our populations show independence from each other. The best models of human evolution show that all non-sub-Saharan Africans are derived from sub-Saharan Africans. Thus, their genes did not all arise independently and the population's histories are not independent from sub-Saharan Africans. This problem can be fixed by nesting the non-Africans within the Africans during the calculation, and when this is done for some sample genetic sys-tems the value increases slightly, but still not enough to approach Wright's arbitrary threshold. So, even with this added sophistica-tion, the study of subdivisions produces no evidence for genetic lineages. Some scientists claim to have found such evidence an-other way, however, so we'll look at that next.

Your Genetic Family Tree

In the same way that people trace their genealogies to see if a line goes back to someone famous, scientists trace molecular information to find the ancestry of genetic groups to see if

they're related. These genetic family trees of human populations have been examined for evidence of unique genetic
lineages.

This is how we found out that humans and chimpanzees have
a more recent common ancestor than either have with gorillas. In
a genetic tree diagram, humans and chimpanzees are on one
branch, and gorillas on another. The lengths of the branches are
used to show how long it's been since the species separated. This
procedure works well for tracing evolutionary histories between
species, because the genes in one species don't recombine with the
genes from the other species, since separate species can't mate.

It's another thing altogether to create a reliable genetic tree
within one species, especially humans. During recombination, the
father's and mother's DNA can exchange segments of genes with
each other. If this occurs, the gene in question has two different
evolutionary histories. And this is just in one individual: When
that individual mates with another in their own species whose
DNA has also recombined, it's much harder to trace a definitive
evolutionary history. Multiply that by billions of individuals, and
you can see the problem.

So, while a genetic tree can be useful for more general things
like showing when different migratory groups of humans started
developing geographically adapted traits, it can't reliably be more
specific than that, and certainly can't show independent genetic
lineages.[4]

All Roads Lead To . . .

More reliable methods of studying human populations can be
used, such as *neighbor joining* techniques, which allow relative genetic distances between groups to be shown. The data from these
studies show that humans vary in small increments from group to
group, rather than differing drastically depending on where they
originated.

Humans have been on the move since we first left sub-Saharan Africa 80,000 years ago, combining our DNA at the same time as we were adapting genetically to our local conditions. Distinct genetic lineages cannot be traced within or between human populations because we've been mixing with each other since we first evolved. We're the only species of the *Homo* genus to have survived into modernity—an analogy would be if the only members of *Canis* to survive were domestic dogs (no more coyotes, jackals, or wolves). Genetically, we're not even separate breeds: We're all mutts.

Aren't Physical Differences Proof that Races Exist?

We kind of look like separate breeds, though. Observable physical features are what people point to first to justify their belief in different races. After everything you've read so far, you know that's a dead horse but, just to make the point, let's beat it a little longer.

What determines physical traits in populations? Genes do this in combination with environmental factors. So, if genetic variation can't be divvied up evenly into races, neither can physical traits. Skin color, hair type, body stature, blood groups, or tendencies to get certain diseases do not alone or in combination define the racial groups that have been socially constructed in North America.

It's absolutely true that these physical traits vary among geographical populations. What most people don't realize is the way that they vary. For example, Sri Lankans of the Indian subcontinent, Nigerians, and aboriginal Australians share a dark skin tone, but differ in hair type, facial features, and genetic predisposition for disease. If you try to use characteristics such as height, body proportions, skull measurements, hair type, and skin color to create a tree showing how human populations are related, you get a tree that doesn't match the measured genetic relatedness and known evolutionary history of our species.

A tree like that would say, "all short, extremely dark-skinned people with thick curly hair are the same race," and would link Papuans from New Guinea and aboriginal Australians most closely to sub-Saharan Africans. We know, however, from genetic analyses, that Papuans and aboriginal Australians are the group most genetically distant from sub-Saharan Africans. And that makes total sense, because sub-Saharan Africans and aboriginal Australians are two of the most geographically separated human groups, so intermarriage has been minimal. Australia, after all, was cut off from human migration for most of its history.

We also know that within sub-Saharan African populations, everything from skin color to skull types to total genetic diversity is more variable than in any other of the world's populations.[4] In other words, a person from the Congo and a person from Mali are more likely to be different genetically from each other than either is from a person from Belgium. Yet, if everyone from this region got up and moved to the United States, we'd call them all African Americans and see them as members of the same race.

Physical traits fail to define races because local populations produce traits that adapt to climate and other environmental factors wherever those factors occur. This means that, however genetically or geographically distant they are, tropical populations will have physical traits that match tropical conditions, like the sickle cell message. Kenyans and Peruvians will have greater lung capacities and red blood cell counts from living at high altitudes. These features are completely independent of the other genetic aspects of their physical makeup, and cannot be used to determine membership in a socially defined race.

Taking It Back Home

America has perfected the concept of socially defined races. On first inspection, it might have seemed that these races had biological legitimacy. The English colonists, the native peoples they called *Indians*, and the West Africans they brought as slaves all came from different places along the range of genetic diversity. It is entirely possible that the social construction of race in America would have proceeded differently if the full spectrum of the world's populations had immigrated to America along with western Europeans and Africans. Certainly, things would have been different if the prior history of the world had allowed these groups to come together under conditions fostering social equality.

But, as we know, cultural rather than biological traits were used to define our races. The rules of cultural evolution differ from those of biological evolution, but sadly scientists, doctors, philosophers, and law makers have for the most part, not yet acknowledged the difference. We must stop masking the real social issues with racist ideologies in order to build a truly just society.

CHAPTER 2

"Great Is Our Sin": A Brief History of Racism

Nineteenth-century naturalists believed that race or biological features determined a person's position in society. They saw these positions as natural, the result of special creation, fixed and unchanging. These ideas were not new or original. We know that this idea goes back as far as the Greek philosopher Plato (c. 428–347 B.C.). Plato created the concept of the natural scale. Every species and every individual within a species had a rung on the scale. The scale began with inanimate objects, to simple life, humans, and finally to the gods. The gods revealed the scale to man and it was as fixed and eternal as the heavens and as the gods themselves. The Greeks did not create a system of racism or racial slavery; however, they did believe that some people were born with more noble natures. Plato espoused that it was the natural order for more humbler folk to serve the more noble.

For close to two thousand years, Plato's ghost haunted Western science. The universe and all in it was thought to be fixed and unchanging. Newton saw the universe as an orderly machine. Geologists thought the earth was essentially unchanged since biblical creation. However, by the beginning of the eighteenth century, Platonic thought was fading. Uniformitarian geology had proposed that the earth was ancient and that it had gone through consistent change. Platonic ideals held on the longest in biology.

Life was still specially created in essential forms, fixed, unchanging, and hierarchical.

In the tradition of Plato, nineteenth century American scientists sought to find objective means to prove the inferiority of nonwhite races, and to that end the most credentialed of them labored to find objective means to prove a fact that all learned whites already knew. Louis Agassiz theorized about why, Samuel Morton measured skulls, and Josiah Nott and George R. Glidden popularized the results. Agassiz and Morton were amongst the most respected scientists of their age, while Nott and Glidden were amateur naturalists. Charles Darwin threw a monkey wrench into all this when he showed that natural selection was responsible for both the origin of species and for their varieties. Few people realized that Darwin also wrote about how the processes of natural and sexual selection might be responsible for the evolution of our species, particularly its unique characteristics. Yet even before he wrote On the Origin of Species, Darwin questioned the prevailing logic concerning the origins of human social institutions. While aboard HMS Beagle he wrote about the evils of slavery: "If the misery of our poor be not caused by nature, but by our social institutions, then great is our sin." Here Darwin provided us a tremendous insight. In this statement, he asks to what degree do human societies derive their features from innate or genetic attributes of humans, which are therefore difficult to change, versus cultural features that are learned and are therefore easier to change. Yet, by invoking either mechanism genetic or cultural, Darwin differs from Platonic or creationist thinking in that for him change is inevitable. There is no scale of nature, neither are the social conditions in our world fixed and eternal.

This question is at the core of what most people think about race. The human species does not contain biological races now nor has it at any time in the past 250,000 years. Yet America's entire history is intertwined with racial injustice. As Gil Scott Heron once lamented, "From Plymouth Rock to acid rock . . ." Even today, most people still believe that races exist, routinely describe individuals by their perceived race, and engage in racist behavior. Institutional racism is still a major impediment to social democracy.

How Can This Be True If People Don't Belong to Races?

To understand this contradiction, it is important to study how human cultures and societies evolve. Cultures change through time and space, but in ways very different from genetic evolution. Consider the fact that once Latin was the most widely spoken language among scholars in the Western world. Or that once there was only one Christian church. Aspects of culture change through time. There are scientific rules that govern cultural change through time. Modern racism, just like any other cultural behavior, is not the result of some deeply ingrained human instinct. Racism, as we live it today, is an artifact of ancient behavior that evolved for a different purpose. The good news is that the solution to our racial quagmire flows from precisely this revelation.

Cultural Versus Genetic Evolution

Most people believe that there is a direct or simple relationship between genes and culture. They also believe that the genetic composition of our species is unchanging, and many people have difficulty with accepting the fact that cultures also change. What most people consider as genetically determined, innate aspects of human behavior, particularly with regard to race, are artifacts of cultural evolution. A *culture* is a complex whole of the beliefs, art, morals, customs, and other capabilities and habits acquired by humans as members of their society. All human cultures have roots in our biology. But the relationship between biology and culture is complicated. This complex interrelationship allows for seemingly broad cultural variation throughout our history. Yet this diversity is still based on biological constraints. All humans had to find a way to gather or grow food. All developed language. All had to reproduce, develop forms of marriage, and rear their children through kin networks. All developed music, art, dance, myths, and religion. Men dominate the political hierarchy of almost every human culture. The current focus on cultural diversity is laudable, but the pendulum may have swung so far that we have forgotten how fundamentally similar the world's cultures really are.

Parents give their offspring two things: its genetic material and its culture and social position. Human genes and cultures must have evolved in association, however, they evolve by slightly different rules. The small difference in mechanism is profound and this accounts for why cultures can evolve much faster than genes. Appendix 3 summarizes and contrasts features of genetic and cultural evolution.

Genetic evolution occurs because the genetic code DNA is replicated in each generation and passed on to offspring. It is impossible for any physical mechanism to copy anything without making mistakes. The code is resistant to change because most genetic change *(mutation)* is bad. What would happen if a person reached under the cabinet of their television set and switched any two parts at random? It is not likely that this would make the television work better. A mutation in DNA is like switching parts at random. The DNA code consists of four chemical nucleotides. Along a single strand of DNA, groups of three of these nucleotides spell out the code of a specific amino acid. Amino acids are the building blocks of proteins, and these proteins carry out the business of the living cell. If the code were changed, these proteins might not function properly. For example, changing just a few nucleotides causes valine to be substituted for glutamic acid in hemoglobin. The result is that the protein changes shape and produces sickle cell anemia. Fortunately living cells actually have a complicated set of enzymes that replicate, proofread, and repair DNA, precisely to preserve the code, but these mechanisms are not perfect and some mutations are missed. Very few changes are better than the original, although a larger fraction are neutral, thereby escaping the purifying power of natural selection. The neutral and few positive changes provide the genetic variability that allows evolution to respond to new environmental conditions.

Biologist Richard Dawkins proposed an analogous mechanism for cultural inheritance. He coined the term *meme* (pronounced meem) to describe the smallest unit of a replicable aspect of culture. Memes are passed on among individuals both within and between generations. Reading this book means that you are acquiring memes. If you like its ideas, you might tell a friend, allowing some of these memes to replicate into their minds. If you don't like this book, its memes may cease replicating within your circle of friends and family. If some memes are particularly useful to individuals or groups within a given society, they will replicate differentially, either because of their utility, or the fact that people seem to copy popular ideas.

The flat earth meme seemed to make sense to every educated layperson in fifteenth century Europe. By the middle of the sixteenth century, the European voyages of discovery had pretty much shown that earth was a sphere. In the twenty first century this meme has succeeded in persuading virtually every culture and every individual within them of its truth. Yet even today, the Flat Earth Society insists that the world is flat, and that the moon landings were faked. This proves that while some memes may have the ability to spread through cultures, they may never be able to completely eliminate old or false ideas.

Even if Dawkins were wrong, and we could not profitably reduce complicated ideas to some kind of discrete unit, it is undeniable that ideas do get passed from individual to individual and between generations. The difference between the meme and the gene are clear and apparent. Cultural ideas are not as rigorously proofread, and thereby can become more variable. Another difference is that for memes, major change can happen within one generation, and the altered concept can be passed on to the next generation. Humans who might have been born to a generation that gathered naturally occurring fire, could have learned how to make fire, then taught this knowledge to their children. Their children may have bartered that information to nonrelated individuals for some reciprocal benefit. The knowledge of how to make fire drastically changed human society. All of a sudden, humans had more security at night and with that security more time to think and wonder about the nature of the universe. This also meant that there was more time to value mental ability and creativity as sexually desirable traits, ensuring that these would be passed down genetically to future generations. Originally, this sort of rapid change could not happen with genes. Only genetic changes that occurred in the germ line (ovaries and testes) could be passed on to the next generation. Mice with tails will always produce mice with tails, even if the adult mice have their tails cut off every generation. We now know how to alter genetic evolution within one generation. We can use genetic technology to give new genes to any species, by implanting the new gene into a fertilized egg. For example, fruit flies given the bovine superoxide dismutase gene live 50 percent longer than flies without it, and pass the gene on to their offspring.

There are also going to be differences between the mutability of specific memes depending on what concepts they represent and their use. We might imagine that memes that deal with how to successfully build suspension bridges will be applied to rigorous tests. Flawed designs that don't work will be exposed, even if through tragedy, and thereby be limited by their lack of utility. The art adorning the bridges could be radically different. Since the art is not constrained by the function of holding up the bridge, other aspects of culture may decide how a specific bridge is decorated.

Ideas that deal with more intangible concepts, like the nature of God, can be far more variable by the fact that they need not be tested by natural means. Consider the evolution of the three Abrahamic religions: Christianity, Islam, and Judaism. All three religions can trace their faith back to Abraham, yet have diverged from each other on key elements of theology and profound differences in doctrine exist within each group. Since human minds are the repositories of culture, if cultural groups disappear for whatever reason from human history, so might many of their memes.

Some archaeologists believe that the settlement of Easter Island took place about eighteen hundred years ago by people from the coast of Chile. However, the ancestors of the present Polynesian population came by canoes from the Marquesas Islands, and possibly massacred the original inhabitants. The megaliths for which the island is famous were built by the Polynesians. We know very little of the culture of the original inhabitants of the island because none survived.

Another important difference between biological and cultural evolution is the relative importance of the individual, kin, sexual, and group levels of selection. In biological evolution there is overwhelming evidence for the importance of individual, kin, and sexual selection. Selection exists that favors genes which improve an individual's reproductive success, or for genes that engender altruism toward relatives, and for genes that help males and females become more attractive to the opposite sex. In biological evolution, group level selection is rare. The only strong case that has been made for its importance is in human social evolution. Human social evolution is inextricably linked to culture, so group level selection processes are crucial to explaining how cultures evolve.

Original Sin, Animal Behavior, and the Evolution of Human Culture

Human behavior evolved by descent with modification from behavior exhibited by previously existing animals. That means that closely related animals such as monkeys, apes, and chimpanzees share behavioral features with us. We should not think of our behavior as more advanced than theirs; each species has a set of its own unique adaptations that are relevant to their ecological circumstances. Neither should we believe that behavioral adaptations represent some perfect and all encompassing set of mechanisms that will be forever relevant to an everchanging universe. The vast majority of large-bodied species in the history of life on earth have gone extinct, possibly because their behaviors simply couldn't keep up with the changing circumstances.

In some cases, contradictions between forms of selection might have caused the extinction of species. Biologists believe that in addition to natural selection, which always operates at the level of the individual organism, *sexual selection* (what mates choose in the opposite sex), *kin selection* (selection that favors altruism toward close relatives), *reciprocal altruism* (altruism toward unrelated individuals that is repaid in kind, e.g., do unto thy neighbor), and *group selection* (selection between groups that are in competition), also play a key role in the evolution of social species.

During the Pleistocene period, the great Irish elk, a species never found in Ireland, roamed the forested terrain of northern Europe. Males in this species may have improved their individual reproductive success by the size of their antlers. If females were more likely to mate with males bearing bigger sets of antlers, then female mate choice (sexual selection) would have driven an increase in the size of male antlers through evolutionary time. (Yes, size did matter to the female elk!) This produced a runaway process where female mate choice drove male characteristics. The females' sons would inherit the genes for their father's antlers, and their daughters would inherent the genes for their mother's choice, which accentuated female mate choice. This produced males with racks of antlers so big that they got caught in trees while walking through the woods, and females that preferred such huge impractical antlers. Thus, natural selection against antlers that were too large could have caused this species to go extinct, even though sexual selection favored males with larger racks. This proves that evolution cannot foresee the future. Adaptation occurs on a local time scale with no guarantee that what is produced in the short term will insure the long-term success of any species. Witness the fact that we alone remain of the many intelligent hominids that once lived on earth. Even now, the expansion of our species is threatening to cause the extinction of other large-brained organisms with complex social behavior, such as the whales and the apes. This indicates that having a large brain, or complex behavior, is not a guarantee for long-term survival in the history of life.

A Light in the Dark

We make too much of ourselves. We deny, forget, and resist the idea that all animal behavior is rooted in reproductive or Darwinian fitness. We do not want to recognize that we are still animals, albeit animals with complex cultures and societies, but animals nonetheless. Our vanity and anthropomorphism insists that we operate on planes of consciousness dominated by rational thought and morality. Our entire jurisprudence system is premised on a belief that our behavior is driven by free will.

Modern social science ignores the implications of evolutionary reasoning at its own peril. In doing so, it has produced mainly correlative models of social processes that only weakly predict outcomes in the real world. In the absence of a powerful unifying theory of human behavior, it is like someone searching for their lost keys in a dark field. He searches only under the light post. Evolutionary reasoning is really the only way to turn the light on the entire field, and thus to understand social questions, in particular the persistence of racist ideology. This theory clearly explains why racism could not have evolved in the human species (in the same way that natural selection did not design aging). However, behavioral features designed for solving other social tasks were most likely co-opted to serve racist ideology. If we can outline the evolutionary mechanisms that predisposed humans to respond to racist indoctrination, we might actually outline how we can control, retard, or even eliminate it in modern societies.

✻   ✻   ✻

Social behavior is one of the defining features of large-brained animals. We see it in all of our close relatives. This includes lemurs, new world and old world monkeys, gibbons, orangutans, gorillas, and chimpanzees. All these organisms have evolved social behavior and culture shared by all species in this group, although each species has its own unique set of adaptations. Because genetic evolution is slow compared to cultural evolution, human minds continue to operate utilizing core behavioral mechanisms that evolved well over one hundred thousand years ago. It may be that the key adaptation achieved by our species was its behavioral plasticity, the ability to co-opt various aspects of our brain to solve new problems. However, there is no guarantee that every short-term accommodation will produce behavior that is adaptive in the long run. Some behaviors that worked well when we were hunter/gatherers could have become maladaptive at any point along the road to our modern societies.

The Devil Is in the Details

Our evolutionary goal is essentially the same as that of any other animal: differential reproductive success. Differential reproductive success means that genes producing more copies of themselves in a breeding population will eventually dominate that population through time. In a sexual population, finding a mate to reproduce with is a crucial aspect of this process. This is not the crude formulation that most people refer to when speaking about evolution's so-called survival of the fittest. We are all descended from individuals who were capable of both surviving to reproductive maturity and also capable of finding someone who was willing to have enough sexual intercourse with them to procreate. In rare cases offspring are conceived in just one attempt, but most of the time children result from prolonged relationships. In our species, sexual selection (whom females and males choose for their mates) played an important role in the evolution of our behavior and resultant culture.

Humans are unique in how much we rely on our brains to decide on our mates. Very simple organisms, such as flatworms, do not rely on their brains for reproduction. Our nervous system and brain shares features with even the most distantly related animals, including flatworms. All animals need to gather information from their physical environment. Some animals are limited to just sensing light and following chemical gradients. We have similar senses and our brains integrate their inputs. Our brain is one of the most complex organs found in any animal on this planet. It does more than just integrate our sensual inputs. We learn, reason, and imagine. This happens because we have a set of evolved information processing systems which, taken together, make up what we call *the human mind*. Our ancestors' minds allowed them to solve problems related to survival but ultimately to successful reproduction. These problems included things such as learning language, making tools, locating food, avoiding danger, kin relations, cooperation with unrelated individuals, and navigating our ancient African social environments and mate selection. Remember, we are descended from individuals who were good at these things. Humans who failed at these died early, leaving no offspring.

Social Hierarchy in Animals

Racism plays a major role in maintaining social hierarchy. A logical question might be why social hierarchies exist and how they operate. Are they a necessary feature of human society resulting from ingrained genetic behavior? Or are they a maladaptive remnant produced by the evolutionary pressures that shaped our species's evolution? Might they result from specific aspects of human cultural evolution with no relationship whatsoever to genetically programmed behaviors?

While social hierarchy results from some past evolutionary pressures that helped to shape our species, racism is not a necessary feature of social hierarchy. In other words, genetically encoded behavior resulting from past hominid evolution may have shaped human cultures. We developed a variety of mechanisms throughout our history that sort individuals into different positions within society. However, human beings are different from virtually every other organism that has existed in the history of life. We can be cognizant of our actions. We have the capacity for abstract thought. We have developed codes of morality and law that restrain individuals from exploiting others, or groups of individuals from controlling society. We, of all the animals on earth, are capable of recognizing that while a given action might improve our Darwinian fitness, its consequences may be in opposition to our moral codes. Previous generations of evolutionary thinkers saw in nature what they wanted to see in human society, and then used their anthropomorphic interpretation of nature to justify their support for their own antidemocratic and genocidal policies. There are no genetically determined reasons for maintaining social injustice, based on purported race or any other feature of human biology one wishes to choose.

Social hierarchy is widespread in animals. Gray wolf packs *(Canis lupis)* have a strict hierarchy in which some members are dominant and others are subordinate. This is exemplified in greeting: When two members greet each other, the dominant one stands erect, while the subordinate one crouches. In this species, social hierarchy plays its greatest role in mating. Gray wolves usually mate for life and, within each pack, only the dominant male and female reproduce. One has an incredibly hard time using individual selection alone to explain such a system. Why should the subordinate wolves accept their lot in the pack? Shouldn't each individual attempt to reproduce? Shouldn't male and female pairs of equal social rank find ways of pairing and producing offspring? The only way this system can be explained is if the pack consists of wolves who are related to each other by varying degrees. In addition, the chance of successfully rearing offspring by subservient members of the pack is very low. This system can be explained if individuals passed on more copies of their genes by aiding their socially dominant relatives to reproduce and thus adhering to the social dominance system. An interesting corollary of this idea is that this social system might be the product of specific environmental conditions. One could imagine that, if resources were at very high levels for sustained periods of time, different pack behavior might evolve, allowing a greater fraction of the wolf population to reproduce.

The only logical explanation for the existence of social hierarchy in animals is to determine which individuals will reproduce the next generation. The social organization of elephant seals is an extreme example of such a system (the northern elephant seal, *Mirounga angustirostris,* and the southern elephant seal, *Mirounga leonina*). In these species, dominant males battle almost to death to determine which male can control the harem. The dominant male is more likely to successfully mate with females. However, on the fringes of a male's territory, subordinate males may be able to gain access to females. These patterns are seen throughout the mammals. The primates are characterized by their complex social behavior, and all primate societies show various degrees of social hierarchy. These hierarchies are also more pronounced in males than in females. This indicates that sexual selection played a role in their origin. Sexual selection theory predicts that males will display and that females will choose, hence social position is a means by which females choose which males with which to mate. The fact that all primates share these features means that these were fixed early on or that each species within the group underwent parallel evolution.

We know that primate evolution was not completely parallel, since each species differs in a number of characteristics, including how their social hierarchies are manifested. With monkeys, there is a much larger difference in mating success between the older and more powerful versus the younger and weaker males. With gorillas *(Gorilla gorilla),* the dominant male garners the vast majority of successful matings within a troop. His dominance is achieved by physical strength, thus evolution of successful gorilla males proceeds by producing greater muscle mass, as opposed to testes size (dominant male gorillas rarely face sperm competition in the vaginal tracks of the females with whom they mate). Yet, with bonobos *(Pan paniscus)*, chimpanzees *(Pan troglodytes)*, and humans, there is more social and mating success equality in males. Successful chimpanzee males are more likely to achieve this by manipulating the social environment, as opposed to utilizing simple brute strength. These males, however, are more likely to face sperm competition; evolution in this species has produced very large testes to win in the sperm competition game. Humans are most closely related to chimpanzees. We also observe that human social relations are also closer to what we see in chimpanzees, as compared to monkeys or apes. Human males have much larger testes-to-body-weight ratios than apes, but not quite as large as chimpanzees.

Why are humans different from chimpanzees? After all, humans and chimps shared a common ancestor over five million years ago. Recent studies have also shown that the vast majority of the genetic difference between chimpanzees and humans occurs in genes expressed in the brain. This amounts to about 12,000 active genes, which accounts for the 1.3 percent difference between the two genomes. Human culture evolved at a rate much faster than our genetic evolution. This was facilitated by the acquisition of superior language abilities early in the hominid lineage. Amazingly, this ability has been tied to just two nucleotide substitutions in a single gene found between us and the other apes!

In the summer of 2002, Svante Paabo and his coworkers at the Max Planck Institute for Evolutionary Anthropology published results from their study of the FOXP2 gene. People with mutations in this gene have difficulties articulating speech and applying grammatical rules. Paabo's group sequenced this gene for the apes and compared it to the mouse. There were only three total changes in the gene, but two of them occurred after the split between humans and apes. This indicates that these two small genetic changes played a significant role in the evolution of human speech. Once humans had the ability to speak, its importance might have been amplified rapidly through sexual selection, as were other aspects of the human mind. Thus, these simple genetic changes explain the immensely greater capacity that humans have for complicated behavior and culture compared to our closest relatives, the chimpanzees.

Ghosts of the Evolutionary Past

Descent with modification explains the increase in our behavioral sophistication. This is the general method by which organisms acquire new traits. Natural selection does not invent entirely new things. It co-opts old things to serve new purposes. Once beneficial behaviors that may be harmful in modern human culture persist. For example, eating fatty or sweet foods may have been exceedingly useful when we were hunter-gatherers in the Pleistocene. Both female and male reproductive fitness is related to body weight. In a world of scarce food and constant physical exertion, we would have benefited from consuming these foods. A behavior that made us crave these foods would rapidly spread through our gene pool. Alternatively, if some general mechanism for experiencing pleasure evolved, it might be linked to a number of behaviors, such as eating sweet things, enjoyment of romance and sex, or even general accomplishment. Either way, depending upon the advantage the trait conferred, individuals carrying it would outreproduce those without it. The future generations would be made up of the progeny of people with these traits. Such genes would therefore be found in all humans.

Today, the vast majority of living humans have these cravings. However, in modern industrial societies, the widespread availability of these foods may cause obesity, and other health problems. This is due to our adopting a sedentary lifestyle while we consume too many calories. The increase in type II diabetes and hypertension in African Americans and American Indians may result from the over inclusion of sweet and fatty foods in the diet. Type II diabetes is virtually unheard of in western Africans, who are much leaner in body mass than African-Americans. This illustrates gene by environment interaction. Genetic variants associated with type II diabetes in African and Euro-Americans are present at very high frequency in western Africans, but this disease is virtually absent amongst them.

Some features of human cultures have not changed at all. Males and females still reproduce offspring, and this constrains many of the aspects of modern human culture. For example, the vast majority of sexually active couples are heterosexual and produce children. They live together precisely so that they can rear their children. This means that much of our culture is going to reflect this, at least until technology is developed that allows children to be created by some other means.

Even some of our present day mental disorders may result from behaviors that were useful in early human evolution. The obsessive-compulsive disorder spectrum includes obsessive-compulsive disorder (OCD), body dysmorphic disorder (BDD), *trichotillomania* (hair pulling), *onychophagia* (nail biting), and compulsive skin picking, among other behaviors. It is thought that these disorders may be related to primate grooming behavior. Individuals with these disorders compulsively engage in things like counting or checking behavior (OCD), or fear of disease contamination or body defects (OCD, BDD, hair pulling, nail biting). These symptoms occur in at least 2.5 percent of Americans, are inherited, and are related to sertonin reuptake in brain neurons. In unaffected people, serotonin is released from one neuron and taken up by the connecting neuron, allowing the chemical message to path through the brain. In this series of disorders, serotonin is reabsorbed by the secreting neuron before the connecting neuron can receive it. The effect on the person is that they replay a specific behavior over and over again (hence the obsession). Checking and grooming behavior may have played a role in resisting skin-borne disease or, more important, rejecting possible mates that could be observed to be unhealthy. Today, unaffected individuals have brains that allow them to engage in this behavior without obsession; however, in the OCD spectrum, gene defects turn a formerly adaptive behavior into an illness. During our evolution, genes associated with unsuccessful behavior were reduced in frequency or eliminated. This may explain why OCD disorders are rare. Yet it is entirely possible that the frequency of OCD might vary between different ethnic groups.

The capacity for racist behavior is also a ghost of our evolutionary past. It results from mechanisms that evolved to distinguish friend from foe, under social conditions that were very different from our modern world. Surprisingly, racism did not result from neural machinery designed to classify or distinguish differences between objects. Rather there is now strong evidence that it results from behavior designed to assess coalitional alliances.

Early humans probably lived in small groups of fifty to two hundred people. Kinship and some sort of reciprocal trust between nonrelated individuals formed the bonds of these coalitions. The advantages of forming such groups were twofold. Individuals have different skills; combining multiple skills increased the efficiency of many activities related to the survival for all individuals within the group. Forming coalitional alliances also helped provide protection against other groups. Most humans would have never traveled more than fifty miles in their entire lives. Therefore, it would have been impossible for humans to evolve behavioral mechanisms to choose allegiance that revolved around what we think of today as racial difference. Furthermore, these mechanisms would have been in place before any anatomically modern humans left Africa.

Ultimately, any characteristics of individuals within the coalition would be linked to improving the reproductive success of its members. One study asked modern humans to identify characteristics that they would wish of a coalition member. The respondents ranked being hardworking, being intelligent, being kind, being openminded, being able to motivate people, having a wide range of knowledge, having a good sense of humor, and being considered dependable, were ranked as highly desirable. Sex differences appeared in the study, with the traits being brave in the face of danger, being physically strong, being a good fighter, being able to protect others from physical harm, being able to tolerate physical pain, being able to defend oneself against physical attack, and being able to physically dominate others, ranked as more desirable by men than women. Men also rated traits such as being poor at athletic activities and being physically weak more negatively than women.

These traits gives clues as to why ancient humans formed coalitions. Humans did not evolve under conditions of food abundance. This is made clear by the fact that, for the vast majority of human history, our population did not exceed a growth rate of 0.0002 individuals per year. Coalitions with more individuals possessing the highly desirable traits stood a better chance of survival and, ultimately, reproductive success compared to groups lacking such attributes. It is highly likely that small groups of early humans often died from starvation, drought, natural disaster, or disease. In addition, groups might have been exterminated or overwhelmed by larger, more effective groups. This is supported by the fact that recorded human history is composed of a series of conflicts between groups. There is no reason to believe it was otherwise at the dawn of our species. These conditions would have placed a premium on the ability of individuals to choose their coalitional allegiances carefully. Good allies would help one with both within-group and between-group survival.

If such behavior persists in humans, we should be able to detect it. Humans should be able to assess the rules of a society and then determine whom they want as their ally and whom they should ignore, avoid, or see as an enemy. In a stratified society, individuals of the dominant group should understand the rules of stratification, who is part of their social group, and who is not. In particular, if the society's stratification is antagonistic (and virtually all stratified groups should have social antagonisms), then individuals should be more likely to choose coalitional allies from their own group.

Two years ago, a paper was published by researchers at the University of California, Santa Barbara, showing that modern humans do behave in this way.[1] However, it also showed that if an individual is exposed to a world with different social rules, their coalitional allegiance can be rapidly altered. Their experiment involved 400 university students. It used pictures of men and women that were supposedly either black or white. The subjects were told that the people in the photos were members of two rival teams that had fought with each other at a game held in the previous season. The pictures were matched with a verbal allegiance cue. This was a quotation from the team member that identified him or her with one side of the fight. The players were identically dressed, so that there was no other obvious way to classify them by team. When the students viewed the pictures with only the verbal cues, race proved the most significant factor in how the students remembered the photos and the captions that went with them.

However, when the same subjects were exposed to the experiment modified to show the two teams in different color jerseys, coalition became a stronger force than race. This was not true when gender was varied. It was consistently the strongest associating factor. Thus, this experiment was able to weaken the importance of race as a classifier within a matter of minutes. However, it was not capable of changing the way the students viewed gender. This is simply because there are clear reasons for why humans evolved to be able to distinguish gender, such as identifying a potential mate, but the same was not true for race. Races and racism are socially constructed. Our historical records validate this idea.

This experiment shows that racism is a recent offshoot of survival mechanisms that helped early humans quickly recognize potentially hostile coalitions and alliances. In our society, the lines between coalition and race have always been indistinguishable. America began with physically distinguishable groups in positions of clear social antagonism. Soon after English colonists landed in North America, they were in a state of warfare with the American Indians. African slaves were imported to provide labor for the plantations. Initially, one's membership in America's social coalitions was clearly distinguishable by physical cues. Europeans exploited both Indians and Africans to increase their own material and ultimately their own reproductive fitness. Racist ideology grew to reinforce the identity and membership of the coalitions. As American social and cultural evolution proceeded, it was no longer clear that allegiance to this scheme would guarantee European-American success. America's social coalitions became more complicated. As these social relations changed, European genetic ancestry did not guarantee that an individual might not profitably ally with someone with genes from Africa or Asia.

The evolutionary theory suggests that individuals will continue to recognize coalitional alliances. Still, the form and function of these allegiances will change over time. Socially dominant groups may use a variety of physical or cultural markers to manipulate coalitions to their benefit. After the Civil War, the most socially dominant white men used their control over the government to create conditions in which subordinate whites would act to the benefit of both groups against nonwhites. Despite the pleas of the newly freed Negroes in the south, President Andrew Johnson and Congress did little to nothing to curb violence against them being used to reestablish former slaveholder control. In a letter dated March 25, 1871, a committee of grievances recounted 116 acts of Ku Klux Klan violence over four years directed against Negroes in Kentucky.[2] Similar atrocities occurred throughout the South; although Congress did eventually enact legislation against the Ku Klux Klan in 1871, the provisions of this bill were never enforced. In this way, dominant whites used the power of the Klan to terrorize Negroes and benefited themselves by keeping the subordinate whites focused on nonwhites, rather than the other inequities in southern society. Racist ideology glued together the white coalition.

Unfortunately, the present social conditions are not conducive to shifting coalitional allegiances away from racial boundaries. Consider that Euro-Americans as a group own the vast majority of America's wealth, are the vast majority of the CEOs of America's top 400 corporations, have been every president, and the vast majority of senators and congresspeople. University and elementary through high-school (K-12) education are dominated by Euro-Americans and their views. Ironically, one of the few institutions in which non-Europeans have made significant headway is in the military.

Darwin was right; great is our sin. Our social institutions do cause the misery of our poor. In America, membership in the poor is disproportionately by socially constructed race. So, what is the incentive for Euro-Americans to act on social justice? How will they widen their conception of who is an American? How will the American coalition be widened to include those who are not clearly of European genetic ancestry? Yet there is hope. It seems that under controlled conditions racial bias can be rather easily diluted. Can we alter our real world society to break down racially based conceptions of allegiance? Why is it more dangerous to continue living in a society rife with falsely based antagonisms than to address and eliminate them?

CHAPTER 3

Sexual Selection, Reproduction, and Social Dominance

Approximately 1.7 million years ago, the brain of our ancestral species *Homo erectus* weighed 800 grams. By 100,000 years ago, modern human brains averaged about 1300 grams. The transition from *Homo erectus* to modern humans did not produce new cultural innovations at a rate correlated with the increased brain size. It would take an additional 90,000 years before the increased brain of *Homo sapiens* would invent agriculture. It is safe to say that the genetic basis of our behavior changed very slowly for over 1.6 million years. However, about 10,000 years ago, cultural evolution accelerated, producing many of the features of our modern societies, complete with all their virtues, vices, and follies. This anomaly suggests that natural selection alone may not be sufficient to explain the evolution of human culture.

Evolutionary psychologist Geoffrey Miller has argued quite convincingly that much of what is unique in human behavior originated in sexual selection. Darwin began the discussion of sexual selection in 1871 in *The Descent of Man and Selection in Relation to Sex*. In this work, he documented the existence of and importance of sexual selection in accounting for the seemingly costly displays of male animals. Sexual selection theory was neglected for many years after Darwin. In the 1930s Sir Ronald A. Fisher developed some of the first theoretical models that explained how sexual selection could operate in opposition to natural selection.

The 1960s saw an explosion in the importance of, and interest in, sexual selection. Evolutionary biologist William D. Hamilton and his students led the way, demonstrating how sexual selection might favor the evolution of fitness indicators. Simultaneously, Israeli biologist Amotz Zahavi tossed a bombshell into the debate over sexual selection theory. He pointed out that for sexual selection to work, fitness indicators had to be hard to copy. For example, if people once had a mating preference for blue eyes, it would have been nearly impossible for brown-eyed people to fake the possession of blue eyes. However, with the advent of modern technology, people can buy colored contact lenses. In fact, theory predicts that fitness indicators should be so hard to produce that they could even become a handicap. A well-known case of this is the extra long or brightly colored tail feathers produced by males in many bird species. These feathers may actually impair their ability to fly or to hide from predators.

This principle explained the significance of the peacock's tail and the oversized antlers of the Irish elk. Consider, for example, that blond hair might have been sexually selected in northern Europe. For most of human history, blond hair might be favored in these regions and thus the frequency of genes that produce blond hair and any other genes associated with them would increase above that we would expect by mutation. Some modern biologists suspect that the blond hair allele is going extinct in northern Europe. If this were true, this loss could be explained by the fact that blond hair is now easy to copy. Now, both men and women can dye their hair blond, so that any slight advantage that genetically blond-haired individuals might have had in mating is reduced or even eliminated. If the advantage has been removed sufficiently, we would predict a gradual decline in the frequency of genetic blondness in northern Europeans to the rate at which mutations for blond hair occur in that population. This would occur, unless having blond hair positively favors reproductive fitness by some other means.

Sexual selection theory predicts two very important results.

First, that runaway feedback loops, based on what females prefer and what males can produce will appear and, second, that even in very closely related species that diverse mating preferences will arise. The runaway feedback process involving the production of costly fitness displays could explain why the peacock's tail is so pretty yet absolutely useless, why the Irish elks' antlers might have guaranteed victory in mating contests with lesser elks, and also why the human brain evolved its sophistication, yet did not contribute to new culture or technology for hundreds of thousands of years. If part of that runaway process accounts for our consciousness, and our sense of pleasure and pain, then it could explain a variety of different phenomena that occur in cultural evolution. We do not see such behavior in our closest relatives, the chimps. We can think of the features that closely related organisms share, as the result of natural selection, whereas the things that make closely related species different are likely the result of sexual selection. Miller argues that the complexity of the human brain and its subsequent behavior may be the result of sexual selection, particularly traits such as our larger brain, language, complex culture, kindness, artistic creativity, and possibly our susceptibility to belief in mythical versions of the world. Sexual selection produced precisely those traits that make us most different from our closest relatives. On the other hand, complex social behavior, social hierarchy, culture, lethal intergroup violence, and knowledge of medicinal plants, is something that is shared with all our close relatives. Our capacity to engage in behavior that is oppressive to other humans could have been produced by natural selection in some primate ancestor, or by parallel sexual selection in all primates. The specific conditions of early hominid evolution may have allowed group level selection to play a role in spreading oppressive behavior against other groups.

How What Eve Wanted Shaped Adam

Modern humans are derived from people who lived only one hundred thousand years or so ago. This explains the common features of our cultures. Genetic evolution could not have altered the fundamental template for human behavior in such a short period of time, and we know that all groups of living humans share essentially the same genes. The behavioral differences we see between geographically separated groups are actually very small, and result from cultural evolution. For example, we have far more evidence of biologically based differences in behavior between sexes within any purported race than we have ever had between any two races. Female mate preferences differ significantly from male mate preferences, and the pattern of the differences are preserved all around the world. Females have greater preference for good financial prospects in a marriage partner, while males have greater preference for physical attractiveness in a long-term mate.[1] These results show that when it comes to mate preferences, males and females significantly differ, and that so-called racially different populations from around the world have the same preferences.

Male and female brains have profound anatomical differences. These differences are supported by brain imaging, in ways that we never see between same sex individuals chosen from geographically separated populations. We even know exactly which locus masculinizes human fetuses. It is the SRY locus·on the Y-chromosome; this locus only controls the production of the male hormone testosterone. Yet, while profound differences exist in some aspects of male and female behavior, no consistent differences exist between them in general intelligence, however measured. Furthermore, since the successful reproduction of our species requires both sexes, there is no reason to suppose that evolution necessarily favored the social dominance of either sex. Some evolutionary psychologists have proposed that female mate choice in early humans shaped male propensities for social dominance. Social dominance is thought to be associated with the tendency of males to oppress other males and women. Males may be disproportionately violent today because our past and present social conditions arouse resistance to social domination. In other words, in a world that has been dominated by social injustice, should we not expect some, if not the majority of, men to react violently to unfair conditions?

Alternatively, there is very good evidence that a key trait that ancient human females chose in men was kindness. Then, if kindness to one's own offspring is genetically wired, it is entirely possible that the capacity for kindness toward all humans could result, particularly if such behavior resulted in social conditions that were beneficial to the rearing of one's own offspring. This suggests that human social conditions might have a crucial impact on individual male psychology. Thus, to end violence, should we not invent different social conditions under which males can exhibit more of the positive characteristics for which women originally selected them?

Understanding our evolutionary heritage shows us that we share far more common cultural traits than we want to admit. It is only our own ethnocentrism that insists on nitpicking and splintering around issues of culture. This and the fact that the cultural attributes of individuals are too often associated with the structures of status inequality in our societies. If we lived in a world that had solved the problem of how to fairly distribute its goods and services, no one would get bent out of shape over cultural differences. Such a world would create conditions under which females would no longer gain fitness benefits by choosing social dominance characteristics in males. We could, in a sense, engineer an environment that fosters and rewards the better angels of our nature, such as morality, altruism, and generosity.

A Walk in the Pleistocene

The Pleistocene epoch lasted from 1.6 million to 10,000 years ago. Huge glaciers covered much of what are today's temperate zones, thus sea levels were lower. *Homo sapiens* first appeared sometime from five hundred thousand to two hundred thousand years ago, and modern *Homo sapiens sapiens* appears no earlier than 120,000 years ago. We suspect that there was no movement of modern humans out of Africa until at least seventy thousand years ago, and no movement into Europe until around fifty thousand years ago. Therefore, the genetic basis of our modern behaviors evolved in eastern Africa, well over one hundred thousand years ago, and all modern humans took those behavioral templates with them when they left to inhabit the rest of the world.

Early humans lived in small bands that subsisted on gathering and hunting. Conditions of life were undoubtedly much harder than they are now. The harshness of Pleistocene life would have made it impossible for many of the fitness-reducing traits we observe in people living in modern societies to spread. There would have been no obesity. The scarceness of food and the constant activity would not have allowed anyone enough calories to exhibit the trait. Neither would obese individuals have been able to keep up with the band. Lone individuals would have been easy prey for other large-bodied predators. Nearsightedness would not have been observed in the Pleistocene either. We believe that this trait was actually produced by the appearance of the printed word. Certainly nearsighted people in the Pleistocene would have been in trouble. If they could not see predators or enemies coming, they were at higher risk for death. The genes that caused nearsightedness would have existed in our species before anyone ever observed the trait. This is an example of gene-by-environment interaction. That is, some environmental stimulus must be present before the genes in question produce a given result. Thus, in cultures where close work is required of children early in life we observe greater frequencies of nearsightedness. In modern societies, there is virtually no selection against the trait so it will be found at variable frequencies depending upon a population's evolutionary history.

These societies were not anonymous as they are now; people in a band or tribe would have known all its members from childhood. Consider how reproductive prospects might have been affected by inheriting a trait that interfered with the ability to gather food, hunt, avoid danger, or to negotiate within the group. Assuming that with such deleterious traits one lived to reproductive age, in such a small society public knowledge of those deficiencies may have seriously impacted one's fitness. If the problem was too severe, most likely such individuals did not leave many offspring. They might not have left offspring because of early death, or because of not attracting a person with which to have children. A male who always bullied and got into fights with other members of the social group would have been suspect. Even the biggest, strongest, and most aggressive members of the group still might not be successful in evolutionary terms. Why? People would band together to resist such individuals, possibly driving them out, or even killing them. Another likely scenario might be that women would avoid such men and not choose one of them for a mate. They would fear that they might pass on those destructive traits to their offspring, or that the male might harm any children she already had (serial polygamy was probably common in human prehistory). It could be argued that physical prowess would have allowed such men to sexually assault women. However, women in the Pleistocene would have been in better physical condition than most modern professional athletes. They also knew how to use weapons, and were often living in groups of close female relatives. These conditions would have made a physical assault highly dangerous for the attacker, and retaliation by the family of the assaulted a certainty.

If such inappropriately violent males did have greater success reproducing, the fact that they lived in small groups would mean that very soon the group would be dominated by their offspring. Such a group would increase the frequency of males always at each other's throats, suffer from more violence, greater attrition, and would be no match for a rival group that had greater internal cohesion. We would expect such a group to die out. Conversely, people who had good negotiation skills, were helpful to group welfare, and found ways to make themselves attractive to the opposite sex, including showing kindness to children of previous mates, probably left the most offspring. Successful behaviors meant that the bearer reached reproductive age and attracted more mates. We are the descendants of these people. Their genes spread through the world's populations. So, if modern behavior is genetically determined, it includes the ability to learn how to navigate living within a group and cooperating with relatives and nonrelatives alike. We are singularly unique among the social primates in that regard. Why? The evolution of our larger brains, with the capacity for abstract thought, meant that we could invent ethics and morality in ways that chimps could not. We evolved the least hierarchical reproductive system of all the primates and, therefore, as a result have the capacity to institute cultural systems that minimize other aspects of social dominance and oppression.

Reproduction and the Origin of Class Societies

It seems that the origin of hierarchy and despotism in our species is related to the increase in the size of human societies. This increase is directly tied to the invention of agriculture and the domestication of animals. These two technological achievements, the former by women, the latter by men, are probably the most important events responsible for the evolution of modern societies. For the first time, human populations could accumulate a socially produced surplus. Once agriculture was established, groups had to stay put to tend their fields and crops. It was now possible to grow far more food than small groups could eat. This food surplus was a prerequisite for the development of complicated technology, social stratification, centralized states, and professional armies. Scientists have evidence that major crop plants, such as rice, wheat, barley, rye, as well as animals, including horses, camels, and dogs, were being selectively bred between ten thousand and one thousand years ago. This drastically increased the rate of population growth and spurred the development of trade between the new small villages that began to grow in this period. It is likely that male behavior changed drastically over this period, creating both a greater social hierarchy within the male sex to control the surplus and trade, and also implementing greater domination over females than had existed in hunter-gatherer society. These conditions also led to the spread of farmer culture and language; even diseases that evolved in domestic animal reservoirs may have led to the inadvertent elimination of the hunter-gatherer populations. Here, feminist scholars are correct in supposing that the first socially constructed oppression in human societies was patriarchy resulting from male dominance over surplus agricultural production.

The roots of the capacity to implement social oppression go deep into our evolutionary history. Early human gatherer-hunters, as did all ancestral human species, lived in environments that were harsh and often limited in resources. Under such conditions, interactions between groups may have played an important role in developing aspects of human behavior, particularly aggression against other groups and social hierarchy within groups. It has been observed, in contrast to long held theories of the benign and peaceful nature of other primates, that both chimp and human societies exhibit lethal intergroup violence associated with capturing territories and resources. Evolutionary psychologists have proposed a number of hypotheses to explain the existence of violence in human societies. These include defense against attack, inflicting costs on intrasexual rivals, negotiating power and status hierarchies, deterring rivals from future aggression, and finally deterring long-term enemies from future sexual aggression. It is argued that the fact that these behaviors are so overwhelmingly exhibited by males and that the pattern is age specific, suggests that in humans these traits may have been produced or maintained by sexual selection. An important difference between chimpanzee and human violence is that the chimps did not invent projectile weapons. These weapons are far more lethal while, in some cases, considerably reducing the potential risk of harm in combat.

Modern warfare results from nations attempting to control material resources. This may seem as if it does not involve improving male access to mating opportunities. However, if we take one step back from the problem we can see how these explanations are not mutually exclusive. Why do male groups within societies send other males off to fight and possibly die? An even more difficult question is, why do they go? How could European princes and kings convince their men-at-arms to recapture the Holy Land? Or bankers and merchants convince European slave traders to risk the danger of capturing and transporting slaves from the west coast of Africa to North America? This can happen because ultimately material resources are turned into reproductive resources. If the risk of death in warfare is perceived to be sufficiently small, men can be convinced to go to war, pillage, and subjugate others, particularly if the others are somehow different from themselves. After the death of Charlemagne, Europe was dominated by attacks from the east (the Magyars, Asian nomads), the north (Vikings), and the south (Islam-controlled southern Spain and the eastern Mediterranean). At the beginning of the eleventh century, Pope Urban II recognized that the best way to unite western Christendom, and simultaneously consolidate the power of the church, was to call for a crusade to free the Holy Land from the Muslims. The First Crusade did not attract major nobles, instead lesser nobles seeking better lands, plunder, and control of the eastern trade routes rallied to the call. Along the Rhine, the First Crusade became the pretext for expropriating and slaughtering Jewish communities within Europe. The individuals in these Jewish communities did not look any different from any other Europeans. They could only be distinguished by their dress and by where they lived. They were different because they practiced a different religion.

Most of the participants in the Crusades were men. If participation in warfare against other groups meant for the survivors increased social status, greater wealth, and therefore ultimately better opportunities for reproductive opportunities within their own group, this activity would not have been inconsistent with archetypical human behavior.

Why There Are No Genes for Racial Animosity

Clearly, we cannot understand the origins of human behavior by examining present day industrial societies. The vast majority of human evolutionary history was spent in small groups, in Africa. It is likely that their coherence relied on division of labor. Individuals have different talents, and a group of people can more effectively hunt, gather, provide clothing and shelter, and defend themselves than any one person could alone. Initially, this had the impact of making life of hunter-gatherer society egalitarian, and limiting the power of individuals. This pattern still exists in many modern hunter-gatherer groups.

These small groups did not range very far and, as such, did not ever encounter groups that would have had physical features drastically different from themselves. Neither did these groups have much in terms of surplus. Resources were scarce, and while aggression might have been a way to gain more, initially cooperation and trade seem to be the more evolutionarily favored way of acquiring additional resources. Individual theft and aggression was not without considerable risk and, certainly, aggression against other groups might have only been favored if one group had large odds of winning against the other. These first intergroup conflicts must have been between groups that had the same physical features. These groups were bonded by kinship, yet they would not have been able to identify friend and foe by physical features. This means that we cannot look for the roots of modern racism in some behavioral trait that was specifically designed to differentiate individuals on the basis of what we call race.

The earliest intergroup conflict occurred between groups that were physically similar, but potentially culturally different. The evidence supporting this idea comes from our earliest recorded history. From the ancient world we find in the King James Bible, the instructions to the Israelites in Deuteronomy 7:1-3:

> When the Lord your God brings you into the land you are entering to possess and drives out before you many nations—the Hittites, Girgashites, Amorites, Canaanites, Perizzites, Hivites, and Jebusites, seven nations larger and stronger than you—and when the Lord your God has delivered them over to you and you have defeated them, then you must destroy them totally. Make no treaty with them, and show them no mercy. Do not intermarry with them . . .

They were commanded to destroy the religious cultures of these tribes, this same command is repeated again in verse 16, and finally with the statement that the Israelites were God's chosen people out of all of the peoples of the earth.

These instructions are consistent with maintaining both their culture and kinship. Intermarriage is not to be allowed with the other tribes since in verse 4 it says ". . . they will turn your sons away from following me to serve other gods." The people are promised that if they follow these commandments, that they will be blessed, herds increased, crops bountiful, that none of their men and women would be childless, and that they would be kept free of disease. They are promised both an increase in their reproductive fitness, and also in the expansion of their culture, a culture based on obedience to the word of God. Between 800 and 700

B.C., these would have been powerful inducements to follow the law. Conversely, the wrath of God was nothing to trifle with, so that together these rewards and punishments could be seen as a form of powerful internal group indoctrination. We know today that the enemy tribes were very closely related to the Israelites genetically. Again, we cannot view this combat as racial in any sense of the word, but it was clearly a conflict of religious cultures. The Israelites were the smallest and the weakest of these tribes, having just come out of bondage in Egypt; without strong internal cohesion they would have never defeated their rivals, their culture would have been destroyed, and they would have been rapidly assimilated in the new land.

Cultural animosity between people who are genetically and physically similar can still lead to bigotry, prejudice, and warfare. Bigotry and prejudice are similar. *Bigots* are intolerant of anyone different from themselves in any way and *prejudice* results from prejudging individuals or groups before you have any factual knowledge about them. Physical differences could be used to reinforce cultural differences and to allow people to utilize appearance to actualize their prejudices. Consider how the Mongols must have treated the Europeans they conquered in the thirteenth century? Their empire spread from what is today Outer Mongolia, south to China and India, east to Poland, and the Adriatic Sea. The Mongols would have appeared physically different from the Poles, Iraqis, Indians, and even southern Chinese. In addition, there would have been even greater differences in culture within their empire.

Cultural Conflict

Abundant evidence exists showing that human cultures share an important feature in common: Individuals within a cultural group are to practice benevolence and generosity toward all other members of the group. Evolutionary biologists Eliot Sober and David

Sloan Wilson examined a sample of twenty-five randomly chosen cultures from a comparative ethnographic database. They found that love-thy-neighbor characteristics were found in all groups. The groups spanned the genetic and cultural diversity of all living humans. This could mean that genetic mechanisms that facilitate this behavior were fixed in all humans before they left Africa, or that all successful cultures independently arrived at this conclusion. Either way, it is clear that an evolutionary pressure existed that required groups of individuals to behave like a unified and cohesive whole. The evidence we have from written history suggests that there might have been strong selection for groups to evolve internal cohesion as a means of survival against other rival groups. Throughout our ancient histories, we first encounter conflicts between groups that have cultural but not racial differences. This occurred all over the world. Much of the struggle occurred within societies, such as the patrician and plebeian classes in Rome, and the struggle of both of these against their slaves. There were also struggles between outgroups who were physically similar, such as the Athenians and the Spartans, Greeks and the Trojans, or the Greeks and the Persians.

Even war and conflict between cultural groups such as the Christians and the Muslims from the twelfth to fifteenth centuries were not based on concepts of race. In various times throughout this conflict, Christian states warred with Christian, Muslim with Muslim, and various allegiances that crossed cultural affiliation also appeared. No theories of racial hierarchy grew out of these conflicts, because there was not a strict relationship between any physical features and adherence to either religion. Slavery at the beginning of the conflicts had more European captives entering the Muslim trade than vice versa. As the Christian states began to consolidate their victories over the Muslims in the fifteenth century, the slave trade began to change its character, with more sub-Saharan Africans entering the Christian trade. These slaves were both physically and culturally different from their European masters. This begins the confusion that suggests that physical and cultural differences are the source of social position.

Race as Culture

What we think of as race today is really a surrogate for membership in cultural groups. Remember that cultures actually evolve much faster than genes do and, therefore, cultural differences can become much greater than genetic ones, even in relatively short periods of time. Given the complexity of the factors that contribute to cultural evolution, there should be a wide variety of potential outcomes, even though the genetic basis of behavior is completely conserved across all groups of humans. These points have particular importance for understanding the evolution of racism as a feature of modern culture. Consider the fact that conceptions of socially constructed race differ depending on the particular history and groups involved in the construction. Neither are physical differences between groups required to develop theories of racial superiority. Socially defined racial categories between conquerors and conquered have arisen in populations that are relatively uniform. The bigotry against Jews in medieval Europe was essentially no different from modern socially constructed racism, yet these individuals probably did not differ genetically or physically from their oppressors. This explains why the Nazis had to determine who was Jewish by legal records and force them to wear yellow stars as the means by which to identify them.

There are other examples of racial ideology that do not require or depend on the existence of physical differences between oppressors and oppressed. Japanese culture coined the term *minzoku,* which means pure blood. This concept conflates the ideas of culture, ethnicity, and race. This term represents cultural features as secondary to and derived from an imagined biological essence of Japaneseness. Prior to World War II, the Japanese imperialists saw the Japanese as a distinct racial group. They asserted that Japan had a homogeneous racial composition. Thus, all Japanese were thought to stem from a single bloodline and they described it as *junketsu no minzoku* or pure blood people. This master race ideology justified their colonization of the island Hokkaido. They displaced and mistreated its inhabitants, the Ainu. The Ainu have physical features that suggest they originated in eastern Europe or western Asia. The Japanese also used this ideology to justify their invasions of Korea and China. While some small physical differences might exist between these groups, recent genetic studies show that the Japanese, in fact, are descended from immigrants from the Korean peninsula, who are in turn descended from immigrants from northern China. Yet the genetic and archaeological evidence for these facts is actively suppressed in Japan.

This ideology helped to spawn the master race of Asia theory. This idea was used in World War II to justify driving the white man out and conquering Asia for Japan. During the war, this cultural attitude helped to sanction the mass rape of Korean women by the Japanese officer corps, the use of biological weapons on civilian populations in China and on European and American prisoners of war. The Japanese high command boasted that the Rangoon to Burma railway (the subject of the immortal Hollywood film *The Bridge on the River Kwai*) would be built on the backs of the white man. Unfortunately, the Hollywood epic grossly underrepresented the cruelty that the Japanese inflicted on their allied prisoners, and thousands of captured British and Americans died in the work camps to build that railway.[2]

There is evidence that some factions of Japanese culture and political leadership have not changed their views of race. This can still be seen in the lack of official acknowledgment of ethnic minorities such as Koreans and the Ainu still living in Japan. Another example of this kind of thinking appeared in 1986 when Japanese Prime Minister Yasuhiro Nakasone told a meeting of his party in effect that the average IQ of Japan is higher than countries like the United States due to Japan's racial purity. He faulted the lower American IQ scores to the presence of blacks, Puerto Ricans, and Mexicans.[3]

There are many other examples of cultural differences superceding physical differences in the propagation of bigotry and prejudice. These include biblical stories of the Israelites and the

Philistines, the battles between Catholics and Protestants throughout European history, the caste system in India, and modern day warfare between the Tutsi and Hutus in Rwanda.

The genocide in Rwanda was socially constructed. The conflict between the Hutu and Tutsi is not the product of ancient tribal hatreds. The Hutu and Tutsi are not tribes. A tribe is a distinct community with its own language, customs, territory, and religion. In Rwanda and Burundi the Hutu and Tutsi share the same territory and speak the same languages. They also share the same customs, practice the same religion, and frequently intermarry. The majority Hutu (who are between 80 and 85 percent of the population in Rwanda and Burundi) and the minority Tutsi (between 12 and 15 percent in both countries) were created by social hierarchy.

Rwanda's Hutu migrated to the region, replacing the aboriginal Twa people and were well established by the time the Tutsi arrived in the 1400s. This early precolonial society was hierarchical, and the Tutsi became the ruling aristocracy. Ruling status was linked to the ownership of cattle, a common symbol of social distinction in East Africa. A Hutu was not allowed to own cattle unless given to him by a Tutsi overlord. For example, Hutu soldiers who served their Tutsi masters well in war were often rewarded with cattle. Wars in the region were frequent, but not between Tutsi and Hutu. They were similar to the wars of European feudalism, in that they were civil conflicts between high lineage Tutsis who were supported by their Hutu retainers or between different nations in the region.

European colonization of Rwanda began with Germany (from 1894 to 1916), followed by Belgium (from 1916 to 1962). Both Germany and Belgium chose to exercise their rule through Rwanda's existing social system of Tutsi aristocrats and Hutu peasantry.

The colonialists distinguished two races in Rwanda using physical appearances—the Tutsi were generally tall, thin, and supposedly more European in their appearance than the shorter, stockier Hutu. The Tutsi, due to their more European appearance, were deemed the master race and received preferential treatment. It is highly likely that the greater stature of the Tutsi resulted from their control of the cattle. Families with cattle probably had more milk for their children and ate more animal protein. Thus, in Rwanda, social control led to observable physical differences between the two groups. This is an example of how differences in social conditions between groups that are relatively genetically similar can still be the cause of large biological differences, such as in physical appearance, health, and predisposition to disease.

The Tutsi, because of their social dominance, actually led the anticolonial struggle in this region after World War II. This caused the colonialists to switch allegiance, now favoring the Hutus against the more rebellious Tutsi. Subsequent political changes in the region led to a situation by the early 1990s in which the Hutu-dominated government of Rwanda chose to enact a policy of genocide against the Tutsi. The total number of people killed has never been systematically assessed, but most experts believe the total was around eight hundred thousand people. This includes about seven hundred fifty thousand Tutsis and approximately fifty thousand politically moderate Hutus who did not support the atrocities against the minority Tutsi. Many of these killings were carried out by club and machete wielding mobs, and their victims often died horribly. Only about one hundred thirty thousand Tutsis survived the massacres.

The evolution theory of warfare states that one of the spoils of war is greater sexual access for the male winners to women. The war in Rwanda led to thousands of rapes, as did the ethnic cleansing in Bosnia-Herzegovena around the same time. There were also beatings, and psychological damage to those who witnessed but escaped the violence. Over one hundred thousand houses were torn down, businesses were looted, and other property destroyed. The war also destroyed intellectual infrastructure. Many of the country's most important citizens were killed or forced to flee, including its most experienced government workers, judges, lawyers, physicians, and other professionals. Rwanda still suffers from these effects in the form of a poor economy, a broken-down judicial system, and an inexperienced government. This tragedy occurred within a people who would be considered by most as members of the same race. While there were slight physical differences between the groups, they were culturally, linguistically, and religiously similar. Ultimately, race played no role in this conflict. Rather, it was like the Hutu revenge against the historical Tutsi control of resources. This is similar to the motives behind the conflicts in the Balkans, Northern Ireland, and the Middle East. In all these cases, coalitions of closely related and less closely related individuals join together in a battle over material resources, which in the end are ultimately reproductive resources.

Coalitions Can Be Altered and Racism Can Be Erased

Our ability and desire to seek group affiliation may be one of our evolutionary legacies, possibly even an unavoidable one for any social species. But, for the vast majority of human existence, group affiliation had nothing to do with what we call *race*. This means that how we identify group membership and allegiance, and how we act on it, might be quite fluid. For example, every individual belongs to several different groups in any given society. These include their socially constructed race, gender, age, language, social class, and religion. In any given conflict, membership in any of these groups might be most important in determining one's social consciousness and identity. Yet, in the Balkans, the Middle East, Northern Ireland, and in Rwanda, these modern-day conflicts are far more vicious and murderous than present-day American racism. Osama Bin Laden's Al Qaeda sees America as the great Satan not because of our physical features, but because we are not practitioners of Islamic fundamentalism and therefore challenge his social coalition for political and social leadership in the Middle East.

Any individual's consciousness can be changed or altered by

the nature of the particular social conflict they are engaged in. Someone might change their social allegiance or experience at different portions of their life, or by simply crossing national borders. For example, a French-Canadian man of African descent is, in Canada, most concerned with his French-Canadian identity. In the United States, he has to deal with discrimination as a person of African ancestry. Realignments of social identity and allegiance have been common in American history. Factory workers seeking union rights had to realign themselves during the battles in the coal mines and auto factories of the 1930s. The bosses used race and national origin to drive wedges among the workers to prevent unionization, but they failed. White American bomber crews, flying missions deep into Germany during World War II, learned to appreciate the flying skills of their Tuskegee Airmen escorts. Again, there was probably more black-white unity on the battlefields of Vietnam than at any previous time in American history. While it would be simplistic to think that all racism abated in these examples, individuals who survived them undoubtedly had to put their racism aside, at least for long enough to come out of them alive. Clearly, these examples show that conditions exist, even if extreme, that can force individuals to address and even alter their social allegiance. The Republican Party for example, the party of Lincoln and emancipation, capitulated to Southern Democrats to elect Rutherford B. Hayes president in 1876. In doing so, it broke its coalitional allegiance with freed African-Americans to reforge a bond with southern Euro-Americans. Indeed blood is thicker than water, for a few years before they were killing each other in the hundreds of thousands. Around the same time African Americans forged an alliance with Euro-Americans to deprive the American Indians of their sovereignty in the West. Earlier, some American Indians had held African-American slaves. In the late 1950s, leading Republicans like Richard Nixon had better civil rights records and programs than Democrats like John F. Kennedy. After the election of 1960, the Republicans simply conceded the African-American vote to the Democrats. Democrats, unfortunately, now all want to be Republicans, and neither party wants to seriously address civil rights.

We have also seen that researchers could change the coalitional allegiance of individuals experimentally. This happened very rapidly in the experiment. However, we do not know how long the effect of the experiment lasted on the subjects. Did they learn that racism was wrong? Did they realize that their ancient machinery to gage coalitional allegiance was shaping their social activity? Will the students be more likely to choose social coalitions on nonracial traits in the future? Both experimental results and historical experience suggest that other social forces can alter the expression of racist behavior. This is hopeful. However, so long as genetic ancestry is conflated with social or coalitional allegiance, America will never find its way out of its racial quandary.

CHAPTER 4

Jungle Fever: Race, Sexuality, and Marriage

Interracial love, sex, and marriage still gnaw at the American psyche. It is a contradiction we just don't want to face. It stands to reason that life, liberty, and the pursuit of happiness includes the freedom of whom to love or marry without interference from the state. Yet, in what many call the greatest democracy in the world, we have never truly enjoyed that freedom. Even though all official prohibitions against interracial marriage fell in the early 1970s there still is great societal pressure enforcing the idea that marriage should be within one's own race to preserve its purity. The denial of this fundamental freedom is yet another sordid legacy of the social construction of race.

Few people realize how twentieth century America was dominated by this contradiction. Interracial sex arose prominently during the controversy concerning the integration of Little Rock Central High School in 1959. A pamphlet directed to the school board asked several questions. The questions concerned the following:

1. Will the Negro boys and girls be allowed to attend the school dances? If so, will the Negro boys be allowed to solicit white girls for dances?
2. Will the Negro girls be allowed to shower with the white girls?

3. Will the Negro boys and girls be allowed to join the school clubs? If so, will they be allowed to take out of town trips and stay in the same facilities?

4. Because of the high venereal disease rate amongst Negroes will white children be forced to use the same toilet facilities?

5. In the dramatic classes if the script called for the reenactment of romantic scenes will the parts be assigned to Negro boys and girls without regard to race or color?

These questions clearly demonstrate the white fear of miscegenation in the service of segregation. In 1967, director Stanley Kramer took on the theme of interracial marriage in *Guess Who's Coming to Dinner*. The film featured Hollywood immortals Katharine Hepburn (who won an Academy Award for her role as the mother of a young woman seeking to marry a Negro), Spencer Tracy (in the last film of his life, as the father), and Sidney Poitier (as the Negro fiancé Dr. John Prentice). The plot was written in a way that only a true bigot could object to their marriage. Poitier is a handsome, successful young doctor working to set up hospitals for the underserved in Africa. What parents wouldn't want their daughter to marry such a man? The drama in this movie results from the problem that he is not white.

Twenty-four years later, in 1991, *Jungle Fever*, directed by Spike Lee, took a somewhat more realistic and cynical look at interracial relationships and how Americans respond to them. Wesley Snipes stars as a black architect (Flipper Purify). He becomes attracted to Angie Tucci (Annabella Sciorra), a white temporary worker in his office. Tucci, who comes from a working class Italian neighborhood, responds in kind. Their brief affair causes many problems. Angie's father beats her when he hears of the affair, while her jealous boyfriend suffers racist taunts from his friends. Purify is thrown out of his house by his wife, who is doubly hurt by her husband's infidelity because it was with a white woman. Spike Lee's award-winning film tells us that, despite the appearance of modern social liberalism, we still haven't gotten very far past our racialized views of dating and marriage.

In January 2003, President George Bush, Jr. nominated Charles Pickering for U.S. Court of Appeals for the Fifth Circuit. Pickering immediately came under fire because it was suspected that he was soft on upholding civil rights. As evidence his critics pointed to an article he wrote forty years ago in a law review suggesting ways to make the Mississippi law banning interracial marriage constitutional. Pickering undoubtedly thought he was doing the right thing at the time. After all, the segregationists' chief argument against school integration was the fear of interracial sex. Noted eugenicists at the time were arguing that America's greatest danger was the untrammeled reproduction of the genetically inferior races and the potential that they might dilute the superior white race by intermarriage or, more likely, through rape of the white female.

More evidence of how America views interracial marriage comes from how differently African and European Americans responded to the O.J. Simpson murder trial. On the face of it, the trial revolved around the accusation that Simpson murdered his ex-wife Nicole Brown Simpson and her companion, Ronald Goldman. The prosecution presented its case, a celebrity former husband, evidence of previous spousal abuse, and powerful physical evidence placing Simpson at the scene of the murder. However, as opposed to the Rodney King assault trial, this evidence was presented to a disproportionately African-American jury in Los Angeles. Prosecution DNA expert Bruce Weir claimed that the blood found at the crime scene had a less than a one in 3,900 chance of not coming from O.J. Simpson. The defense countered by shedding doubt on the prosecution timeline, proving that the statistical calculations used to evaluate the DNA evidence were incorrect, that it actually was a one in 1,600 chance, introducing the idea that the blood evidence was tampered with by Mark Fuhrman, an L.A. police department officer accused of both racism and brutality, and, finally, that the bloody gloves found at the scene of the crime did not fit Simpson's hands. In summation defense attorney Johnny Cochran issued the immortal line: "If the gloves don't fit, you must acquit!" Mr. Simpson was found innocent in the criminal trial, but was found responsible for Nicole Brown Simpson's and Ron Goldman's deaths in a civil action by the victims' families. The burden of proof required in the civil proceeding was the balance of the evidence, not the reasonable doubt required in the criminal trial.

However, was the burden of proof really at issue in the African- and European-American responses to what was called the trial of the century? Everyone had an opinion on this case. The media focus on this trial was unparalleled and for months it was standard conversation at the workplace and at social gatherings. What was so different about the Simpson case that kept it squarely in the minds of the public? Unfortunately, in America, husbands routinely murder their ex- and present wives. Also there have been an abundance of high-profile celebrity cases. Claus von Bulow, a wealthy Euro-American man was accused of murdering his wife in 1984. Yet this equally sordid affair did not garner nearly the same attention as the Simpson case. The recent murder of Bonnie Lee Bakley and the accusation of her husband, actor Robert Blake, pales by comparison to the Simpson case.

This is because in America our perception of crime and our dispensing of justice depends upon the social identity of the alleged perpetrator and the victim. This is particularly true with regard to sex crimes. Sex crimes committed against white women are more likely to be prosecuted than the same crimes against nonwhite women. If the accused is a nonwhite male then the retribution is more swift and violent. A series of studies over the last two decades has shown that black men who were accused of sexually assaulting white women were charged with more serious offenses than any other race-of-victim/race-of-perpetrator combinations. The least severe sanctions came against black men accused of sexually assaulting black women.

It was also found that sexual assaults against black women were treated the least severely, and that the pattern of race-of-victim/race-of-perpetrator severity did not hold for other felonies such as robbery or assault.[1] Why?

The reason for this is simple. Socially constructed race was invented in a social system that identified precisely who was privileged and who was not. Privileged individuals enjoyed all the fruits of the social acquisition of wealth, including a police and legal system biased to their needs. Conversely, the nonprivileged people produced the social wealth, were expropriated of it, and were controlled and victimized by the police and legal system. All material wealth eventually becomes physical health and emotional well being, and in turn contributes to reproductive wealth. This means that, in all previously existing social hierarchies, privileged males gained greater sexual access to the bodies of both the privileged and the underprivileged either through naked force or social coercion. America began with all the privileged people being of European descent. Under these conditions, social-coalitional allegiance was determined by physical appearance. Everyone in colonial America served the white male masters in a variety of ways. The African slaves, American Indians, and European indentured servants served with their labor, or military alliance, and with their bodies for the master's sexual gratification. A few hundred years later, Chinese and other immigrants would lend their labor to build America's railroads, and their women would be put to work in the white man's brothels. Until the latter portion of the twentieth century, American society belonged to the "white" man, in every sense of the word. Despite all the deranged cries of the white supremacists, there is no attack on the democratic rights of the white male going on today. What we are witnessing instead is backlash against nonwhites because some whites are being forced to relinquish some of their social domination and privilege in favor of greater democracy and inclusion of nonwhites into the American mainstream.

*   *   *

The state of white male sexual privilege created contradictions that the ruling elite had to contend with, for heterosexual activity creates offspring. These offspring were half European and half other. How would they be dealt with? What would happen if, by virtue of their ancestry, they attempted to claim the rights of their fathers? How would the wives and offspring of their legitimate marriages deal with their half kin? The solution was simply to classify them as nonwhite and thereby deny them the rights of their fathers. The master had property rights to his female slaves, squaws, or China dolls. This was not rape, and their children were not his but hers. And as hers, they were "other." To legitimize this state of affairs a social mythology was created to blame the victims of this oppression for their own wretched state. They were temptresses, whores, and harlots. White men could not be blamed for succumbing to their wiles; their seductiveness was part of their subhuman, animal natures.

In contradistinction to the white male's morality was the depravity of nonwhite men. European males had manufactured the sexual bestiality of the African from at least the seventeenth century. Richard Jobson wrote while traveling in Gambia in 1623 that the Mandingo tribesmen he met there were "furnisht with members so huge as to be burdensome." The English physician Charles White wrote in 1799 that the penis of an African is larger than a European had been shown in every anatomical school in London. To the European mind, the larger sexual apparatus of the African was proof positive of his bestial sexual nature. Therefore all conceivable steps had to be taken to protect the white woman from these animals. The rules also had the effect of keeping the ruling elite white by protecting it from the incursion of foreign racial seed. The social customs and conventions developed to legitimate the purity of the white race were simple: Other races were inferior, race mixing produced inferior progeny, nonwhites were lecherous and degenerate, nonwhite males lusted after white women, and nonwhites carried diseases that would pollute the white race. Conversely, the white race was superior, pure race offspring were healthier, white women were repulsed by nonwhite men, and whites were morally superior.

While nonwhite women were portrayed as sexual beasts, the white woman was placed on a pedestal of virtue. Her beauty guaranteed that she would be desired by all men, including the degenerate nonwhite brutes that stalked the earth. European men fought to protect and control the womanhood of Europe. For virtually all of America's history the sexual rules were enforced under the power of law and the lynch rope. The civil rights movement ended the power of law but lynching would remake itself in the guise of the criminal justice system.

O.J. and Nicole Brown Simpson brought to the surface all those American stereotypes of sex and race. O.J. had risen from obscurity to become an American hero, first in sports, then in films. He had made a point to distance himself from African-American issues as his film career and celebrity advanced. There were those who argued that he only regained his African-American identity once he was accused of murder and was fighting for his life. The prosecution presented evidence that Simpson was a spousal abuser. His jealousy toward Nicole intensified after their breakup. He was presented as a frequenter of white women. Conversely, elements in the media attempted to paint Nicole Brown Simpson as a loose woman, a woman with *jungle fever,* purporting a possible affair with Raider Marcus Allen. Middle-aged African-American women interviewed by the defense team before the trial began deeply resented her—particularly the fact that she had been living such a lavish life with a black man's money. L.A. police officer Mark Fuhrman supposedly discussed her breast enlargements with other officers. Questions were raised as to why Ronald Goldman needed to make a special trip to her house late at night to return her sunglasses.

The verdict reminded us of how immense the divide is between black and white America. The defense team knew this going into the trial. Their focus-group interviews had broken down directly along racial lines. On the day the verdict was issued, the L.A. media showed images of African Americans shrieking for joy, while European Americans expressed horror and disbelief. The shock on the white faces reflected their disbelief that a jury could acquit Simpson, despite what they saw as overwhelming evidence of his guilt. They could not grasp the irony of this situation. They did not realize that they were experiencing the rage and frustration that African Americans had always experienced at the hands of the criminal justice system. They had forgotten that just two years ago an all-white jury in Simi Valley, California, had acquitted policemen who were shown, on videotape, beating Rodney King. While many had understood that race was a key factor in determining one's guilt or innocence, they never had known what it was like to be on the other end of the racial equation. For them, it seems that the world had been turned on its head. If they had Simpson at hand, they would have taught him what he should have already known. He should have known that as a black man, he would never get away with violating a white female's innocence, physically, and emotionally abusing her and finally depriving her of her life.

America had always dealt with such transgressions severely. Data from capital murder cases show that blacks convicted of killing whites are twice as likely to face the death penalty compared to whites killing whites, whites killing blacks, or blacks killing blacks. Euro-American faces after the Simpson verdict showed what many were thinking. They wanted a return to the good old days before desegregation, when black men knew their place, and American social life revolved around the sanctity of the white woman. In those days, accusation was enough. In such cases, black men would be hunted down with all the power the state and the white community could bring to muster. Many never saw a trial, murdered at the hands of white mobs enacting vigilante justice. The most graphic images we have of American racial violence involve lynching, and lynching was linked to retribution against black males for violating white womanhood. It made little difference what the actual offense was, a sure way of dispatching a Negro was to accuse him of eyeing, sassing, or touching a white woman. Things haven't changed much since then. African-American men accused by white women of any sexually related transgression are still more likely to face dismissal, punishment, or imprisonment than white men accused of the same acts. In 1939, Lewis Allen wrote, and Billie Holliday sang, of the lynching of the black male in America. The song described Southern trees that bore a strange fruit, with blood on the leaves and blood at the root. This imagery conjured up the image of an African-American man, brutally murdered and hanging from a lynching tree.

Lynching became an American institution; we don't have accurate numbers of how many lost their lives to white vigilante justice. In 1890, Ida Wells Barnett, an antilynching crusader, estimated that 10,000 African Americans had been lynched since the civil war. She also showed that, in the vast majority of cases, the charge of raping a white woman was untrue. Furthermore, that the charge had been added after the fact to incense the white crowd, or to cover up the fact that the man's real sin had been to have consensual sex with a white woman.

In cases in which the state did bring the accused to trial, it was not uncommon for black men to receive death sentences if they were convicted (and they always were) of raping a white woman. One of the most infamous examples of this injustice was the case of the Scottsboro Boys. On March 9, 1931, nine young African Americans were arrested in Scottsboro, Alabama, for the alleged rape of two white girls. The evidence against them consisted mainly of the testimony of the girls involved. Despite the fact that, within a month, one of the girls recanted, eight of the accused were sentenced to death and the ninth, only thirteen years old, to life imprisonment. The claims against the boys were so outrageous that many Americans, including prominent lawyers, such as Clarence Darrow, came to their aid. The case of the Scottsboro boys garnered international attention. In the next six years of appeals and retrials, the U.S. Supreme Court declared two mistrials. Finally, five of the original indictments were dropped. The remaining four men received long prison terms. The Alabama prosecution regarded Heywood Patterson as the leader of the group, and sentenced him to seventy-five years. By 1946, all of the Scottsboro boys were paroled except Patterson. Two years later, he escaped to Michigan, where the state government refused to extradite him to Alabama. In light of this example, we should consider that no white man in the history of America has ever faced or received the death sentence for raping a black woman.

The asymmetry of these facts suggests that sexual behavior brings out the most violent responses of the oppressive race caste system in America against its subordinates. Researchers concerned with the structure of social domination have proposed theories and collected data to explain why and how this happens. Sociologists Jim Sidanius, Shana Levin, and Felicia Pratto proposed the following rules of social domination.

1. When society's laws are violated, the expected level of negative sanction directed against members of subordinate groups will be greater than the expected level of negative sanction directed against members of dominate groups.
2. When members of subordinate groups are accused of acts of violence against members of high-status groups, the accused faces a particularly high risk of being found guilty and of suffering particularly severe punishment. This is called the *out-of-place* principle.
3. The level of social dominance orientation among hierarchy enhancing people of the criminal justice system will be relatively high, whereas the level of social dominance orientation among hierarchy attenuating people of the criminal justice system will be relatively low.
4. The degree of negative sanctions against the security forces for abuses of power will tend to be exceedingly small, espe-

cially in cases of abuse against members of socially subordinate groups.

5. The greater degree of social hierarchy, the greater the use of terror will be.

The data supporting their hypotheses was drawn heavily from the experiences of African Americans.[2] Why should this be so? European-American males display violence and have institutionalized terror against African-American and other nonwhite males because of the link between human heterosexual behavior and social structure.

Sex Is Fundamental

Reproduction is a necessary attribute of all organisms. In the absence of this process, life as we know it could not exist. Even if we could engineer an organism that was immune to biological death, it would still need to reproduce, or it would certainly become extinct. Over a long period of time, all such organisms would succumb to accidental deaths. In actuality, nature is far from benign, and biological causes of death are abundant. For this reason, natural selection has always focused on features that enhanced reproduction. Sex evolved very early in the history of life, possibly to diversify the genotypes that can be produced in any given species. Whatever the reason, sex worked so well that in the modern world sexual reproduction occurs in the vast majority of organisms. In biology, sex simply refers to the uniting of genetic material from different individuals to produce offspring that are genetically different from either parent. Generally, organisms that produce eggs are female, and those that produce sperm are considered male. Some species exchange genetic material between individuals of identical sex, yet many others have evolved separate male and female sexes and are called sexually *dimorphic* (two forms). Sexually dimorphic species may be able to switch sexes (remember *Jurassic Park?*), or can be born as one sex and remain that way for life. In species that can switch sex, social cues play a primary role in determining which individuals will become male or female. In some reef fishes, if the dominant male is killed, the socially dominant female will change sexes and become male. In other species, cues to sex ratio may determine which individuals become a given sex. In opposition to the creation story found in Genesis, in this sense, all living things were first female, and males were derived (taken from Eve's rib, as it were). Even in human biology, every male begins life as a female, until the gene products from the testes determining factor (tdf) found on the Y chromosome channel development to produce a male.

Sexual reproduction has taken on different levels of prominence in evolution. Most of the organisms we see and are familiar with display obligate sexual reproduction, with organisms that are definitely male or female. The characteristic that most clearly defines the class *Mammalia* is the presence of mammary glands in females that produce milk for their young. Certainly, the behavioral features of primates have been strongly influenced by their obligate sexual reproduction. This means that the choices that females and males made to increase their evolutionary fitness profoundly influenced both the physical and mental adaptations of all primates, including our species. Much of the evolution of our societies has been and still is driven by our sexual behavior. If you're still unconvinced, Madison Avenue is convinced enough for you. Simply turn on the television during prime time and examine the main themes found in advertising. Herbal Essences commercials say to women that if you shampoo your hair with their product your sexual pleasure will increase and the man of your dreams will fall on his knees before you. The Miller Lite catfight commercial begins with two supermodels debating the virtues of Miller Lite beer: "Tastes great, less filling!" This is followed by a wild tussle that includes both falling into water, wrestling each other's clothes off, and finally falling into a trough of cement. A male in the spot summarizes the ad's effectiveness: "Now, what guy wouldn't watch that!"

Even the wildly popular *Tonight Show* host, Jay Leno, jokes frequently that men are attracted to women with large breasts and women are attracted to men with lots of money. In fact, without human sexual behavior most comedians (Rodney Dangerfield, Eddie Murphy, Chris Rock, Margaret Cho, and Dave Chappelle) wouldn't have any material! These examples of popular culture are effective because they tap into the deeply ingrained sexual mate choice behaviors that made us humans and are very much still with us.

Human mate preferences result from sexual selection. For sexual selection to operate in any species there must be variation in traits desirable to the other sex, the variation must be heritable, and mates must choose the traits that lead to greater reproductive success in those that carry them. Long- and short-term mate preferences in our species would have evolved hundreds of thousands, if not millions, of years ago. They have been modified in form, but not in essence, by human cultural evolution.

Human females needed to solve some key adaptive problems in choosing a mate. Women needed to be able to gauge both the present and future potential of men. Sexual selection favored women who could choose men who possessed attributes that conferred fitness benefits, such as physical prowess, athletic skill, industriousness, kindness, empathy, emotional stability, intelligence, social skills, sense of humor, kin network, and social status, and disliked men who imposed fitness costs, such as having children already, bad debts, bad temper, selfish disposition, and promiscuous proclivities. Women needed to access these characteristics accurately, particularly if men were able to deceive women. Appendix 4 illustrates the adaptive problems faced by females and how a mate preference might have solved them. Males faced different problems from females. Females, as the choosers in the human species, become the limiting sex. Also, because female fertility occurs over a fraction of the female lifespan, men must be concerned with accurate indicators of a female's fertility, often relying on youth, beauty, body fat, commitment cues, kin networks, and other variables (Appendix 5).

Adaptation, Aggression, and Sexual Selection

Aggression in animal behavior evolved as a way to solve certain adaptive problems. For example, every animal species engages in some form of aggression to find food, defend itself, or to acquire mates. Some species are known for mating aggression, such as sheep, elephant seals, and gorillas. Indeed, even species that are commonly thought of as peaceful are aggressive in mating, including the capture of females by male dolphins, and the raiding and warfare carried out by chimpanzee bands against other males to capture females.

There is evidence that much of the basic structure and context of human social organization may have been already fixed in the ancestor of all modern day primates. Studies of the primates most closely related to us (gorillas, bonobos, and chimpanzees) show that their social structures have several common elements. These include the existence of social networks, lone males, females dispersing to mate in other groups, interaction quality, males as the parties of outgroup hostility, stalk/attacking outsiders, and territorial defense. *Social networks* refers to the organization of groups into families, subsistence groups, and tribes. *Subsistence groups* are made up of relatives and nonrelatives that work together for survival purposes. *Tribes* are composed of several smaller subsistence groups. *Lone males* refers to whether males travel alone, a potentially dangerous activity since there is risk of violence at the hands of hostile male groups. In all four species, females leave the subsistence group they are raised in to mate in another group (this is true in human hunter-gatherer societies). Interaction quality refers to the range of hostility that males in a group show toward outsiders, usually to protect members in the group from attack, capture, or the loss of scarce resources. The hostility can range from physical assault to lethal attacks. Males in all four species engage in stalking and attacking outsider males and in territorial defense. Females do not engage in territorial defense, since they are often immigrants to new groups.

The evolutionary heritage of human behavior entered upon a new context once we began to accumulate surplus agricultural production. This technological feat accelerated the development of the oppressive characteristics of our societies. There was little reason to incite warfare against neighboring tribes if all tribes were living at subsistence level. Any spoils you might recover would not recoup the energy expended in the war. It could be argued that males might have incited wars to kidnap females. However, observations of modern hunter-gatherers such as the Yanamamo indicate that these conflicts often escalate out of control, and yield no net gain in females transferred between each group.

Once surpluses are created it is possible to now steal what one cannot produce alone. Furthermore, if stable villages and cities exist it becomes conceivable to reduce some outgroup members to servitude. This produces greater sustenance that also makes your group stronger and larger. Male slaveholders also get greater sexual access to their female slaves. The ancient Mesopotamians, Indians, and Chinese developed slavery very early in their history. Slaves played indispensable roles in large-scale construction or agriculture. The ancient Egyptians, Hebrews, Aztecs, Inca, and Maya used slaves on a mass scale to build the royal palaces and monuments. Some cultures allowed their laws to free slaves of their own nationality under special conditions. What is clear is that slavery in the ancient world resulted from conquest of an outgroup, punishment for a crime, payment of debt, but never was associated with biological features remotely related to race. Slavery in the ancient world was a social construction just as real and brutal as modern racist chattel slavery and modern racism.

Finally, surplus food allowed individuals the time to specialize in warfare and to develop the technology of warfare. More skilled soldiers with better weapons became the means by which to acquire more territory and slaves. The first class societies consisted of rulers or big men, priests, warriors, merchants, artisans, farmers, and slaves. Women were rarely rulers, priests, or warriors.

They were most often merchants, artisans, farmers, and slaves. The formation of classes with the invention of surplus agricultural production was a new context for social dominance. Evolutionary theory would predict that males would use class structure to increase their individual and inclusive fitness.

The evolutionary prediction can be seen most clearly in the behavior of despots in ancient societies. Men of high social status often had several wives, concubines, and mistresses. Even Abraham was allowed to have his wife's handmaiden to bear a son. Ramses the Great (II), reputed to be the pharaoh of the Exodus, had over six hundred wives, and additional concubines. Roman society depended on the exploitation of slave labor to increase the wealth and well-being of the patrician class. The empire used its army to seize the resources of weaker nations, either directly or through taxation. Roman slaves were drawn from all these conquered nations, and had no relationship to racial identity. It also gave high-status men unfettered sexual access to slaves (females and males). Also, noblewomen could use their influence to have slave men for their sexual gratification. American chattel slavery operated in a similar fashion, except that physical differences, race, was used to mark the slave class. It also allowed high status Euro-American men unchecked sexual access to their female slaves, yet drastically punished the reverse. Slave codes described the rape of a female slave as a "crime against the master's property." This practice in American slavery was so widespread that it resulted in 10 to 17 percent of the genes in people described as African American originating in Europeans.

It is still true that men of higher social status marry more desirable women and also desire and achieve more extramarital affairs then men of lower status. This is generally not true for women. High-status women marry more desirable men, but do not have more extramarital affairs than low-status women. This has even been shown in the lives of American politicians (Thomas Jefferson, John F. Kennedy, William Jefferson Clinton). The pattern of social status and greater access to sexual opportunities has been validated crossculturally.

Evolutionary theory also predicts that there are a number of ways that individuals can increase their reproductive success. Males should be competitive because male fitness is limited by access to females. Males should compete among themselves over opportunities to mate. Conversely, females should be choosy. Their fitness is not limited by the opportunity to mate, however any given mating entails a substantial commitment by the female to a large investment in the offspring. This means that females will be selective about with whom they mate. One of the most important traits that human females choose in a long-term mate partner is access to material resources. So, males who control wealth are more likely to win the woman they desire. An extension of this thinking also predicts that males may attempt to institute social dominance over females to curtail their reproductive choices. We have seen this throughout history and unfortunately this still continues. The degree that human females have reproductive choices is directly tied to their economic independence. There are extreme differences in this, from the situation in Scandinavian countries where women have strong political rights, economic independence, and state-supported child care to some northern African and Middle Eastern countries, where women have no political rights, are relegated to domestic work, and their sexuality is controlled by genital mutilation.

Male competition will be manifested in different ways, in species where males can monopolize access to females, then we should see intrasexual selection, that is, males directly fighting other males. In species where males cannot monopolize access and females choose between advertisers, we will see intersexual selection. The key aspect of this system will be female choice, so males compete against each other (sort of like the interactions we remember between Bluto, Popeye, and Olive Oyl). Human social structure results from both intersexual and intrasexual selection.

Males in our species exhibit adaptations such as sperm competition, variations in the volume of ejaculate, and killer sperm. Killer sperm are sperm cells that cannot fertilize eggs but instead attack other men's sperm, thus protecting a mate's vaginal tract from fertilization by another man. The existence of killer sperm is strong evidence for both male competition and female promiscuity.

Males inflict costs on intrasexual rivals. Individual males may bully, derogate, and use violence against same-sex rivals. We also see human males forming aggressive coalitions to co-opt the resources of others and steal or rape their reproductive-aged women (throughout human history and in modern-day Yanomamo). Social dominance hierarchies can also achieve this end for groups of high status males. High-status males use their status to marry desirable women, to have short-term liaisons with lower-status women, and also to prevent access to higher-status women by lower-status men. Social dominance allows this to be achieved under code of law and by vigilantism if required. Psychological experiments show that dominant males may want to punish subordinate males who compete with them for females they desire. In one experiment, dating from the early seventies, white male students were placed in a situation where they could cheat at a task to prevent pain being inflicted on a test "victim." The white male test subjects were allowed to observe the person before they are shocked and to determine the "race" of their girlfriends. The test victims fell into four groups, white males, white males with black girlfriends, black males, and black males with white girlfriends. The white male test subjects were upper middle class, with liberal political leanings, from southern California. The results show that black males with white girlfriends received the most shocks, followed by black males, followed by white males. The group that received the least shocks was white males with black girlfriends. This last result proves that the students were not just allowing pain to be inflicted due to their abhorrence to interracial dating, but rather due to their feeling of sexual threat from the black males with white girlfriends! A followup questionnaire was used to rate the sexual security of those males who allowed shocks to be administered in this experiment. The survey found that a significantly higher percentage of males with low sexual esteem administered shocks at a lower threat level than high-sexual-esteem males. This study could not show how much of a male's sexual esteem relates to his social position; however, other studies validate that higher status social status males tend to be more confident. This would explain why lower socioeconomic status white males were involved in much of America's racially motivated violence.

Feudal Europe clearly illustrates how social dominance influences reproductive success in humans. Loose political unions characterized feudalism. Aristocrats maintained their position by oaths of fealty and acts of homage from their followers. This was primarily a military system with the nobility ruthlessly exploiting the peasantry. Nobility was a right of birth and in post-Roman Germanic society the aristocracy consisted of a limited number of families, distinguished by descent or deeds. Eventually, these families would become landed through gifts of land from a king. Later, in the medieval period, commoners could be given title for some outstanding service to the noble class. This practice was actually quite rare, and noble families married into other noble families. Women and their offspring took on the names of their husbands.

Feudalism allowed the enrichment of a small subset of families at the expense of the vast majority of families. The seizure of the social produce of the peasantry increased the health and emotional well-being of the noble class, while simultaneously degrading those traits in the peasantry. In humans, material wealth ultimately is translated into reproductive fitness so, initially, the nobility would have displayed higher average fitness than the peasantry. In ninth century England, the nobles justified their right to do this by providing military protection for the peasants from violent raiders such as the Vikings. The Vikings adopted this raiding lifestyle, because their own soils were too barren to support large-scale agriculture. Their culture glorified warfare, gave entry into heaven to only the brave, and instituted a reign of terror over western Europe that lasted for several centuries.

This reproductive system over the course of seven hundred years or about forty human generations would have allowed the gene frequencies of the European nobility to become slightly different from the peasantry. This would happen simply because the genes of the noble families, who were a very small group, could not have represented the entire genetic diversity of Europe. Furthermore, these families intermarried exclusively over this period, leading to an increase in homozygosity in the royal family lines. *Homozygosity* means an individual inherited the same genes for a given trait from both their mother and father. Genetic studies validate this and show that the royal families accumulated rare genetic defects over the course of centuries. For example, King George III and others in his family suffered from porphyria. This disease causes urine to appear blue, hence the origin of the term *blue blood* to describe royalty. Later on, the hemophilia mutation that was passed to the young Tsar Alexander Romanov came directly from Queen Victoria of England. This means that a system that first enhanced the reproductive fitness of the noble classes broke down due to the practice of intermarriage among the noble families.

We could have also followed the genetic contributions of the European nobility by tracing the inheritance of Y-chromosomes. In theory, all the royal males should have had Y-chromosomes that originated from royal fathers. Sometimes this did not happen and a commoner might have fathered a noblewoman's son, but we should not expect that this happened too often. On the other hand, many royal Y's would have ended up in the peasantry due to the practice of nobles having their way with the common women.

The differences in nutrition and conditions of life probably meant that observable physical differences existed between the two classes. It is likely that a medieval intelligence test would have proven the nobility to have a greater average IQ than the peasants.

So, one group's superior social conditions, won by military force, gave it greater health and reproduction, provided it greater material wealth, while simultaneously producing observable physical differences between it and another group that differed slightly in gene frequencies. Noble males also had the pick of noblewomen based on their family's wealth and political power, while having their way with common women. The analogy between the medieval European noble class (the exploiters) and its peasantry (the exploited) can explain what we see today in American society (although not on the same scale).

In modern-day America, our social conditions and past mating practices have continued to produce a dominant social group. Americans whose ancestry is primarily European have greater health and psychological well-being, (although presently not greater average reproduction), greater material wealth, differences in physical appearance, and slight differences in overall gene frequencies compared to Americans whose ancestry is primarily African, Hispanic, and American Indian. The trick is that medical scientists (who are mainly of European origin) continue to operate as if the differences in psychological and physical health we observe in America that favor Europeans are the result of their superior genes. They steadfastly refuse to explain to the public why this is really not the case, but instead the result of their historical domination of the society.

Evidence that white male social hierarchy in America is harming black males can be seen from census data. Americans have recently been made aware of health disparities that plague minority populations. The social dominance system in America is largely responsible for those health disparities. When it comes to African Americans however, the system is not gender blind. It disproportionately strikes men. Comparing the male–female sex ratio for African Americans and European Americans revealed striking disparities. In humans, more males are conceived than females due to the lighter male sperm, however, females survive better than men, so we expect more females than men (97–99 men per 100 females). The male–female sex ratios for European Americans was between 103 to 96 men per 100 women and, for African Americans, 100 to 88 per 100 females between 1830 to 2000. Appendix 6 shows this disparity. Whites have maintained a higher percentage of males in their population over the last 180 years. These results have profound implications. First, they say that the American social system's bias against African-American males had real effects on their survival relative to European American males. It also means that, since males are the primary wage earners, that the African-American community is at a disadvantage simply due to the fewer number of males, let alone the fact that the average African-American male still makes only 81 percent of a European American male's income. Furthermore, in a racialized marriage market, African-American females face a higher probability that they will not find a suitable male to marry. Recently, *Newsweek* ran a cover story concerning the difficulty professional African-American women have finding suitable African-American husbands. The article did not bother to investigate or suggest that white male social dominance was at the root of the skewed sex ratios. This problem, while subtle, has multiple and complex effects on the African-American community. Most of those effects are negative especially given the role that males play in American society.

Modern racist behavior is tied to adaptations linked to the evolution of social hierarchies in the human species. Social hierarchies require various forms of aggression to maintain them. Aggressive behavior in the human social context allowed human males to co-opt the resources of others, defend themselves against attack, inflict costs on intrasexual rivals, negotiate status and power hierarchies, deter rivals from aggression, and deter long-term mates from sexual infidelity. We can see all these factors in operation today in the American social system.

However, let's be clear on this point. Recognizing the origins of this behavior does not excuse or defend it. The racial/sexual system of the United States was and still is inhumane and brutal. It has condemned thousands, if not millions, of people to tortured and unfulfilled lives. Its continuance is a powerful danger to our democracy and the security of our nation. These behaviors, remnants of our evolutionary legacy, are definitely maladaptive in our modern world; just like craving sweets when we no longer live a hunter-gatherer life. Fortunately, other byproducts of our past evolution, our intellect, our capacity for altruism, and our capacity for morality, allows us to evaluate which behaviors are no longer useful or now harmful. By understanding the origins of racism, we can confront it as rational beings, design social safeguards that curtail and discourage it and thereby dismantle it forever.

How Does Racialized Sexual Oppression Operate in Modern America?

American history illustrates this principle very well. Law and social convention placed the Euro-American female on a pedestal. High-status Euro-American men could vie for the most beautiful women of their race and, at the same time, also had access to lower status women (such as European indentured servants, African slaves, American Indians, and Chinese immigrants). Conversely, men of the lower social categories were violently denied access to high status white women. Ironically, in many instances, African, American Indian, and Chinese men were even denied access to white prostitutes. Modern patterns of marriage show that sexual social dominance is ongoing in American society.

Through it all I discerned one clear and certain truth: in the core of the heart of the American race problem the sex factor is rooted, rooted so deeply that it is not always recognized when it shows at the surface. Other factors are obvious and are the ones we deal with; but regardless of how we deal with these, the race situation will con-

tinue to be acute so long as the sex factor persists . . . It may be innate; I do not know. But I do know that it is strong and bitter . . .
——James Weldon Johnson, in *Along This Way*.

Johnson was correct in suspecting that American racism was closely linked to sexual domination. American patterns of marriage and reproduction have always reflected white male social dominance. It began with the use of American-Indian women by the Spaniards under Columbus for their sexual pleasure. Racial slavery in the French and English colonies also gave white men greater access to nonwhite women. Conversely, there was no greater crime than for nonwhite men to be in union with white women, consensual or not. The gravity of this particular crime can be traced to the particularly English view of the depravity of African sexuality. Europeans had engineered tales of the bestial nature of African sexuality, particularly males, since the sixteenth century. In 1623 Sir Francis Bacon described Africans as the "spirit of fornication." About 150 years later, the Englishman Edward Long wrote Africans were brutish, bestial, had a fetid smell, and inferior faculties of mind. He also wrote that their reproductive apparatus was primitive, yet clearly superior to that of whites. African women gave birth without pain, thus had escaped the curse on Eve, and therefore could not be human. Long suggested that African females mated so readily with their macrophallic men, that they sought even greater satisfaction with apes. Long wrote: "I do not think that an oran-outang husband would be any dishonor to an Hottentot female." Indeed there was no limit to the absurdities the white mind could generate about black sexuality. Tennessee clergyman Buckner Payne wrote the Negro had been created before Adam. Beliefs such as this allowed Charles Carroll to write in 1902 that it was a Negro-ape rather than a serpent that tempted Eve in the Garden of Eden. Carroll described the apple as a metaphor for a large black penis and that man's fall from grace was really caused by Eve's having sex with an animal.

The twentieth century began with the white man preoccupied with the fear of the black sexual animal:

> The southern woman with her helpless little children in a solitary farm house no longer sleeps secure . . . The black brute is lurking in the dark, a monstrous beast, crazed with lust. His ferocity is almost demoniacal. A mad bull or a tiger could scarcely be more brutal.
> ——George T. Winston, President of the University of North Carolina, 1901.

Lester Ward, called the Father of American Sociology, produced an academic theory to legitimate this view. He wrote of his four laws of race mixing:

1. Females of any race will freely accept the males of a race they regard as higher than their own.
2. Females of any race will vehemently reject the males of a race which they regard as lower than their own.
3. The males of any race will greatly prefer the females of a race that they regard as higher than their own.
4. The males of any race, in default of females of a higher race, will be content with women of a lower race.

Modern sociologists simply write off Ward's ideas as racist. But they actually make some sense, if we employ the evolutionary theory of human mating and substitute the concept of social status for that of race. The structure of female and male mate preferences (Appendices 4 and 5) explains the way Ward's rules operated in the racist context of early twentieth century American society. There is overwhelming evidence that human males primarily select females on signs of fertility and evidence of sexual loyalty. This has been shown in existing hunter-gatherer tribes and in modern societies around the globe. Additionally, there is a great deal of uniformity around the world for certain features that are correlated to reproductive fertility. Males uniformly prefer youth, physical beauty, and body proportions that indicate fertility. Remarkably, men find the same general traits, particularly facial symmetry, as attractive, without regard to the geographic origin of the face. These preferences indicate a deep evolutionary origin and thus genetic predisposition for them in our species.

Cultural evolution will affect how these preferences are manifested in any given society. In particular, standards of beauty may be influenced by the social structure. Thus, in America whiteness became beautiful because of its association with social stature. Yet, during chattel slavery and Jim Crow, while white men adhered to the official rhetoric testifying to the unparalleled beauty and desirability of the white woman, we know that, in practice, white males took sexual liberties with African, American Indian, Hispanic, and Asian women. Indeed this practice has been true throughout the entire history of despotism and slavery in the world. This occurred because the evolutionary legacy of mate choice mechanisms in our species collided with social convention. Do we really believe, as comedian Lenny Bruce once chimed, that Sheriff Bull Connor, if marooned for life on a desert island, would have preferred his old and unshapely wife to Lena Horne or Lola Falana? In the America of Jim Crow and hypodescent, white men were not free to publicly make a choice other than that dictated by social convention. Yet the evidence shows that throughout Jim Crow, white males consistently had greater access to black women than black men ever had to white women.

Ward's points 3 and 4 follow from the social construction of race in America. The highest-status males (coded by wealth and race) would have first choice at the most desirable women (coded by youth, beauty, and race). Evidence that whiteness once defined beauty can be shown by the color castes that developed within Jim Crow African-American society. High-status African-American males often had wives who were light-skinned. In African-Americans, we can show that light skin tone is correlated with the percentage of genes of European descent. Generations of this practice developed sons and daughters who were light skinned and the disproportionate representation of this group amongst the African-American elite caste. This skin-color caste system also developed in the Caribbean. These ideas of beauty held sway amongst African Americans until the emergence of Black Nationalism, starting with Marcus Garvey, through the black power and cultural nationalist movements of the 1960s. Black power called for pride in one's African heritage and thus also in one's African appearance. Black power was probably the biggest cultural event that changed the beauty standards sought by high-status African-American men, and thus displayed by the most desirable African-American women.

Ward's points 1 and 2 are explained by the premium that women place on acquiring financial resources for their future offspring. This is often translated through social status. The preference that women have for social status in a long-term mate is evidenced through all existing human cultures. We also see this preference in all closely related primate species, again indicating that this trait is genetically fixed in our lineage. Ironically, even women who are financially independent seek long-term male partners whose financial resources are greater than their own! In a racialized society, where social status was determined by your membership in the white race, very few high-status women would risk lowering their status by marrying a nonwhite man. The genetic programming of women would suggest that whenever possible they should seek a higher-status mate. This is consistent with modern data that show when white women marry black men, a disproportionate number of black-white marriages involve pairings between lower-status white women and higher-status black men.

The choices of high-status women were also constrained by the penalties exacted against women or their lovers who dared to stray outside social norms. In 1892 Texarkana, Arkansas, an unnamed white woman who loved black man Edward Coy was forced to implicate him and participate in his lynching. While, in another example, from Florence, South Carolina, a white woman's intercepted love letter led to the lynching of her black lover Ed. She escaped to the swamps and sought protection from the lynch mob in another town. Beyond the extreme penalty of lynching, white women who married outside of their race would be ostracized by their own community or labeled as mentally ill or sexually depraved.

Given that women marry to improve the fitness of their offspring, interracial marriage in a racially stratified society would not be a wise strategy for higher-status women. Their children would face alienation because they would no longer fit into the neatly defined social categories. Hypodescent does not work for white women with children fathered by nonwhite males. The children of interracial unions have been denigrated throughout our history and called mulattoes, half breeds, or mixed. Even in today's society these children are often forced to choose their racial allegiance. The multiethnic American movement developed out of this frustration. One of the movement's victories was the change in the 2000 census form that allowed individuals to check off multiple categories. However, the census bureau still analyzed the data by assigning any individuals who checked off black ancestry to the darker category. Hypodescent is still alive and well.

Ward's points 1 and 2 explain why Euro-American men routinely had sexual relations with African-American and Indian women during colonialism and slavery yet, at the same time, placed the white woman on a pedestal. But Ward confused long- and short-term mating in these points. Socially dominant males should seek the most highly desirous women for long-term mating (marriage). Yet, at the same time, their social dominance allows them access to other highly desirable women, and also women who do not meet their definition of attractiveness. During chattel slavery, white men proved their manhood by taking black women, but almost always married white women. Their wives understood that their husbands lived in a state of polygamy on the plantation, since their husbands would sire children from the slaves who could be identified by their physical resemblance to the master. To justify this state of affairs, slaveholders created the hypersexual black female and her alternative, the *mammy*. White men could not be blamed for their transgressions because the black women craved satisfaction constantly. The institution of the mammy was further created to free the white woman from the burdens of motherhood. In this way, the black woman satisfied the master's sexual desires, and also raised his children, both legitimate and not. The end of slavery gave greater protection for African-American women from the sexual assaults of Euro-American men. However, European-American men still actualized greater opportunities for sexual choice due to their social dominance. Nonwhite men who may have imagined such freedom were controlled by both their lower social standing and, if that failed, the power of the state or the lynch rope.

In 1944, Swedish sociologist Gunnar Myrdal wrote that Negroes and whites had the same concerns about integration, except that they were in reverse order. Whites listed:

1. intermarriage and sexual intercourse
2. social equality and etiquette
3. desegregation of public facilities, buses, churches
4. political enfranchisement
5. fair treatment in the courts
6. economic opportunities

African Americans listed interracial marriage as their least concern. They were more interested in economic and political opportunities, including fair treatment in the courts and the vote, along with the desegregation of public facilities. The fear of interracial sex and marriage was at the core of the segregationist argument against economic, political, and social equality for blacks in America. Again, the segregationists were correct, but for the wrong reasons. If males were given equal economic opportunities, then female choice would eventually no longer be based on socially constructed race. It would only be a matter of time, assuming no innate differences between the races preventing males from taking advantage of the equalized economic and political environment. So, if American racists were confident in their belief that members of the opposite sex between races naturally abhorred each other, they should never have been opposed to economic, political, and social equality. On an equal playing field, the races would have remained segregated and marriage would still have taken place within each racial group. The fact that the racists have fought so hard to maintain white social dominance structures is an indication that they don't believe their own propaganda. Instead they realize that maintenance of white male social dominance is their strongest method by which to prevent "race mixing."

Sociologists use a group's willingness to allow marriage to an outside group as a key variable in their calculation of social distance. Groups could be differentiated by nationality, religion, socioeconomic status, or socially defined race. The social distance scale, coined by Emory Bogardus in 1968, includes in rank order:

- Close kinship by marriage
- Membership in clubs as personal friends
- Living on my street as neighbors
- Employed in my occupation
- Citizenship in my country
- Visitors in my country
- Would exclude from my country

Modern studies of social distance still show that the attitudes of Euro-Americans toward African-Americans have changed little over the twentieth century. In 1926, American whites ranked Negroes twenty-sixth on the social distance list that included ten Western European ethnic groups, six eastern/southern European groups, American Indians, and, finally, Mexicans and four East Asian groups above them. The same rankings in 1966 showed Negroes in twenty-ninth out of thirty possible places (only East Indians were ranked lower). Finally, in 1991, African Americans were ranked twenty-first of thirty, with Mexican-Americans, and some

East Asian and Middle Eastern ethnicities ranked below them. These data indicate that while Euro-Americans were becoming generally more tolerant of non-Europeans over the last century, their ranking of these groups changed little. For example, American cities are still as segregated as ever.[2] The average segregation index between blacks and nonblacks for nine American cities with populations in excess of 450,000 was 83 percent. This means that 83 percent of the cities' populations would have to be moved to achieve representative integration of the cities' neighborhoods (the figures were 55 percent and 46 percent for Hispanics and Asians, respectively.) Since social distance measures are calculated from seven variables, it is possible to change the value of social distance without changing attitudes toward marriage. For example, modern Americans would state that they are more willing to allow minorities into their professions, without being supportive of interracial marriage. There is still strong opposition to the idea of interracial love, sex, and marriage. In 1958, 96 percent of Americans disapproved of interracial marriage. In 1997, this figure had dropped significantly, but 39 percent of white and 23 percent of black Americans still disapproved of interracial dating or marriage. In 1998, a South Carolina referendum to remove prohibitions against intermarriage was opposed by 38 percent of those who voted.

Responses to interracial marriage were more negative when people were asked about whether they would support the interracial marriage of a close relative. A National Opinion Research Center poll in 1990 asked Jews, blacks, Asians, and Hispanics how they felt about a close relative marrying someone from outside their racial or ethnic group. In opposition to their response to the question in general, blacks were most strongly opposed, at 57.5 percent against interracial marriage for a close relative. Other ethnic minorities were similarly concerned, with Asian-Americans at 42.4 percent; Hispanic Americans at 40.4 percent; Jews were the least opposed, at 16.3 percent. Jewish Americans also had the largest response neither favoring nor opposing intermarriage of a close relative (63.1 percent) and slightly over 46 percent of Asian and Hispanic Americans were neutral on the question. These results suggest that some ethnic minorities may fear cultural dilution from intermarriage. In the case of African Americans, the fear of intermarriage for a close relative may come from their understanding of how the dominant society responds to relationships that challenge the color barrier and the difficulty that interracial children still face in American society. Also, since the African-American male–female sex ratio is biased toward more females and most interracial marriages are between higher-status black men and lower-status white women, there may be resentment to the potential loss of African-American husbands to white women.

Counterbalancing the fear of cultural dilution for some ethnic groups is the potential benefits of marrying into the dominant social group. This has been accomplished by some sectors of the Asian-American population. One recent study has shown that Japanese and European Americans intermarry at rates high enough to indicate that they see each other as social equivalents. The Japanese–European-American intermarriage rate is asymmetrical by gender and social status, with marriages more likely to occur between European-American men and Japanese-American women. Educational attainment for women in either group lowers the probability that they will marry outside of their ethnicity.

Despite the recent increases in interracial marriage, the vast majority of American marriages are still within socially constructed race (95 percent whites) and (92 percent blacks). However, within the interracial marriage category, certain pairings are less likely than others. Whites and blacks show the greatest marriage distance with the odds in the 1990 census of 11,222 to one of a black married to a black, rather than a white, as compared to a white being married to a white, rather than a black. White–Hispanic odds were only 270, and or Japanese–white odds were in 873 (Appendix 7). These data suggest that there are still strong social taboos against interracial marriage. A 2002 study of the attitudes of racist whites from an internet chat room indicated that the two most likely "threats" to which the participants would respond to with violence were first interracial marriage and second blacks moving into their neighborhood. The respondents did not seem to be threatened by job competition with blacks. Results such as this beg the question as to why interracial sex, marriage, or reproduction are still such challenges to the existing social order? After all, why should we care who loves or marries whom?

This enigma is more problematic once we realize that the resistance to interracial marriage isn't just from the dominant racial group, but also from many in the subordinate groups. There seem to be two sorts of answers. The dominant groups oppose interracial marriage because it threatens to dismantle the existing social order by eliminating the racial categories. If Americans were to marry and have children without regard to socially constructed races, the physical distinctions within our nation would disappear within eight generations, or 240 years. The resultant population would be a mixture of all the physical features exhibited from humans around the world. The racist should oppose such mixing precisely because they believe in racial hierarchy. The eugenicists of the early twentieth century opposed both the untrammeled reproduction of the genetically unfit and the pollution of pure northern European races with the genes of inferiors (southern Europeans, Africans, or Asians). Conversely, ethnic minority political movements with strong cultural identity, such as the Afrocentrics, the Nation of Islam, La Raza, and others, also resisted intermarriage. For example, the Garvey movement formed allegiances with local Klan movements to suppress both sexual race mixing and trade unionism in the 1930s. Again, interracial marriage if practiced at a sufficient rate would consolidate cultures and erode the rationale for such groups to exist.

Yet, despite the warnings of the eugenicists, the amalgamation of the American population began a long time ago. This was driven by the fact that humans always mix their short- and long-term reproductive strategies. Males, in particular, will mate with people they might not consider for marriage, even across socially constructed racial barriers. Until the advent of modern birth control, heterosexual activity always has had a significant probability of producing offspring. It also has had the power to break down the socially constructed barriers. For example, there were free white women who married African slaves or American Indian men even in colonial times. Conversely, many more white men took American Indian wives or sired children with African women in slavery. So, we should not be surprised to find that there are people socially described as "black" or "yellow" who are descended from the Mayflower pilgrims. The average person described as "white" in Louisiana may have as much as 20 percent African heritage. We already know that African-Americans and American Indians are strongly mixed with each other and Europeans. Hispanics have ancestry from Africans, American Indians, and Europeans whose common bond is that they speak Spanish and are generally Roman Catholic.

Thirty-six years after official miscegenation laws were struck down we are still a long way from marriage patterns that would produce complete physical integration. Only about 3 percent of official marriages were interracial in 2000, although a greater percentage of cohabiting heterosexual couples are interracial. This means that it is easier for people to ignore racial barriers in short-term sexual relationships, as compared to long-term ones. This is not surprising, since both sexes have been shown to lower their standards in short-term mating on a variety of preferred mate characteristics.

Several mechanisms could explain the rarity of interracial marriage. It could result from some natural preference for marriage within biological races. This might be true particularly if mechanisms of sexual attraction were somehow cued by differences in the physical features that were used to socially construct races. Alternatively, the rarity of interracial marriage could result from females and males marrying along the social hierarchy. This would be more likely, particularly if all Americans were taught the unofficial social-dominance relations. There is ample evidence that, by adolescence, children have learned the dominance relations of American society. Under these conditions people would sort out by social status, with the higher-status members of each social group finding each other, with some high-status individuals of subordinate groups marrying less desirable members of higher-status groups. This mechanism predicts that the fraction of interracial marriages should be clearly related to the perceived social distance between groups. Still, this scenario also allows for very high-status individuals from the socially subordinated groups to marry very high-status individuals from the socially dominant groups. African Americans like R&B artist Lou Rawls, or basketball player Charles Barkley, or singers and actresses like Mariah Carey or Angela Bassett could marry into any social group they desired. Finally, cultural differences and opportunity might be conspiring to make marriages between groups that display different cultural features less likely or stable. Spousal compatibility may have a lot to do with shared cultural experiences, political, and religious beliefs. In that sense, the rarity of European- and African-American marriages may be explained by their diametrically opposed experiences in America. The evidence suggests that there is some support for the second and third explanations, but not a lot of support for the first.

Evidence against the first explanation can be found from data that show that the probability of interracial marriage is inversely related to the percentage of your so-called racial group in the population. Thus, whites, the largest group in our population, have the lowest percentage at 1.0 percent, blacks at 3.3 percent, Hispanics 23 percent, Asians 14.7 percent, and American Indians at 47.6 percent. The general pattern of interracial marriage by the proportion of the population says that people marry based upon the opportunity to meet a suitable mate. This means that groups that are the smallest have the lowest probability of meeting someone they wish to marry within their own ethnic group, thus, are more likely to intermarry. The difference between the percentage of interracial marriages exhibited by blacks and Hispanics could be support for the physical appearance explanation. In 1991, Euro-Americans ranked blacks slightly higher than Hispanics on social distance, yet there is a much higher percentage of Hispanic intermarriage (most Hispanic intermarriage is from Hispanic men with non-Hispanic white women). A recently published paper showed that Americans still judge the social status of blacks by their skin complexion. In a survey of 150 Boston area college students, both black and white students were given pictures of black students that differed in skin tone. They were then asked to write their own character judgments of the pictures. Not surprisingly, both black and white students wrote significantly more positive descriptions of the blacks with lighter complexions. The preference of white Americans for lighter skin complexion would partially explain both the higher rates of intermarriage of European-American males with Asian and Hispanic as opposed to African-American women, but also the higher frequency of adoptions of Chinese, Korean, and Russian children into white families when an abundance of ethnic minority children are available in the United States.

There is overwhelming evidence that men choose their mates more on physical appearance than do women. International data on male mate choice has shown that men choose women based on physical cues of fertility, such as youth, beauty, waist–hip ratio, general body proportions, and facial symmetry. The global uniformity of male and female mate preferences is evidence that they evolved early in the history of our species. The actualization of the genetically encoded mating preferences with our species is clearly influenced by culture, but there are limits to how far culture could possibly mold such fundamental behavior. Males and females pretty much are constrained to what they could ever want in a long-term reproductive partner.

In our racialized society, in which men are generally presented women with European features as the images of beauty, we would expect that men of every ethnic group would find such women desirable. In this light, Ward's claim that men of a lower race would want to have women of the so-called higher race is correct in the sense that all men would want the women whom a society deems are the most attractive. In the white supremacist America of the early twentieth century that would have been the white woman. But this does not mean that Asian, black, Hispanic, or American-Indian men would have displayed uncontrollable criminal sexual impulses to force themselves upon white women. Men of all social strata would be motivated by the same desires to successfully reproduce. Given the social and political force arrayed against minorities seeking sex with white women, no one in their right mind or unwilling to face imprisonment or be killed would have openly taken on that challenge. This only means that the great African-American boxer Jack Johnson, who openly consorted with white women, was either very heroic, crazy, or suffered from a death wish! Jack Johnson's courage was never in doubt, but his sanity could have been questioned given the power of the social forces aligned against him.

Many of the ethnic minority political movements of the time responded against the idea that whiteness and sexual desirability were equivalent, as illustrated by the black pride, racial purity ideology of Marcus Garvey and UNIA. Yet the dominance of the cultural icon of the white woman continues to this day. This explains the predominance of African-American or Hispanic male–European-American female marriages within the interracial marriage category. Most likely, both the physical appearance and social status explanations are at work in this case. European-American women in such marriages are generally less educated than European-American women who marry European-American men. If education is an indicator of economic status, then this would support the social distance explanation. I am not aware of any studies of interracial marriage that have evaluated the physical attractiveness of the women involved compared to women who marry within socially constructed race. However, the evolutionary theory would predict that women who are most physically desirable would be married to socially dominant men, without regard to the racial identity of the men. However, since in American society race is a surrogate for social dominance, most of the socially dominant men will be of European-American ancestry. Such men include CEOs, political figures, doctors, lawyers, actors, and professional athletes and so forth. We know that European-American men dominate these professions (except for sports such as basketball and football) and, therefore, they should be the ones married to what our racialized society considers the most desirable women (whether by beauty, social status, or wealth without regard to race). Conversely, the theory predicts that European-American women married outside of their race should be less desirable overall (based on youth, beauty, or social status) compared to those married inside of the socially dominant group. This does not mean that individuals of great desirability will not defy the social trends. Of course they do! But one of the great crimes of racist society is that it decides who is and who is not sexually desirable based on their racial identity. It even steps in to deny and oppress people who find themselves in love across the social status hierarchy. White people are not intrinsically more desirable than anyone else; their desirability results from their social dominance.

Neither are nonwhite people sexually frustrated and unhappy in their marriages because they are not married to a member of the dominant social group. Nothing could be further from the truth. Our history illustrates that those born into socially subordinated groups do not just accept their oppression. The struggles to overthrow both the infrastructure and the ideology of oppression add to the richness of American history. Much of what is best in African-American culture results from that struggle. Among these are music, poetry, literature, and art that have been shared with the entire nation. Individuals have lived, loved, and raised their families as best they could under the oppression of institutionalized racism.

European American social dominance did control many parts of African-American life. W.E.B. Du Bois wrote about it in *The Souls of Black Folk*. The process of social subordination cannot help but create "dual consciousness." For years, the black cosmetic industry made its money off altering appearances to look white (hair straightening, skin lightening cream, and so forth). This was possible because there was a skin-color caste system within African-American society. Many African-American leaders displayed their lighter skin color and processed hair as a badge of their social status. The reach of European social dominance has also spread internationally. In Japan, men pay high prices for the sexual favors of blonde women, Japanese women dye their hair blonde, and some even dye their pubic hair. These practices all resulted from the social and, hence, sexual dominance of whites in the Japanese mind.

It might seem strange to talk about the sexual dominance of whites, especially given the American mythologies concerning the bestial sexuality of blacks. The white myth of black male sexuality begins and ends with the African macrophallus. This myth might be of some importance if women actually choose their long- or short-term mates on the basis of penis size. However, studies of female mate choice have conclusively shown that women seek men who can provide resources for their future offspring. Indicators of this are economic potential, social status, and perceived willingness to invest those resources in that woman and her offspring. In American society, it has been white males who have dominated those resources, without regard to any supposed difference in sexual apparatus. The sexual desire for social dominance is rooted in the evolved mate choice mechanisms of our species. If we change the social relations, our culture would respond with new hierarchies. Finally, if we eliminated social hierarchy altogether, then we would find new traits to choose our mates. In such a world, the macrophallus might have some significance!

Evidence that cultural factors operate to influence intermarriage also comes from the percentage of marriages between ethnic groups. Recent studies have shown that, at least for Japanese-Americans, the marriage boundaries between them and European-Americans are disappearing. Additional evidence is that within socially dominant groups the probability that a woman married outside her group is inversely related to her own education. If education is a measure of social status, then higher social-status women have the opportunity to choose males of higher status, and in the racial status hierarchy they rarely choose down. There is also a strong correlation between employment status and marriage rates. The evolutionary theory of mate preferences predicts this result directly. Rates of marriage have declined in the Western world since 1940. In the United States in 1965, 97.3 percent of women who had survived to age fifteen would marry, with an average age of marriage at 21.1 years. Yet, in 1983, for this population only 89.7 percent married and the average age of marriage was 24.5 years. Greater opportunities for women to acquire education and participate in the workforce clearly influence their marriage patterns.

The decline in marriage rates has not been uniform. There has been a much greater decline among African Americans. Currently marriage rates among African Americans are declining more rapidly than amongst European Americans. Is this because women choose social status and economic prosperity in their mates? Are African-American males not measuring up for the more upwardly mobile African-American woman? One study of marriage propensities in Wisconsin found whites twice as likely to marry as blacks by age and educational level. It also showed that African-American males were slightly more likely to marry a nonblack woman than a black woman (1.02 times). Conversely, white men were 15.02 times more likely to marry a white woman than a non-white woman. Employed African-American men were twice as likely to be married than unmarried African-American men. This illustrates how cultural and social factors may alter the outcome of mate-choice mechanisms. Abundant evidence shows that women desire to choose men with good financial prospects, thus declining rates of employment and wage earning by African-American men would make them less viable for marriage.

Despite the rarity of interracial marriage, there is an unanticipated outcome of its increase over the latter portion of the twentieth century. Even with the low rate of interracial marriage a substantial portion of Americans belong to multiracial extended families. One-fifth of adult Americans currently belong to multiracial kinship groups. For the smallest ethnic groups, Asians and American-Indians, the exception is not the multiracial family but the monoracial one! Fewer than one in five Asians belong to an all-Asian kin group and only a few percent of American-Indians belong to a kin network in which everyone has the same racial identity. Blacks and whites still retain the most homogeneous kin groups, but one in seven whites and more than one in three blacks have close relatives of a different socially defined race.

Studies indicate that there are different responses of the dominant social race to its genetic versus its legal kin. The most intransigent simply disown the intermarried relative and their offspring from their social group. It is more common that the discord continues between the parents and intermarried children until the appearance of grandchildren. Evolutionary theory explains this phenomenon well. Racism is a social construction, but grandchildren carry the grandparents' genes. Altruism toward genetic kin is deeply ingrained in human behavior. In many cases, this is sufficient to alter the behavior of the estranged parents, at least to where they are providing support for their genetic relatives. This also has the impact of forcing coalitions with members of the racial outgroup. Grandparents from both races share equal genetic contributions to the grandchildren. To the extent that both have a common interest in seeing those children thrive, they may enter into liaisons of convenience. There is also the possibility of the interest in their grandchildren expanding to larger opportunities of understanding for kin on both sides of the family.

In the thirteenth century, the French nobleman Pierre DuBois argued that intermarriage of the Christian and Muslim nobility was far more sensible than the Crusades. He was right . . . love really is the answer. As the social classes of America diversify, neighborhoods, schools, and churches will become more diverse. In the absence of overtly racist ideology, children will increasingly marry between socially constructed races. Yet the kinship networks between racial groups will expand at an even higher rate. Under these conditions, the genetically ingrained altruism toward kin will foster a greater understanding or our shared heritage. This is why the racists fight so hard to maintain their dominance over our social infrastructure. They know that social equality will lead to the genetic amalgamation of our species through marriage. If this happens they will be forced to recognize the genetic uniformity of our species, and they will cease to have a reason for being, for there will be no one left to single out, stereotype, and hate!

CHAPTER 5

America Is Enough to Make You Sick: Differential Health and Mortality for Racial Minorities

Life, liberty, and the pursuit of happiness are guarantees that the founding fathers wanted to provide for Americans. The founding fathers were all of Northern European descent and they saw their children as the same. They had no moral opposition to producing these freedoms on the backs of non-Europeans. Yet, over our history, we fought to make these promises more inclusive. Some of us are under the impression that we have succeeded. After all we can see the Huxtables on television, Lucy Liu as a Charlie's Angel, and, in Arizona, we can rename mountain peaks after fallen American-Indian heroes. Unfortunately, despite all these cosmetic advances, we still aren't there yet.

Certain socially defined racial groups are still more likely to be deprived of their liberty, suffer from depression and impaired cognition, suffer from infectious or genetically based disease, poisoned environments, and die at rates higher than others.

Biomedical science is now beginning to tackle the problem of ethnic and racial health disparity. Researchers and clinicians are beginning to ask why different groups suffer from diseases at different rates. On the surface, it might seem that the obvious explanation is that these groups are genetically different. We know that people have different cultures and lifestyles, and we expect them to manifest disease at different rates. This seemingly benign and value-neutral set of explanations seems to be at odds with the data on health disparity. If we were to follow the logic of these ideas, we should expect that there should be no discernable pattern to the mortality rates of different ethnic groups. After all, why should any one group have all the best genes for disease resistance and simultaneously maintain cultural and lifestyle practices that combine to provide them greater health? However, an examination of age-adjusted death rates shows a striking pattern (Appendix 8).

If both genetic and environmental factors produce these results, a pattern such as this is not too surprising. We would expect that groups that differ slightly in gene frequencies and have different cultural practices would therefore have different patterns of disease prevalence. However, when examining the overtly biological causes of death we see that Asian Americans are lower in 100 percent and, conversely, African Americans are higher than whites in 83.3 percent of the categories. These differences have created a huge problem in defining the meaning of health disparity.

Originally, researchers defined the problem in a very narrow scope. They viewed the problem only from the differences that existed between socially defined whites versus blacks. Once additional ethnic groups were included, the pattern of health disparity becomes more complex. Hispanics have individuals whose genetic ancestry includes people who are almost purely Asian, African, or European, and mixtures of all three (such as Puerto Ricans, other Caribbean populations, and Mexican Americans). American Indians have genes that originated in eastern Asia, with significant European and some small African admixture. By genetic distance arguments alone, one might expect Asian and African mortality rates to be more distant from each other and European, Hispanic, and American-Indian rates to be in between. We would not expect that all the bad genes would be exhibited by people of African descent and all the good ones to be found in East Asians, particularly given that African Americans have significant European and some American Indians (hence East Asian) admixture (10 to 21 percent)? So, at this time, it is impossible to truly evaluate the genetic distance argument because the social environments of these groups are not equal. This introduces complications of gene by environment interaction.

Ironically, blacks have a lower rate of mortality from Alzheimer's disease compared to whites (0.70). This is also an indication of health disparity. Alzheimer's is a late age disease so, if fewer blacks are living to advanced ages, we would expect to see fewer dying from this disease. Whites exceed blacks in suicide rates, yet the ratio of mortality from homicide and police intervention is 6.2 times higher for blacks than whites. These differences also reflect social oppression. While one may be driven to suicide by external circumstances, ultimately, the decision to take one's life is personal. On the other hand, homicide and police intervention results from decisions that others make concerning how much your life is worth. The case of the African immigrant Amadou Diallo is case in point. Diallo was shot over forty times by a special unit of the New York City Police Department while reaching for his identification in the vestibule of his own apartment. The officers claimed that they thought he was reaching for a weapon. Virtually every major metropolitan area can cite a case involving a nonwhite citizen gunned down or otherwise killed by excessive police force, and that the officers involved were white. I am not aware of an example of a white citizen gunned down by a group of Asian, black, or Hispanic police officers. In a truly democratic society we should expect that membership on the police force would be independent of socially constructed race. Furthermore, we would expect that the distribution of honest versus corrupt police officers should be independent of race. We have never seen such democracy in the United States. The Christopher Commission was convened in the wake of the beating of Rodney King. It examined allegations of excessive force by the overwhelmingly white L.A. police force between 1986 and 1990. Of the 3,419 complaints, only 3 percent were shown to have enough merit to warrant further investigation. Of those meriting investigation, only 7.6 percent resulted in the removal of the offending officer.

This amounts to a virtually zero chance of a corrupt police officer being removed from the force by civilian complaints!

The consistent pattern of differential mortality for Asians and blacks compared to whites is puzzling. Why should Asian mortality be so much lower and African mortality be so much higher? Particularly if we believe that genes or lifestyle are the causes of the mortality rate differences. This pattern cannot result if blacks and whites are equally likely to be predisposed to any specific disease. Could it be that black genes and cultural lifestyles are simply worse than those of whites? This is precisely what the official rhetoric from the biomedical community is saying. But, in reality, there is no intellectual justification to think that sub-Saharan African genes were any less preadapted or that Asian genes are more adapted to life in the Western hemisphere than those of Northern Europeans. Neither is there any reason to believe that East Asian are superior to Northern European cultural lifestyles which are in turn inherently superior to sub-Saharan African ones.

The historical pattern of superior white health outcomes results from their social dominance over blacks and other nonwhites in North America. Basically, nonwhites have died and continue to die at higher rates to improve the prospects of life, liberty, and the pursuit of happiness for the dominant group. It is highly doubtful that Chinese immigrants enjoyed greater health status than European Americans during the building of the Transcontinental Railroad. If we truly wish to actualize the American dream we must address the reasons for ethnic health disparity. We already know the source of depressed African-American health. This disparity results from and simultaneously reinforces multifaceted social inequalities. This is the most serious civil rights issue we must address at the turn of the twenty-first century.

See, Hear, and Speak No Evil

The official discussion of health disparity refuses to see, hear, or speak about the role of social dominance in producing disparate health outcomes. This is particularly alarming given that the scientists and public policy makers involved in formulating the program to redress health disparity understand this point very well. We must implement a program to address health disparity. It is of crucial importance. Things are not getting better.

In 1994, the American Cancer Society reported that the cancer incidence rate was 454 out of 100,000 and 394 out of 100,000 for African and European Americans respectively. Over the preceding four years, the African-American rates had increased by 1.2 percent, while the European-American rates only increased by 0.8 percent. These data indicate that the health disparity gap for African Americans is growing. President William Jefferson Clinton recognized this danger when he announced his health disparity initiative in the last term of his presidency. The health disparity initiative was confused from its very start. The problem was that it began with biomedical researchers still lacking understanding of the difference between biological and socially constructed races. The race concept once again . . .

Racial apologist Sally Satel wrote that she was a racially profiling doctor in *The New York Times Magazine* dated Sunday, May 5, 2002. She argued that this made sense because races had unique diseases and responded to drug therapies differently. Her piece was partially in response to a debate between two physicians, Robert Schwartz and Alastair Wood, that had appeared a year before in the *New England Journal of Medicine*. Schwartz argued that racial profiling in medical research was unsound because no biological races existed in the human species. Schwartz cited the 1999 statement of the American Anthropological Association that declared that human populations are not unambiguous, clearly demarcated, biologically distinct groups. He pointed out that most clinicians still labored under the assumption that races were real. As evidence of that fact he showed that the term *Negroid race* appeared in 13,592 papers in a 2001 search of current medical literature. The papers included studies of race-based lipid metabolism, renal function, responses to vasodilators, sexual maturation, drug metabolism, neurodegenerative diseases, and even a very rare disease called *Dupuytren's contracture.* This proves that most biomedical researchers still assume that races exist and therefore should differ in virtually every aspect of disease. This misconception continues in spite of fifty years of genetic research debunking the existence of biological races in the human species. Schwartz explained how and why populations differ in gene frequencies. He made the crucial point that the existence of geographically based genetic variation is not sufficient reason for classifying biological races. For example, at least one major research journal, *Nature Genetics,* no longer subscribes to racial thinking and requires authors to explain how and why specific ethnic groups or populations were included in their studies.

In the next few pages Alastair Wood attempted to rebut Schwartz, but Wood reiterated all of the standing confusions concerning biological theories of genetic variation and socially defined races. He pointed out that specific populations had different frequencies of genes. Black Americans and Africans have a high frequency of a cytochrome P (CYP2D6) allele that encodes low activity for that enzyme, and that this allele is virtually absent in whites and Asians populations. The cytochrome enzymes are important because they play many roles in general metabolism, particularly of drugs. If someone has an enzyme that has low activity, a particular medicine may not work or have toxic side effects. Wood's essay continues with several examples of this kind, yet Wood never addresses how biological races are defined and whether, under those definitions, we can identify races in our species. He, like most physicians, relies on nineteenth century typological thinking that goes back to the essentialist ideas of the Greek philosopher Plato. In this scheme, all things are shadows of perfect eternal ideas. The essence of the duck, revealed to man by supernatural means, defines all ducks. *Typological thinking* looks to measurements of central tendency such as the average to describe the entire group and ignores variation within groups. For the typologist of race, blacks are blacks, whites are whites, and yellows are yellows. A racial typologist will claim that African Americans and Western Africans are both blacks. They will ignore the fact that African Americans have genetic admixture from Europeans and American Indians (10 to 21 percent or more), since according to them, 90 to 79 percent black is still black. They do not recognize how admixture complicates the probability that any given person will have the most common allele from the suspected region of their origin. They forget that the chromosomal theory of inheritance shows that genes for skin color segregate independently from those for any specific disease. They will ignore the fact that African Americans and Western Africans have different cultures, diets, and social circumstances. To the racial typologist, in the end, black is still black. They do not grasp that all populations have variation within them. Africa, Asia, and Europe are continents with many ethnic groups. Genetic variation in them is a function of the distances between population groups. Racial typologists may be willing to admit that for Europeans. They may realize that Italians may have different gene frequencies from the English. However, Africa is Africa, and Africans are all the same. So they will not realize that Nigerians have different gene frequencies from Thosa or Zulu, and fail to realize that Algerians or Egyptians are also Africans. Neither will they recognize that Northern Africans may be similar to Spaniards. In the typologist's mind, North Africans are Arabs and Spaniards are white. The fundamental error of typological thinking is that it refuses to recognize both the existence of genetic variation and its continuity. This means that depending on the criteria chosen it is possible to define any number of statistically defined genetic groups in the human species.

Appearing in the same journal of the *New England Journal of Medicine* as the Woods–Schwartz debate, a paper was published purporting that *enalapril,* an angiotensin-converting enzyme (ACE) inhibitor is more effective in whites than it is in blacks, while another paper claimed that *carvedilol,* a beta-blocker, had similar effects in both groups. ACE inhibitors work by interfering with the enzymes that convert an inactive chemical known as angiotensin I to an active form, angiotensin II. Angiotensin II increases the retention of salt and water in the body, raising blood pressure. Inhibiting the formation of angiotensin II results in relaxed arterial walls and lowered blood pressure. Beta-blockers are properly known as beta-adrenergic-blocking drugs. These drugs interfere with actions of the *sympathetic nervous system,* which controls involuntary muscle movement. They slow the heart rate, relax pressure in blood vessel walls, and decrease the force of heart contractions.

The report by cardiovascular researcher D.V. Exner and his co-workers that enalapril did not work as well for blacks prompted the formation of companies whose goal was to discover drugs that could be tailored to specific so-called races. There was support for this from some sectors of the medical and African-American community. The enalapril result was widely publicized in the popular media. I spoke to *The New York Times* on the issue of racial medicine shortly after the enalapril report. I pointed out that it was not possible to create race-specific drugs because human genetic variation did not partition itself into specified racial groups, and it was certainly not organized according to our socially defined groups. However, my voice was in the minority. The racial typologists had garnered the lion's share of the media's attention. Was all this attention and support warranted? Did they capture the media because of the validity of their ideas? Was it the prestige of their academic appointments and think tank associations? Or was it more insidious? Was it because they were saying what our racialized society wanted to hear?

A Rose by Any Other Name

The dawn of racial medicine has been championed as a way to reduce health disparities and save lives. How can this work when biological races don't really exist within the human species? Many biomedical researchers answer that biological races can be found in our species. They say that anthropologists and geneticists have abandoned racial classification only as a capitulation to political correctness. This is hard to believe. American scientists are amazingly resilient to fads, political pressure, or to ethical or moral imperatives. Most of them come from social strata least likely to be sympathetic to racial progress. The idea that scientists have abandoned racial typology for these reasons is absurd. The problem was in the concept itself, not any liberal social agenda. The data gathered to test for racial division in our species has not held up.

Racially based medical differences just do not exist. The enalapril results began to unravel shortly after the paper was published. A year later, a paper appeared in the *Journal of the American College of Cardiology* showing that enalapril was equally effective in preventing heart failure in black and white patients. The lead author, Daniel Dries, had been a co-author on the earlier paper. However, the second paper disproving the original results did not receive the same amount of media attention. The proponents of racialized medicine still cited the first enalapril paper well after it had been shown to be wrong. For example, well-respected Stanford epidemiologist Neil Risch cited this paper in his opinion piece published in *Genome Biology* in July 2002. This paper declared that self-identified racial labels were legitimate categories mirroring human genetic variation. While the example he discussed in this paper did not require the enalapril report to be correct, he did not state that the Dries study had shown that those results were incorrect.

Risch's *Genome Biology* piece did hit upon an important point. Self-identified ethnicity does not map into discrete racial categories, but it can often mirror the genetic distance between populations. This effect results from the social history of the United States. People who represented the complete spectrum of the world's genetic diversity did not found our nation. Initially, we had Northern Europeans, indigenous North Americans, and Africans. As our history progressed, immigrants from southern and eastern Europe, along with East Asia, came to America. Finally, immigrants from more regions such as the Middle East and Southeast Asia began to arrive. However, numerically, the majority of Americans still derive from Europe. Gene frequencies in the United States reflect that bias.

American social customs have kept most of these people from intermarrying. Thus, a person who can state their cultural ancestry for the most part still has a genetic makeup that reflects origin in that portion of the world. A person whose says they are Scots-Irish, Japanese, or Russian will most likely have some genes that are specific to that region of the world. This fact is still different from the idea that races exist within the human species and that we can learn important things about individuals within them or by identifying their ethnic group as if it were a biological race. Biomedical research has not been interested in human genetic diversity until recently. Most of what we know comes from populations that fit into the socially constructed races. Scientists collect genetic data from American blacks, Afro-Caribbeans, Hispanics, American Indians, an amorphous group know as *whites,* and Asians. The way genetic information is sampled and compared gives the impression that there are ways to legitimately cluster people into biological races that just so happen to correspond to our socially constructed races.

For example, a 1997 study examined 109 DNA markers in sixteen populations to determine the within-group versus between-group genetic variation. This study found that only one of the DNA markers gave evidence of having more genetic variation between groups than within groups thus, overall, the results of this study have been taken to be evidence against the existence of races in modern humans. Yet this study is illustrative of a general mistake in how human genetic variation has been gathered. It looked at four sub-Saharan African (Senegalese, Mbuti Pygmies from Zaire, Lisongo from Central African Republic, Biaka Pygmies from Central African Republic), two central European (North Europeans and Northern Italians), three East Asian (Cambodian-born from San Francisco, Chinese-born from San Francisco, Japanese-born from San Francisco), three Australian and Oceania (Australians from the Northern territory, New Guineans, Nasioi Melanesians from the Solomon Islands), and four Central and South American populations (Maya from Yucatan, Karitania from Rondonia, Brazil; Surui from Rondonia, Brazil, and mixed Karitania–Surui). This sampling is not systematic nor was it a random sampling along the genetic continuum of the human species. Three of the African populations are clustered within 1200 miles of each other, anthropologically interesting, but not really representative of the population of central Africa. The European samples came from around four hundred miles apart and, over historical time, people could move between the European sites far more easily than anyone could between any of the African, Asian, or Australian/Oceania locations. Finally, by simple geographical distance or along the proposed routes of ancient human migration the distances between the sampled groups are enormous. The distance between the Africans and Europeans is at least five thousand miles, Africans and East Asians, greater than seven thousand miles, Africans and Australians, greater than eight thousand miles, and by land Africans and Central or South Americans greater than fifteen thousand miles! More important, the sampling scheme omits populations that are between the groups examined in the study. For example, no data are included from Northern Africa, Spain, the Middle East, Asia Minor, or the Balkans. These populations exist in places where the contact between Africans and Europeans throughout history would have been the greatest. The data we currently have concerning human genetic diversity is actually biased toward finding racial clusters because it comes from populations that are very far apart geographically. Despite the bias in favor of identifying racial groups, it is notable that in this study examining 109 genetic markers the authors still did not find evidence of racial clustering!

A more recent study examined single nucleotide polymorphism (SNP) diversity for fifty noncoding genetic sequences in individuals from three continents, Africa, Asia, and Europe. Remember that SNPs are nucleotide substitutions in a sequence of DNA. Most humans share the same sequence but, at any specific point, some individuals will have a different nucleotide from the population majority. This study utilized one individual from ten different population groups on each continent. The ten Africans included one Biaka Pygmy, one Mbuti Pygmy, one Ghanaian, one Kikuyu, one !Kung, one Luo, one Yuroba, one Rivers, one South African Bantu speaker, one Zulu (also Bantu speaking). The Europeans included one Finn, one French, one German, one Hungarian, one Italian, one Portuguese, one Russian, one Spaniard, one Swede, and one Ukrainian. Finally, the Asians included one Cambodian, one north Chinese, one south Chinese, 1 Han Taiwanese, one Punjabi, one Bengali, one Japanese, one Mongolian, one Vietnamese, and one Yakut. It examined genetic diversity utilizing samples that more effectively covered the geographic range of these continents than usual. The study found that SNP diversity was greater within the African populations than it was between Africans and Eurasians. The entire sample revealed 146 SNPs, of which fifty-three were observed only once (singleton) and twenty-two only twice (doubleton). The African populations showed 118, of which sixty-eight (thirty-six singletons, fifteen doubletons, and seventeen others) were not found in Eurasians. In contrast, the Eurasian sample showed only seventy-eight variants, of which only twenty-eight (seventeen singletons, four doubletons, and seven others) were unique to Eurasians. These results mean that, with the exception of some rare minor genetic variants, Eurasian nucleotide diversity is a subset of African. This is consistent with the idea that modern humans originated in Africa, then subsequently migrated to Europe and Asia.[1]

These results tell us that while there is human genetic diversity, all populations are much more alike than they are different. A much larger study examined 26,530 SNPs from African Americans, East Asians, and European Americans. It found that 79.5 percent were common in more than one population, 56.6 percent were common in more than two populations, and 29.8 percent were common in all three populations. Remember that this study is different from the previous study in that it did not specify where the individuals within each of the three populations came from and used individuals from population clusters whose origins are geographically distant from each other (Africa, Europe, Asia). Nonetheless, when the study examined the statistic that allows us to examine the genetic variability of subpopulations versus the total population, it showed that there was very little subdivision between Africa, Europe, and Asia. The highest value for subdivision was found in the noncoding region of the genes, which are not subject to natural selection.

Once again, we find that in a very large sample of genetic markers there is no evidence for the existence of biological races. The study shows that natural selection operates both to diversify, but also to limit the amount of diversity our genome can accumulate. This can result because noncoding DNA sequences do not produce proteins and therefore do not face natural selection, so they can accumulate mutations that will be unique to specific populations (Appendix 9).

These sorts of results do not dissuade those who insist there are discrete groups in our species. They simply attempt to develop more sophisticated statistical techniques to partition humans into groups that make some sense in the guise of our socially constructed racial view. For example, Rosenberg and his coworkers examined the diversity of 377 microsatellite DNA markers in 1056 individuals from fifty-two populations. They found that within population, differences accounted for 93 to 95 percent of the genetic variation, while only 3 to 5 percent of the genetic variation existed between groups. These results correspond to what geneticists have shown over the last twenty years, that is within group genetic variation is much larger than between group variation. However, this study also employed a computer program called STRUCTURE to determine if it was possible to clearly identify clusters of human populations. The program worked by placing individuals into a number of predefined clusters based on the overall genetic similarity of the individuals. They varied the number of clusters and found that there were several statistically significant ways of partitioning the human population. For example, using two clusters, they partitioned the human species into a group rooted in Africa, and a second group rooted in the Americas (the groups with the largest amount of genetic distance between them). Alternatively, using an analysis with five clusters, they found that they could partition the human species into groups that matched the indigenous populations of the five inhabited continents. In the analysis using six clusters, an additional major group (or race) emerged, which was comprised solely of a population from Kalash in Northern Pakistan.

Most damaging to the concept that the discrete clusters were legitimate divisions of the human species, they found that many of the individuals in the analysis could be placed in more than one of the supposedly discrete groups! This means that if we thought of these clusters as *races* there are individuals who would belong to more than one race. These results show that there are actually several logical ways to divide the human genetic variability into groups, if groups are what you must have. All this data really does is allow us to get a better handle on the past migratory history of our species, as opposed to identifying or assigning individuals to discrete racial categories.

Unfortunately, the popular press overstated the results of the Rosenberg study. Nicholas Wade, a well-known science writer for *The New York Times,* reported on December 20, 2002, that the paper's results "broadly corresponds with popular notions of race." He further asserted that "the new medical interest in race and genetics has left many sociologists and anthropologists beating a different drum in their assertions that race is a cultural idea, not a biological one." However, he never pointed to the result that there were five statistically significant ways to cluster the individuals in this study, and that only one of them corresponded to the five continents. Neither did he say that in these analyses an individual could belong to more than one cluster! Thus, Wade's trumpeting of the racial implications of this paper flew in direct contradiction to the editorial accompanying that same paper when it appeared in *Science*.[2] The *Science* editorial stated that the results helped us to better understand the migratory history of our species and said nothing about the study overturning the social construction of race.

Individualized Medicine and Race

The new field of pharmacogenomics is interested in providing medicines that react well with each individual's genetic background. This seems like a laudable goal when one considers that the majority of human genetic variation (85 pecent) resides within populations, thus, even two people whose ancestors are from Central Europe could differ significantly as a genotype responsible for metabolizing any specific drug. Yet the adherents of racial biology immediately muddied the simplicity and clarity of this idea. Sally Satel claimed that racial profiling was required to offer patients better medical care since races were biologically different. Shortly after this, Neil Risch and Noah Rosenberg and his coworkers at Stanford claimed that so-called self-identified ethnicity sufficiently matched biologically defined racial groups in the human species. Others vehemently rebutted their arguments, claiming that a reversion to racial thinking in medicine would be disastrous.

Genes that are involved in intermediary metabolism are most likely to influence an individual's drug response. An individual whose genes do not metabolize a drug well are likely to not receive its full benefit or to suffer toxic side effects. In the best of all worlds, a doctor would profit greatly if he could call up a person's drug-metabolizing genotype, along with social and cultural information before prescribing a particular treatment. Since individuals who share common ancestry are most likely to share common genes, it is likely that sharing origin from a specific portion of the world might be a powerful clue to an individual's genetic identity. If people can be legitimately classified into discrete racial categories, it follows that their drug responses should also, and thus might not corporations be more responsible if they manufactured race-specific drugs? This is precisely what enalapril was supposed to be.

The trouble is that humans do not have discretely defined racial groups. However, we have seen how the sampling of human genetic diversity can give the appearance that such groups are legitimate. A study published in 2001, utilizing data from the International Project on Genetic Susceptibility to Environmental Carcinogens (GSEC) suggested that there were major and significant differences in allele frequency at eight metabolic gene loci between Africans, Asians, and Europeans. The data was gathered from fifty-two laboratories representing seventy-three separate studies and contained data from 12,525 Caucasians, 2,136 Asians, and 996 Africans and African Americans (pooled). The authors did not explain from what countries or ethnic groups the sixty Africans in the pooled sample originated. Neither did they make it clear that the Caucasian sample was also pooled, containing North Americans of European descent and Europeans. The Asian samples were from East Asia: Japan, Korea, and Singapore. Again, the samples in this study were biased to show large differences in gene frequencies between the races. They came from groups whose ancestral homes are very far apart and not from populations that are found along the intersection of Africa, Europe, and Asia (Appendix 10).

If we are concerned about finding the correct drug for any given patient, we do not really gain any more information by knowing the fact that the frequencies of these groups differ by alleged racial group. A physician armed with different variants of a given medication would still have to either determine the genotype of his or her patient, or utilize trial and error to see which drug works best for that individual. Even if large frequency differences between groups existed, a racial profiling physician would still be irresponsible if he stereotyped a patient's drug therapy based on their race. Why? Simply because the data clearly show that there is within population variation at virtually every locus responsible for drug metabolism.

James Wilson and his coworkers recognized this point in a paper they published for *Nature Genetics* in 2001. Their study found that commonly used ethnic labels were both insufficient and inaccurate representations of population genetic clusters. They suggested that the distribution of drug metabolizing enzymes differed significantly between clusters based on gene frequencies. They used individuals from the following racial/ethnic groups in their analysis: South African Bantu speakers (forty-eight), Ashkenazi Jews (forty-eight), Ethiopians (forty-eight), Norwegians (forty-seven), Armenians (forty-eight), Chinese (thirty-nine), Papua, New Guineans (forty-eight), and Afro-Caribbeans living in London (thirty).

Six of the eight populations examined had greater than 80 percent of their population falling into a given cluster: Askenazi Jew; Norwegian; Armenian; Papua, New Guinean; South African Bantu; and Chinese (Appendices 11 and 12). At first examination, this result might seem to support the idea that the genetic clusters are just another way of approximating the racial division that some believe exists in our species. However, this study suffers from the same problem of the previous research on human variation. Sampling populations separated by rather large geographic distances biases the results. What the study is missing is samples taken from populations that bridge the distances between Africa, Asia, and Europe. If more of these populations were included, we might see a very different result. Unlike the six populations that are predominantly associated with one cluster, the Ethiopian and

Armenian samples show more dispersal among the different clusters. Ethiopia is located in northeastern Africa in an area thought to be near the origin of anatomically modern humans and along migratory routes out of Africa into the Middle East and Asia Minor in historical and recent times. The Ethiopian sample had more individuals that are classified as part of the European as opposed to the sub-Saharan African cluster. In addition, it had significant representation in the New Guinean and Chinese clusters. Armenians were similarly dispersed, due to Armenia's location in Asia Minor, a region between Europe, Africa, and Asia. Finally the dispersal of the Afro-Caribbean population living in London is most likely due to admixture between Caribbeans, who would have been predominantly of sub-Saharan African origin, and Europeans. This could have occurred both in slavery, or in modern times, since the rule of hypodescent operates in England similarly to the way it operates in America. A racially profiling doctor in England would have a 27 percent chance of giving an Afro-Caribbean patient the wrong drug, if they assumed that they necessarily belonged to the African cluster.

The Essence of Contradiction: Genetic Variation, Socially Constructed Races, and Health Disparity

Still, the question remains: If genetic differences are not responsible for health disparities, what is? The proponents of racial medicine never tire of making case examples of rare genetic diseases such as Tay-Sachs, Crohn's Disease, BRCA1, or cystic fibrosis. They say if races don't exist, why do certain groups have such disparate frequencies of genetically determined diseases? The differences in the frequencies of rare genetic diseases are not as disparate as they would have you believe. The frequency of cystic fibrosis carriers (heterozygous for normal/CF) is 1.5 percent in African Americans, 2.1 percent in Hispanics, 4.5 percent in European Americans, and about 1 percent in Europeans. Similarly, the frequency of the phenylketonuria (PKU) allele in the Irish, Scots, and Yemenite Jews is identical, at 0.02 percent. Swedes have this allele at a frequency of only 0.003 percent and Chinese even lower at 0.0006 percent. The rarity of these diseases results from the fact that they are so severe. Such diseases ensured death or sterility before the advent of modern medicine. Therefore, individuals with these genes could not pass them on to the next generation. Their frequency would result from chance mutation and unique events of population history. Swedes do not have less PKU because they are better people than the Chinese; the differences in frequency result simply from chance events in each population's history.

Rare alleles cannot be the source of health disparity, because they are by definition rare, and thus would only affect a small percentage of the population. What we know about the human genetic diversity predicts that localized populations will differ in their frequency of rare genetic variants, hence of rare genetic diseases. It is a much bigger problem to understand how the essential genetic uniformity of the human species can produce the glaring disparities in the ten major sources of death in America, such as heart disease, diabetes, kidney disease, and cancer. We cannot answer this question discussing genetics as most people think of it. The common conception of genes and disease tell us that bad gene equals bad disease. The popular literature discusses the gene for cancer, the gene for hypertension, the gene for schizophrenia, or the gene for violence. Instead, we must understand that most fitness-related traits are under the control of several genes. In addition, all genes are expressed in relation to specific environments. Trees that grow straight and tall in nonwindy environments become twisted and short in windy habitats. Mutations exist that have no effect at one temperature, but are lethal in another. Many genes are expressed in response to social interactions. Genetics is complex. For example, the life span correlation for identical twins, who share 100 percent of their genes in common, and who lived in very uniform environments was only 20 percent. Complex genetic traits are strongly influenced by environmental factors. The problem with examining the genetic basis of health disparity in America is that our ethnic groups have never enjoyed environmental equality. Our history is one in which the social dominance of one group provided them supportive environments and toxic environments for those it oppressed. This is the real source of health disparity, not subtle differences in gene frequency.

Genetics of Complex Diseases 101

At the turn of the twentieth century, two great intellectual powerhouses squared off concerning the mechanisms of evolution. One group was called the *biometricians,* who felt that the inheritance of traits related to Darwinian fitness followed statistical distributions rather than qualitative descriptions. The second faction coalesced around the new principles of Mendelian particulate inheritance, which shows how qualitative traits such as eye color, tongue rolling, or widow's peak segregate in predictable ways in families and populations. The dispute between the two schools became furious, often with professional appointments hinging on what theory an academician believed. However, it would soon be shown that the biometricians and Mendelians were talking about the same mechanisms of heredity. The Mendelians were researching what were single gene traits while the biometricians were studying traits influenced by multiple genes. The inheritance of traits determined by multiple genes worked by the same Mendelian principles, but the interaction of the multiple genes produced many more phenotypes than single genes could. This meant that for traits such as height, weight, fingerprint loops and whorls, or behavior, statistical analysis was required.

Consider a simple disease like sickle cell anemia. It is produced by a mutation that substitutes one nucleotide for another and thereby causes a different amino acid to be included in the hemoglobin protein. The sickle cell mutation is associated with the presence of malaria. Individuals that receive a normal hemoglobin allele from both their mother and father will have normally shaped red blood cells. It is also possible that someone might receive a normal hemoglobin allele and a sickle hemoglobin allele. Their red blood cells would appear partially sickled. Finally, someone might receive two sickle hemoglobin genes. In this case, only three phenotypes are possible, normal, partially sickled, and severely sickled. If we knew the percentages of each gene in a population we can readily predict the percentages of the three possible phenotypes, normal, partially sickled, and severely sickled (Appendices 13 and 14).

Traits that result from more than one gene are called *complex* or *quantitative* and can produce many more possible phenotypes. For example, a trait controlled by four or five loci would have nine or eleven potential phenotypes in ratios of 256 and 1024, respectively. Environmental influence complicates things even further (Appendix 15).

The Victorian eugenicist Sir Francis Galton was one of the first to recognize that many biological traits could be described by normal curves. We now know that these are the traits determined by multiple genes, and that complex traits such as Darwinian fitness are normally distributed in many organisms, including humans. Darwinian fitness is composed of differential reproductive success and differential survival. Virtually every genetic system in organisms is related to fitness; therefore, to understand the distribution and variability of disease in any species we must approach it from an evolutionary perspective. For example, evolutionary theory predicts that many modern diseases result from a mismatch between human genes selected under very different conditions operating in modern environments. Unfortunately, this perspective is not widely understood among medical practitioners. This is one of the greatest failings of our modern biomedical research and clinical practice, and is also the root cause of the persistence of racial thinking in medicine. This failure is amply illustrated by examining how the medical community has approached the concept of race and complex diseases such as hypertension, diabetes, heart disease, and cancer.

Just-So Stories of Race, Natural Selection, Salt, and Hypertension

Current medical literature is rife with reports of supposedly racially based differences in disease prevalence. Most clinicians and researchers assume that the differences in disease rates should exist, because race has a genetic basis and genes contribute to specific diseases. However, the genetic explanation is antitheoretical when we compare the amount of genetic difference to the magnitude of the health disparities, particularly when it comes to complex diseases. The simple genetic explanations do not hold water. They are just-so stories, tall tales that hold together only so long as we uncritically accept every assumption they contain.

Research concerning race and hypertension risk is a prime example. The observation of elevated blood pressures in African Americans goes back to the early 1930s. Within thirty years, there was extensive evidence reporting that the average blood pressure of African Americans was nearly twice that of European Americans. By the 1960s, similar observations had been made of Afro-Caribbean populations. These results suggested to many that hypertension was a racial feature of Negro, even as data was accumulating showing that no such elevated blood pressures could be found in Africans from West Africa and that European populations existed that had similar rates of hypertension as African Americans.

Sodium retention plays a crucial role in hypertension. Researchers began to devise theories that posited a greater ability of Africans to retain salt due to their evolution in hot and humid climates. They further argued that salt supplies in western Africa were limited, thus providing an even greater selection pressure for individual retention of salt. Given the greater hypertension rates in western hemisphere blacks compared to Africans, it was proposed that survival in the middle passage required greater salt retaining capacities. In 1988, the slavery hypothesis of hypertension was complete, including additional mechanisms that would deplete individual salt supplies during the long voyage (vomiting and diarrhea). Major media immediately picked up the slavery hypothesis for hypertension. On October 22, 1991 *The New York Times* ran an article linking hypertension to the hormone *norepinephrine,* a byproduct of melanin produced during stress. Blacks had more melanin and presumably more stress than whites, which would explain the hypertension difference. There was no published scientific data to support this assertion. Things got worse in the early 1990s, after several prominent scientists came forward supporting the slavery hypothesis as reasonable, despite the number of unproved assumptions it contained.

Biological anthropologist Fatimah Jackson was one of the first to raise severe criticisms of this theory. She pointed out that even if high mortality had occurred in the middle passage due to salt retention, that genes predisposing to hypertension would not have been maintained in novel environments and there was substantial genetic admixture from Europeans into African Americans. Historian Philip Curtin pulled the plank out from the slavery hypothesis by demonstrating that two of its key assumptions were false. First, he showed that western Africa was not scarce of salt. Western Africans had known how to produce salt by evaporating sea water long before the European slave trade began in Africa. Further, Curtin challenged both the magnitude and the sources of mortality in the middle passage required to make the slavery hypothesis tenable. Curtin showed that mortality on slave voyages was not as high as 70 percent, but more in the range of 15 percent. The high mortality figure was essential to the slavery hypothesis. It required very strong natural selection operating in a relatively short period to make any sense. Evolutionary biologists pointed out that it was not likely that salt retention and excretion were controlled by the same genetic mechanism. Neither could such a complex genetic trait evolve so rapidly nor was there evidence of a genetic bottleneck in African Americans that should have resulted from such severe selection. African Americans do not seem to be less genetically variable than western Africans; in fact, Europeans are more genetically restricted, indicating that they were founded from a few thousand individuals thirty to fifty thousand years ago. Finally, the available evidence suggested that other sources of mortality, such as respiratory infection, on slave vessels might have been just as prevalent as salt retention. However, despite all the evidence to the contrary, the slavery hypothesis is still widely cited by researchers and clinicians as a cause of greater hypertension in African Americans.

Hypertension could be the poster child for complex diseases. At least thirty-three genetic systems and more than sixty-three gene loci have been investigated for an association with increased risk of hypertension over the last six years. In a recent search on MEDLINE, one of the most popular biomedical research citation services, I examined fifty-seven studies published between 1997 and 2003. These studies concerned genetic variation associated with hypertension and racial variation. The studies revealed some inconsistencies that continue to plague research concerning biological variation, complex disease, and socially defined race. For example, twenty-three out of fifty-seven studies compared genetic variants in only people socially described as black or white in the United States, six out of fifty-seven examined only blacks, while none of the fifty-seven examined only whites. Another twenty-eight out of fifty-seven studies included sub-Saharan Africans, Afro-Caribbean groups, Europeans, or east Asians. The results of these studies show that we are a long way from understanding the complex genetic determination of hypertension or how these are distributed geographically.

The genetic variants were related to hypertension or a related disease in all the populations examined in only seven out of fifty-seven studies. However, fifteen out of fifty-seven and fourteen out of fifty-seven studies found that the genetic variant was associated with disease in people described as U.S. "whites" or "blacks" respectively. Another two out of fifty-seven and six out of fifty-seven found the genetic variant only associated with disease in only Caribbean and African blacks respectively. Finally, two out of fifty-seven and two out of fifty-seven found positive associations of the genetic variants in people described as European and east Asian, respectively. This also means that thirteen out of fifty-seven of the studies found *no* significant associations with the genetic variants they studied. Results such as this are almost impossible to interpret. They could be due to a number of complex genetic mechanisms, including genetic background effects such as linkage disequilibrium, *epistasis* (the influence of genetic background on the expression of any particular gene), or *pleiotropy* (the effect of one gene on multiple physical traits in an organism).

In the case of hypertension there is at least one locus that could have pleiotropic effects predisposing individuals to this disease. Lactose intolerance results from an autosomal dominant gene found in high frequency in Africans, East Asians, and Hispanics. A *gene* is an autosomal dominant if it is found on the non-sex-determining chromosomes and the trait is expressed over the recessive form (lactose tolerant). A lactose-intolerant person cannot digest lactose and, therefore, has a very difficult time eating dairy products. Dairy products are high in calcium, magnesium, and potassium; these minerals have been shown to reduce the risk of hypertension. A study of dietary intake and hypertension found that diets that included three servings of low-fat dairy foods significantly reduced blood pressure; the result was twice as effective in African-American participants. They further showed that African Americans, Hispanic, and Asian Americans have very low dietary intakes of calcium, 600–700 milligrams per day. *Osteoporosis* (bone loss) and hypertension may result below this threshold amount. If African Americans, Hispanics, and Asian Americans are avoiding dairy products due to lactose intolerance, than this gene is having a pleiotropic effect on both genes predisposing for hypertension and osteoporosis. However lactose intolerance alone cannot be responsible for elevated hypertension levels, since Asian Americans generally have lower hypertension rates than European Americans, yet have higher frequencies of lactose intolerance.

Gene frequencies alone do not explain the hypertension differentials; something else must be going on. The disease differential could also be the result of powerful environmental interactions with genetic backgrounds, which are not all easy to decipher. The simpleminded genetic explanations for racial hypertension differentials fail to explain why, in studies that report gene frequency differences between populations, the results do not support this hypothesis. In the studies I examined between 1997 and 2003, only 20 percent had results that were in the direction of genetic variation matching hypertension differential! That means that 80 percent of the studies showed genetic differences between populations, but the differences did not match the prevalence of hypertension in the groups studied (Appendix 16).

There is abundant evidence that the physical and social environments that individuals experience strongly influence their predisposition to disease. For example, if minerals such as calcium, magnesium, and potassium play a role in reducing hypertension risk, then diet alone could be a powerful source in hypertension rates. European Americans could be eating foods that have higher concentrations of these minerals due to cultural reasons, as opposed to such genetic reasons as lactose intolerance. In addition, vitamin D levels are linked to predisposition for hypertension. This may be because vitamin D plays a role in the retention of calcium. Humans can produce their own vitamin D through interaction of Ultraviolet (UV) light with their skin. Individuals with darker skin have greater UV protection but lower vitamin D synthesis. However, vitamin D deficiencies can be corrected by diet. Dairy products such as a cup of whole, fortified milk contain as much 2.5 micrograms of vitamin D, but dairy products pale in comparison to seafood. A 100 gram portion of swordfish, salmon, or tuna contains 45, 12, or 7.2 micrograms of vitamin D, respectively.

Skin-color variation in the United States shows that there is a great range of pigmentation in people of African-American descent. Darker individuals will synthesize less vitamin D than lighter individuals, and skin color is not a racialized trait. However, on the whole, African Americans are darker in complexion than European Americans, and one could argue that many disease conditions result from differences in skin tone (assuming that diets are inadequate). Hypertension rates generally increase further from the equator, so that intense sunlight still allows sufficient skin vitamin D synthesis, even given that populations near the equator are darker skinned. In America, the African-American population is concentrated in the southern areas that receive a great deal of sunlight. Further, if vitamin D deficiency were the sole cause of the hypertension differential, providing affected individuals with better diets and UV radiation therapy would easily eliminate the problem. Both treatments increase vitamin D levels and reduce blood pressure.

Unfortunately, the evidence tells us that the problem is not simply a problem of diet or sunlight exposure. Hypertension, like the predisposition to many other diseases, is related to how our social structure exposes individuals to toxic physical and cultural conditions. Chronic lead exposure is related to a number of disease conditions including hypertension and predisposition for violence. Data from the Third National Health and Nutrition survey showed from a representative sample of 14,952 African- and European-American men and women older than eighteen years that the former had between 22 percent to 13 percent higher blood-lead levels. The blood-lead levels were further shown to increase blood pressure in predictable ways. Other studies have validated the generally higher blood-lead content of African Americans at all ages compared to both Mexican Americans and European Americans. This pattern may also be linked to low cal-

cium intake in the diet of African Americans, but differences in
calcium intake are not the only cause of the disparity, since we
have already pointed out that both Hispanics and Asian Americans have lower calcium intakes, but do not show the same
amount of blood lead or hypertension.

How can social structure be responsible for the higher lead exposure of African Americans? Social structure determines where
you live and the quality of the environment in that location. For
example, most children poisoned by lead were exposed to it in and
around their home. This exposure comes from harmful levels of
lead-contaminated dust, deteriorated lead-based paint, and lead-
contaminated soil. The two key risk factors linked to elevated
blood-lead levels in children are living in older housing and living
in a low-income household. In addition, the widespread use of sil-
icofluoride additives in drinking water have disproportionately affected African Americans. The role of silicofluorides in
transporting heavy metals such as lead and mercury was never
tested before their introduction in the 1950s. Now, over 140 million Americans are exposed to this chemical which, unlike sodium
fluoride, ferries lead into the blood stream via drinking water. The
U.S. Centers for Disease Control (CDC) considers lead poisoning
the foremost environmental health threat to American children.
Almost one million children, 4.4 percent of all preschoolers, have
enough lead in their blood to reduce intelligence and attention
span, cause learning disabilities, and permanent damage to their
brains and nervous systems.

The EPA monitors more than forty compounds present in pollutants that contain lead. Throughout America, toxic exposure is
strongly linked to socially constructed race. Over 53 percent of the
toxic waste sites across the country are located within one mile of
housing projects that are greater than 75 percent minority occu-
pied. New Jersey ranks among the top 20 percent in lead exposure
environments. It shows the same pattern of differential exposure
to toxic materials in the environment for nonwhites (Appendix
17).

In America, the social variables of race and ethnicity, high and low income, and home ownership are related. African Americans still lag behind in home ownership, new construction, density of living units, and quality of plumbing. The quality of African-American housing is behind European Americans in all these standards, yet the former still pay a larger fraction of their income on housing. Housing was the last area of American life civil rights legislation addressed. The National Housing Act created the Federal Housing Administration on June 27, 1934. After World War II, returning GIs faced a shortage of housing, so Congress implemented Reorganization Plan Number 3 which established the Housing and Home Finance Agency on July 27, 1947. The Housing Act of 1949 augmented these measures establishing the national housing objective to provide federal aid to assist slum clearance, community development, and redevelopment programs passed on July 15, 1949. This legislation helped the Federal Housing Authority to guarantee long-term housing loans in ways that had never existed before. Under the new lending requirements, an applicant could put 10 to 20 percent down, and finance the house at very low interest rates for up to thirty years. Between 1934 and 1962, FHA loan programs provided 120 billion dollars in loans, but less than 2 percent went to nonwhites. Furthermore, FHA underwriting manuals warned that even one or two nonwhite families in a neighborhood posed a severe risk to property values. The National Appraisal System for Financial Risk ranked properties as most desirable (marked in green), still desirable (marked in blue), declining in value (marked in yellow), and undesirable (marked in red). Green properties were those farthest away from nonwhites and the inner cities, still desirable communities were described by their proximity to minorities, but the fact that they were still predominantly white, declining in value meant that the neighborhoods had been integrated, and undesirable meant a large percentage of minorities resided in the communities. The effect of this loan program and rating system was to create the modern suburbs and to further segregate whites and nonwhites in American society.

To maintain these conditions, lending agencies systematically denied African Americans and other minorities housing loans. Well into the 1990s, bankers calculated the financial risk of a neighborhood based on the percentage of home ownership and the racial composition of that community. Federal housing reports showed these communities in red, which is the origin of the term *red-lining*, as referring to denying minorities fair housing rights. Research has shown that, in cities such as Atlanta, Baltimore, Boston, Chicago, New York, Philadelphia, and Washington, the neighborhoods of subordinate groups received fewer and smaller bank loans than European-American communities. The race of a perspective buyer also determined their loan, whites in the lowest socioeconomic categories often received loans while blacks with median incomes over $66,000 per year could not receive loans.

The denial of home loans to African Americans has powerful implications. One of them is health, since living in home-owning communities means less risk of exposure to environmental pollutants and older housing more likely to have high levels of lead. It also is directly responsible for the present wealth differential between African and European Americans. Most Americans accumulate wealth through home ownership; in 1990, only 43 percent of African Americans, compared to 68 percent of European Americans, owned homes. Social oppression maintains housing segregation which, in turn, reinforces the coalitional allegiances in our society. For example, private prejudice and discrimination act so that people do not sell, rent, or lend to people of the wrong coalition (socially constructed race). Real-estate companies, controlled by the dominant social coalition, still steer people to the supposed right neighborhoods based on race. The government, also controlled by our dominant social coalition has been predictably slow to enact antibias legislation with regard to housing. Also, public-housing policies and past construction practices reinforce segregation of minorities in poor and inner city neighborhoods. Finally, the policies of banks and other lenders, again mainly operated by our socially dominant coalition, still create barriers based on race to financing or purchasing a home.

Social oppression can directly affect an individual's risk to hypertension. The differential between European Americans and African Americans results from differences located in the higher income categories. If one examines hypertension rates by socioeconomic status, then analyzes these rates deleting the highest socioeconomic class, African- and European-American rates are identical. This means that in the case of hypertension for African Americans, we see an inverse of the usual association between higher disease incidence and lower socioeconomic class. This results because of the out-of-place principle of social dominance. Thus, higher-status African Americans are exposed to greater stress as a result of their social position. The socially dominant group responds with hostility toward a member of a socially oppressed group within their midst, we would expect that the out-of-place person would experience greater stress. There is adequate evidence to support this idea. Ellis Cose's book *The Rage of a Privileged Class,* published in 1993, describes the often horrifying experiences of African Americans in high-status professions. Other scholars point to an epidemic of undiagnosed depression amongst professional African-American men, again indications of the out-of-place principle in action. This means that the hypertension difference results from a biological response to social and cultural factors, as opposed to a genetic predisposition to hypertension. Therefore, if we control societal racism, or African-American responses to societal racism, we could quickly reduce the hypertension differential with European Americans.

There is already evidence that this approach may work. A study of Afro-Caribbean women showed that internalized racism, anxiety, and depression were statistically linked with abdominal obesity. Obesity, in turn, is linked to elevated blood pressure and hypertension risk. Another study of ninety African-American women showed that women who had the risk factors associated

with hypertensive disease were able to avoid using medication because of greater anger coping skills.[3] Finally, a study of rural
southern African- and European-American women found that
when the hypertension rates were adjusted for the body mass
index of the women, race was no longer a risk factor. The only ex-
planatory variables were level of education and body mass index.
African-American women had fewer years of education, and a
higher percentage of them were overweight and obese.

Hypertension has all the ingredients of a complex disease. Yet
when we examine the research on genetic and environmental and
social sources of the differential hypertension rates in America,
simple genetic explanations fail woefully. From what we have
seen, environmental and social conditions seem to be playing a far
more important role in influencing genetic predispositions which,
in turn, produce the health disparities we have observed for
African Americans and other socially subordinated groups over
American history.

Social position is clearly a factor in expected health and life
span. Within social position, education could be a key factor. A
2002 study published in the *New England Journal of Medicine,*
examining mortality rates between 1986 and 1994, showed that
persons without a high-school education lost 12.8 potential years
of life, as compared to 3.6 years for a person who graduated high
school. The income level effect was similar to that of educational
level. The effects were different for African and European Americans, with African Americans losing seven years per category as
opposed to only five for European Americans. Results such as
these could explain why Asian Americans are actually doing better than European Americans in health statistics. While Asian
Americans have also faced degrees of social oppression in the
United States, they have fared better economically and with regard
to education compared to African Americans. In addition, Asian-
American diets are generally healthier in some ways compared to
other populations, although disease statistics for Asian populations have begun to mirror the general population in proportion

to the number of generations they have resided in America. Presumably, this reflects changing cultural values and attitudes.

Despite all the high-sounding rhetoric of the health disparity initiative, it seems that historical social factors do a better job of explaining the racial patterns we see in mortality, as opposed to genetic differences in disease systems. If our goal is really reducing health disparity, then why not address the patterns of social dominance that relegate some people to inferior housing, greater exposure to toxic pollution, lower educational opportunities, and, so, less chance of entering higher-income professions?

The evidence tells us that a death sentence is waiting for minorities who have beaten the odds and successfully played the game. The out-of-place principle guarantees that such individuals are met with frustration, stress, anxiety, and depression. Mr. T once said that he was still in chains, but his chains were fashioned of gold. Social dominance guarantees that the racial coalition in power wins either way. Only two scenarios can change this and they are not mutually exclusive. The first is that the socially oppressed achieve both consciousness of their oppression and the resolve to end it. In this scenario, both peaceful and violent solutions to this injustice are possible. Peaceable change is dependent on how determined the oppressors are at maintaining an unjust society that determines your longevity by the color of your skin. Lincoln tried every avenue he could to preserve the Union, but the Confederates insisted upon the path of violence.

The other scenario is that the oppressors realize that they cannot safely maintain their injustices. The price they pay for today's social dominance is growing social unrest and, if it continues, our society may burst at the seams. They may have been willing to look the other way at the drug epidemic, as long as nonwhites were predominately affected. Now, the data tell us that European-American youth are more likely to suffer from tobacco use, alcohol disorders, marijuana abuse, cocaine, and hallucinogenic use as compared to African Americans.[4] Greater drug use will have cascading effects, including the risk of increasing HIV transmission.

Neither can the socially dominant group allow the social divide between the haves and the havenots to get much bigger. As America's enemies abroad increase, it will be even more necessary to mend fences internally. A country's people is its most precious resource. Can we really afford to poison our own children with lead and other toxic compounds? How many potential scientists, doctors, engineers, and entrepreneurs are lost in childhood due to differential health conditions? The ruling elite will have to decide how much of this carnage it can stand and still maintain its claim to legitimacy. Otherwise, the other scenario will make that decision for them.

CHAPTER 6

Europeans, Not West Africans, Dominate the NBA: The Social Construction of Race and Sports

One of the most pernicious of all the racial beliefs is the idea that blacks are innately superior athletes. Over the last six years, I have given innumerable lectures debunking the existence of our socially constructed racial groups. When the lecture ends, invariably someone from the audience confronts me with the deeply held conviction that races are real because everyone knows that there are profound differences in athletic ability among the races. They cite the overwhelming dominance of African-American professional athletes in basketball and football. They state that black musculature and bone density, while making African Americans great jumpers, means that they cannot float. As proof positive, they talk about the overwhelming dominance of whites in swimming. They go on to state that the emergence of athletes like Tiger Woods in golf, the Williams sisters in tennis, and the Kenyans in long-distance running is further evidence of the general superiority of the black athlete. If social barriers were removed, they predict that sport performance would reveal its racial character, because some races are just better at certain athletic feats than others. Most Americans believe these ideas. But are they really true?

Purportedly scholarly analysis, in recent years, has accentuated the false belief that races exist and that they differ in athletic ability. Predictably, many of the scholars behind this concept are also champions of African-American and Hispanic intellectual inferiority. A decade ago, Richard Herrnstein and Charles R. Murray discussed their ideas on race and intelligence in *The Bell Curve*. Supporting them, Canadian psychologist J. P. Philippe Rushton provided the supposedly scientific rationale for genetically based tradeoffs between intellect, athletic ability, and sexual perform- ance in human races.[1] Rushton invoked the concept of r- and K- selection theory to rank the three broad races of humans (Negroid, Caucasoid, and Mongoloid) on a scale of life-history characteristics. Life-history characters include traits related to Darwinian fitness, such as longevity, reproductive effort, gestation time, and infant mortality. In brief, r-selected species have charac- teristics similar to weeds: fast growth, short life spans, and rapid and copious reproduction. K-selected species, on the other hand, should exhibit slow growth, longer life spans, and reduced and ju- dicious reproduction. Originating in the 1960s, this concept soon became a major theoretical tenet of life history evolution. It ar- gued that, at low population density, individuals with genes that promoted rapid growth and early reproduction were favored, de- spite the fact that they would have deficits in traits related to long- term survival. Conversely, at high population density, traits that fostered survival and competition would be favored, despite the fact that they would interfere with reproduction. Several authors have attempted to describe the features of the human races utiliz- ing the r- and K-scheme. Caucasians and Mongoloids are suppos- edly K-selected, explaining their larger brains and supposed superior social traits, while Negroids are supposedly r-selected, explaining their smaller brains, larger gonads and reproductive ef- fort, and shorter lives. While these ideas may seem to make sense, they are, in the end, hopelessly compromised.

All of the r- and K-selection arguments infer some kind of un- derlying genetic tradeoff between competing physiological needs. By this logic, genes that are beneficial for athletic performance are simultaneously detrimental to the intellect. Although this is a widely held belief, there is no evidence for such a genetic tradeoff between these traits. In fact, what we know about intelligence, however defined, suggests that as much as 40 percent of the genes in our genome contribute to it. There are good reasons to believe that genetically based differences could be either positive or negative for both intellect and athletic ability. If, for example, genetic differences in circulatory capacity exist, they would help both the brain and the muscles. Genes that provide faster neural conduction in the brain could also help movement of the muscles, and so forth. Studies of athletic conditioning, which is overwhelmingly a physical treatment, and its effect on cognitive function suggest that being in better athletic shape increases your cognitive potential, although not necessarily vice versa! At first, this might not seem correct. After all, our society provides plenty of examples of physical or phenotypic tradeoffs between athletics and intellect. We all know the nerdy couch potato who, while very smart, isn't exactly Mr. Universe. Or conversely, we know of the sports programs that discourage their athletes from taking any academically rigorous courses. However, these are culturally and socially induced tradeoffs, not genetic ones. They result from the amount of emphasis an individual gives to either athletic or intellectual pursuits. Most people have the potential to develop both their intellectual and athletic abilities.

In a fall 2000 BBC documentary film about race and athletics, *Black Britain: The Faster Race,* several scientists claimed that blacks (Negroids) can run faster than whites (Caucasoids) or East Asians (Mongoloids) because the black skull is the smallest. The smaller skull, they reasoned, meant that blacks had a narrower pelvis bone than whites or Asians whose babies were born with bigger heads. So, the difference in skull size meant a smaller pelvic aperture in black females resulting in a more efficient stride. This posits that all black sprinters, such as Marion Jones or Australian Cathy Freeman, (who dominated the 2000 Summer Olympic Games), descended from mothers who had narrow pelvises. This is not something that would have happened in one generation, but over hundreds of generations of human evolution, thus giving each race its unique athletic features. There are of course, huge problems with this sort of analysis. The first is that r- and K-selection arguments could easily predict that Europeans or Asians should be athletically superior to Africans. The r- and K-model does predict that K-selected (Europeans and Asians) invest more in the entire body versus energy used for reproduction. There is no reason why this increased investment could not include the development of superior musculature or skeletal features. Furthermore, a tradeoff in female pelvic bone width could be easily compensated for in other physiological systems that might help athletic performance. This general form of argument is once again a story that works so long as we accept all of its assumptions. However, if we challenge any of them, the entire argument collapses like a house of cards.

We can never make claims about an individual's physical attributes based on knowing the average characteristics of a group. People who attempt to calculate average anatomical differences for groups of people to stereotype individuals have never grasped the illogic of this enterprise. Worse still are those who understand what they are doing, precisely so that can denigrate races other than their own. This is another example of racial typology, identical to the reasoning used in racial medicine. This predicts that every person of African descent will be a great runner, but a bad swimmer. It predicts that West African sprinters will usually defeat European sprinters. However, we know that Africans, African Americans, and Australian aborigines did not win every sprint event in which they were entered in 2000, or any other Olympic games, for that matter. Further complicating the racial typologist scheme of athletic performance was the emergence of Kenyan long-distance runners in the last quarter of the twentieth century. This ideology was saved by now positing an overall running superiority for Africans over Europeans and Asians. Yet the East Africans did not win every long distance event in recent years. In fact, the more we examine sports that don't happen to be popular in the United States because they lack major financial rewards (such as soccer), the less case can be made for any sort of African, or African-American dominance of sports performance.

Physiological Differences and Athletic Ability

People still believe the myths regarding race and athleticism, even though physical anthropologists disproved these claims in the 1930s. Today, however, much is still made of the relationship between running ability and the genetic differences controlling muscle-fiber types between so-called blacks and whites. Fast twitch (type IIa and IIx) fibers are good for power and speed, and slow twitch (type I) fibers are best for endurance. We would expect to find that sprinters have more type II fibers and endurance runners have more type I fibers. Empirical studies suggest that the legs of a world-class sprinter would have about 80 percent fast twitch to 20 percent slow, while the average active person would be expected to have about 50 percent fast to 50 percent slow. On the other hand, a world-class marathon runner would have 80 percent slow to 20 percent fast.[2] Racial typologists assume that there are racial differences for the genes that control the distributions of muscle fiber types. They furthermore claim that the genetic factors fix the proportion of fibers and that training cannot drastically alter their ratio. For example, a 1986 study examined fast and slow twitch-muscle types between West African blacks and French-Canadian whites.[3] The authors found that the blacks were 67.5 percent fast muscle, as compared to only 59 percent in the whites. Utilizing these averages, and applying a normal curve based on the variability in the data, they concluded that the black curve would have a greater probability of producing fast-muscle percentages consistent with what we would expect in world-class sprinters (they estimated world-class sprinters should have more than 90 percent fast fibers). Because they believed that the differences in muscle-fiber proportion were genetically determined and therefore immutable, blacks, they claimed, were naturally more likely to produce world-class sprinters.

Once again, this study suffers from the authors' own irrational belief in the existence of the biological racial categories. They made the most elementary error in genetics, assuming that a pattern in physical features necessarily results from an underlying genetic difference. They assumed that membership in a socially constructed racial group was responsible for genetic differences that specified the number and type of muscle-fiber types we would expect to find in any individual. They made this assumption without ever establishing which specific genes were responsible for determining muscle-fiber percentages. Neither did they do any sort of systematic measurement of human populations to determine what the frequency of these reputed genes was for each group. For example, they reported no information that proved that all blacks, or Africans, have 10 percent more fast-muscle fibers than all whites, or Europeans, or whether there was a range of values of these fibers in Africans, Asians, Europeans, or in any of the geographic regions that border these major continental areas. Neither did they consider whether, if they reassigned the individuals in the study into new groups based on other physical characteristics, they might not get similar results. For example, they could have taken all the individuals in the study who were short versus tall, with widow's peaks or without them, or with different blood types and asked do we get significant differences in muscle-fiber proportions? If we do, are the differences on the same order as that produced by membership in a socially constructed racial group, are they less, or are they more? In addition, they didn't perform any of the standard analyses between the socially constructed racial groups in their study required to prove that a physical difference results from a genetic difference. These tests require some kind of controlled breeding scheme, across several generations, with rigorously controlled environments, and require at least two generations to control for maternal genetic effects. During the sixty years of the research you would have had to tell the people whom they could marry, men to sire children from at least four different women, what those children could eat, where they could live, and what exercise regime they could have maintained. We can do this in the laboratory with experimental animals, but we do not allow such studies on humans for obvious ethical reasons. Alternately, if they had taken data on large numbers of identical and fraternal twin pairs in each of the socially constructed racial groups they could have estimated the number of fiber types and calculated its heritability in each group. We have no studies of muscle-fiber distribution that match what would be required to make genetic claims to test racialized or even population differences. The studies that have been published about muscle-fiber distribution only imply a genetic basis to any differences they find, but they are a long way from offering any sort of scientific proof.

Even things as subtle as differences in diet or conditions faced during gestation could influence the expression of various genes, hence producing a physical difference. Diet influences hormone levels and they, in turn, can influence the proportion of muscle-fiber types in animals. Testosterone level is responsible for the different muscle-fiber percentages between male and female mice (females have more type I fibers). If there was no control for those factors in the study, one could not even begin to make a claim that the differences in muscle-fiber percentages resulted from differences in underlying genes. What is worse is that, for a long time, this study was considered the gold standard for suggesting that there are genetically determined racial differences in fiber percentages! A significant amount of biomedical research continues to assume that the findings of this study were valid. Yet, two recent studies of American blacks and whites examining both inactive college-age men and college football players show no significant differences in muscle-fiber proportions and muscle architecture (Appendix 18).

The football-player study did show that the black athletes had a significantly greater quadriceps, hamstrings, and biceps muscle thickness, compared to the whites. However there was no evidence of any difference between the muscle architectures of the two groups.[4] Any number of social or environmental factors could explain these results.

Worse for those insisting that racial identity determines athleticism, their reasoning would not explain the differences we currently observe in the number of world-class sprinters of African-American versus European-American origin. We can understand this point by examining some basic tenets in statistics. The racial typologists suggest that blacks have a greater percentage of people whose range of type II muscle fiber is suitable for producing world-class sprinters. Let us suppose, for example, that blacks would be ten times more likely to produce people with the muscle-fiber distribution of the world-class sprinter range as compared to whites. However, the actual number of people with world-class sprinter muscle distribution we would expect to find would be dependent on the size of the population in question. Using the total population size and the relative proportions of whites and blacks in America, we would expect that 303,118 blacks and 206,672 whites are alive today with the genetic architecture required to be world-class sprinters! Proportionately, there should be only 1.46 times more blacks with the proper genetics to be world-class sprinters than whites. Yet, recently, African-Americans have dominated sprinting in America, in numbers greater than predicted by the theoretical distribution of genotypes that predict muscles of world-class sprinters. Remember that this scenario proceeded under the assumption that blacks were ten times more likely than whites to have the proper muscle distribution, which the most recent data show is highly unlikely. So, we need to find other reasons for why whites have not excelled in sprinting besides predicted differences in genetic ability between the socially constructed races.

The genetic argument for racial dominance in sprinting also suffers from the assumption that muscle-fiber types are fixed and that they cannot be changed during development or by training as juveniles or as adults. We now know that this is false. New research coming out of Sweden suggests that type I fibers can be converted to type II and vice versa.[5] This work has profound implications for the future of athletic training. The laboratories involved in this research see the day when it will be possible to use gene therapy techniques to introduce either the genes or their protein products that allow this transition to occur directly into athletes while training. This would mean a new type of doping before competition, one that might not be detectable by authorities. This type of technology would most likely be available to the richest of nations. It is also clear that the implementation of such technology would soon overturn racial stereotypes in running, since these treatments could produce any desirable combination of muscle fibers, regardless of an individual's genetic composition.

If Athletic Success Is Influenced by Genes, Why Isn't It a Racial Feature?

We cannot apportion individual humans into biological groups determined only by their skin color or any other physical features. If we accept the principle that biomechanical features of individual athletes predict their potential for success in a specific sport, we still could find individuals from most parts of the world that have the physical features to participate in and for some to excel in a given sport because genetic variation determines the amount of physical variation within a specific population group. Since there is more genetic variation within groups than there is among them, we expect that in populations of sufficient size, we should observe virtually all body types within any chosen group, even if the average of the body type features between arbitrarily constructed groups were different. A recent study of bone mass density in boys shows that in three different bones (hip, trochanter, and the femoral neck) blacks had significantly higher bone-mass density than whites (Appendix 19). However, in three categories there was no significant difference, total body bone density, forearm, and lumbar spine. The values for the hip, trochanter, and femoral neck are so close together that there would be many black individuals with white values and white individuals with black values. Neither can we assume that any of these differences were the result of solely genetic differences between groups. We know that diet in midpuberty and activity levels in prepuberty significantly predict bone mass in adults and that lifestyle variables significantly impact bone density in adult humans.

Of course there are exceptions to the rule that all groups will produce the entire range of human body types. Small populations that lost much of their genetic variation in their history will produce a narrower range of physical types. Pygmies of the Central African Republic, whom most people would call black, are not likely to produce people who are very tall, so do not expect them to excel in any sport were height is an advantage, such as basketball or volleyball. Since genetic variation combines with environmental conditions to produce the physical features we see in individuals within populations, we could imagine that some groups exist with all the genes required to produce individuals who would excel in a variety of athletic events, but due to social factors such as poverty and disease can never do so.

A number of general rules come into play when we examine the evolution of the physical features and body proportions in any warm-blooded animal, such as humans. The first is *Bergman's Rule*, which relates body size to average environmental temperature. This principle states that body sizes that evolve in cooler climates will be larger than those in warmer climates. This results from the fact that large bodies retain heat better due to smaller surface area. An extension of Bergman's Rule is *Allen's Rule*, which states that protruding body parts, such as arms and legs, are generally shorter in cooler climates. Finally, *Gloger's Rule* relates to body pigmentation—people from warmer, more humid areas are more heavily pigmented than those from cooler, arid areas. For example, we could use these principles to explain the difference in body features we see in Eskimos versus northeastern Africans. The former tend to be shorter, have thicker chests, are short limbed, and fair skinned, versus the latter, who are taller, leaner, long limbed, and dark skinned.

If northeastern Africans and Eskimos were the only people on earth, it would be rather easy to sort them into two discrete groups. However, it is more correct to understand that people who inhabit the tropical zones and those of the artic zones represent the extremes of the continuum of human physical features. These three physical rules work together and vary continuously in conjunction with changes in climate and altitude. In addition, individuals from various parts of the continuum of human genetic and physical variation move back and forth, between populations. This means that they often (and we have abundant evidence of this) reproduce and thereby move genes that might have originated in the tropics, to populations in the temperate zones. In fact, we can show that it takes very little migration to explain the small amount of genetic diversity we see among human populations. The long and short of this is that for most large populations, there is sufficient genetic variation to produce virtually any body type in conjunction with other specific physiological traits. This means that we could produce great athletes for virtually any sport, anywhere in the world, given the correct cultural and environmental input.

Another consistent theme we see to explain the supposed superior performance of black male athletes is that of their supposedly higher hormone levels. Black males are supposed to have higher levels of circulating sex hormones, called *androgens,* compared to whites and Asians. It was further argued that these hormone-level differences make blacks more aggressive, violent, and lawless. The theory of r- and K-selection that purportedly created the different human races predicted that sex hormone levels should also vary by race. In the early 1990s, a study of racial hormone levels examined males discharged from the U.S. Army sometime between 1965 and 1971.[6] The study examined over four thousand non-

Hispanic whites, blacks, Hispanics, Asian and Pacific Islanders, and Native Americans in their late thirties. They found that the amount of testosterone in the blood was greatest in Asian and Pacific Islanders, then blacks, whites, Hispanics, and, finally, Native Americans. After the samples were adjusted for the both age and the weight of the individuals in the groups, the order of the groups changed to: Blacks, then, Asian/Pacific Islanders, Native Americans, whites, and Hispanics. There were a number of problems with how this data was obtained but, even if we accept these results, they do match the predictions of those who claim that socially defined race determines athletic performance. This study predicted that Asian and American Indian men should be more aggressive than white or Hispanic men. Yet our society sees Asian Americans as the model minorities, and also doesn't view them as likely to be superstars in aggressive and violent sports, such as football or boxing.

Finally, while it is widely known that testosterone levels influence sex drive and aggression in male primates, it is also known that learning strongly modifies the influence of sex hormones.[7] Experiments in which additional testosterone was given to males did not increase their sex drive above normal levels, and testosterone levels are strongly influenced by daily and seasonal rhythms. There is an extensive literature that also shows strong environmental influences on hormone levels. In addition, transient aggression also influences testosterone levels in human males; such things as tennis matches, stress, collegiate exams, or army basic training can decrease the amount of testosterone a male experiences. Studies that have used psychological rating scales to quantify levels of aggression and hostility in human males have found no relationship to their androgen levels.[8]

Even more revealing is that studies of hormone levels in recent years have not found any difference between the testosterone levels of African- and European-American men. One study found that male testosterone level was correlated to age, body mass index (BMI), and waist circumference. When black and white males were compared for testosterone level and only age and BMI were controlled, black males had about a 3 percent higher testosterone level. However, once waist circumference was included in this analysis, there was no difference between the groups. The 1992 study of men discharged from the army did not use body mass index or waist circumference when analyzing their results. Research concerning the genetic controls of testosterone level show that it is a complex trait. A genomewide linkage scan for genes controlling steroid hormones found that over sixteen different genes were involved in the process. The loci were not the same in the black and white families examined. This is strong evidence that many environmental influences alter sex hormone levels.[9]

Once again, we arrive at the same underlying problem that exists in all the biological comparisons of socially constructed races. That is, unless all the subjects in these testosterone measurements experienced the same environments, the same social conditions, and had displayed the same psychological responses to them, such studies are meaningless. We know full well that American society does not treat African- and European-American males equally so, until that is true, we cannot take any measurements of hormone levels in these groups by which we can prove has any relationship to any supposed genetic differences between them, let alone posit that hormonal levels determine success in any specific sport.

Basketball Jones: If Blacks Are Such Great Athletes, Why Don't Africans Dominate the NBA?

So far, we have assumed that the claim that black athletes dominate certain sports on the international and professional level is true. However, when we actually put sport performance under more objective analysis, we see that this just is not true. Playing basketball is a human behavior, determined by a complex interplay between individual genetic ability, culture, and society. If we assumed for one second that there was a black gene for jumping or basketball ability, then we should expect to see that gene in large numbers of people from every population that we call black. Furthermore, we should see more basketball playing ability in people who are supposedly pure black, if there is something uniquely black to that particular athletic endeavor. Thus, since the ancestral home of the African portion of black American genes is in West Africa, we should see more West Africans in the National Basketball Association (NBA), Women's National Basketball Association (WNBA), or the National Collegiate Athletic Association (NCAA—men's and women's) demonstrating amazing jumping ability. Or we should observe West Africans setting world records in the high jump or hurdles in Olympic events.

However, we do not see that because other factors: aspects of culture, environment, and chance also come into play. For example, in the early days of American basketball, Jewish individuals of Eastern European origin were well-represented in the professional ranks. Anti-Semites explained their prominence in the sport by pointing to their craftiness and cunning. These traits were thought to contribute to their success at the game.

The so-called black dominance of the NBA has been well touted. The NBA was founded in 1946 and, after its first fifty years, named its fifty greatest players. Of these, only one was a West African, Hakeem Olajuwon, of the Houston Rockets; thirty-one were African Americans, and eighteen were European American. However, if we examine players whose career peaked before the 1970s, there were no West Africans, six African Americans, and nine European Americans. An examination of the Basketball Hall of Fame, which, by its nature, is biased toward representation of players and coaches from the earlier periods of the sport, shows only thirty-four African Americans, seventy-seven European Americans, and no West Africans, as of 2001. This means the perception that African Americans dominate professional or collegiate basketball is only the result of the last thirty years. The change in the league's composition coincided with social changes in the United States, in particular, the movement of larger numbers of African Americans from the rural south to the Northern cities after World War II. Basketball was suited to become a game frequented by the urban poor because the infrastructure to support it was relatively cheap. Both indoor and outdoor courts sprang up across the predominantly African-American inner cities. Sports had already become an acceptable avenue for the advancement of African-American individuals, in part due to the racist ideology that portrayed blacks as innately superior in some forms of athletic performance, such as running and jumping.

The difference between who participates in American basketball and volleyball illustrates the social construction of sports performance. Both games require the same set of athletic skills, agility, hand–eye coordination, strength, jumping ability, and speed yet, in the main, basketball is currently dominated by African-American athletes, while volleyball is dominated by European-American athletes. There are currently 210 national federations in the International Volleyball Federation (*Fédération Internationale de Volleyball,* FIVB), the international governing body for the sport, which is located in Lausanne, Switzerland. An estimated 800 million people play volleyball throughout the world. World volleyball powers have included Japan, Korea, China, Soviet Union/Russia, Poland, Cuba, Brazil, and the United States. These countries clearly represent all of the world's major population groups, indicating that achievement in this game is not racially biased.

Americans held their first national volleyball championship in 1922. The U.S. Volleyball Association, now known as USA Volleyball, formed six years later. In the United States, volleyball has been one of the main women's sports at the intercollegiate level. Today, there are several hundred NCAA division I programs and the U.S. national team reflects that diversity. Women's volleyball has been both ethnically and geographically diverse. From 1981 to 1984, the U.S. team stayed near the top of international volleyball rankings. This was due in part to the play of Flora (Flo) Hyman, a high-jumping six-foot-five athlete of African-American descent, who had developed into one of the world's top players. At the 1981 World Cup Games, she was named best hitter and was se-lected to the All-World Cup Team, which consists of the world's top six players. After the 1984 Olympics, in which Hyman helped the U.S. women's team finish second to the Chinese women's team, Hyman left the U.S. team to join a club team in the Japan-ese national league. On January 24, 1986, after she was called out of a game, she sat on the bench and fell dead to the effects of Mar-fan Syndrome, a genetic defect that weakens the wall of the aorta. In 1987, the Women's Sports Foundation created the Flo Hyman Award, which is presented annually to the woman athlete with Hyman's "dignity, spirit, and commitment to excellence." A bronze sculpture of her, dedicated in 1988, stands at the U.S. Olympic Training Center in Colorado Springs.

The U.S. national team has women of African, Asian, and Eu-ropean ancestry. Only two have hometowns listed in California. In the United States, men's volleyball has never been as successful as the women's program. There are very few varsity teams. Also, the majority of the U.S. men's volleyball players are from southern California (seven of twelve Californian, one Hawaiian, one south-western, two midwestern, and one eastern) and are of European-American ancestry. A comparison of the men's U.S. basketball and volleyball programs is revealing. U.S. basketball consists entirely of NBA stars; only one of the twelve (Nick Collison) is not of African-American ancestry. There is no intrinsically athletic ex-planation for this disparity. The difference in the sports rosters reflects the different sport socialization of African- and European-American men. Men's basketball is a sport deeply influenced by and influencing African-American culture, whereas men's volley-ball is associated with the beach culture of southern California, it-self a product of European Americans.

It is easier to understand the absence of African Americans from men's volleyball than it is to explain the absence of European-American participation from men's basketball. The lack of participation of European Americans in basketball is not because they are inherently inferior athletes; the performance of and popularity of basketball in Europe vitiates that explanation. What is it about American basketball that makes it a disproportionately African-American game? The popularity of basketball in America has virtually every American youth dreaming of someday playing professional hoops. Yet the odds of making it to the NBA or WNBA are infinitesimal. In 1996, 1,957,000 boys were born in the United States. If the NBA does not expand, then any one of them stands about a one in 5,000 chance of making it into the NBA. If we calculated the number only for African Americans, it would still be just fourteen chances in 5,000!

The representation of the league now favors African Americans. A count of the socially defined races of the 1999–2000 NBA rosters for players who logged more than six hundred minutes in the season (with eighty-two games, this means at least seven and a half minutes per game) showed there were 257 blacks, and forty-nine whites, or 84 percent of the league was black, and only 16 percent was white. This result is not surprising for any reader familiar with the composition of the modern NBA. However, we might come to a different understanding if we examine the league's composition genetically. African Americans have genes that originated in West Africans, Europeans, and American Indians. The average percentage of non-African genes in African Americans has been estimated to vary from as low as 6 percent to as high as 40 percent. The percentage of European genes may be even higher in some modern black professional athletes. Many are the children of men who were athletically or socially successful in the last generation and have married European-American wives. Conversely, our social conventions tell us that most European Americans have no recently derived African genes. Thus, the correct comparison to test whether it is African or European genes alone that are best for basketball performance would be to compare the number of Africans versus the number of Europeans in the league. We shouldn't use African Americans because they have a substantial fraction of their genes that originated in Europeans and American Indians. If we examine the number of Africans playing in the NBA, averaging seven and a half minutes per game in 1999–2000 and compare that to the number of Europeans, we find there were only three West Africans (Mutombo, Hawks; Olajuwon, Rockets; and Olowokandi, Clippers), nine Europeans, and one Australian (Potapenko, Celtics; Nowitski, Mavericks; Smits, Pacers; Nesterovic, Timberwolves; Kukoc, Sixers; Longley, Suns; Sabonis and Schrempf, Trailblazers; Divac and Stojakovic, Kings). Thus, if there were some uniquely West African genes that predisposed individuals for basketball, given both the NCAA and NBA's ability to recruit internationally, we should see it in the representation of its players. An examination of the NBA 2002 rosters shows twenty-one Europeans, one Asian, and only nine Africans in the league. In that same season, Yao Ming, formerly of the Shanghai Sharks, made a particularly dramatic entry into the NBA, finishing second in Rookie of the Year voting. The 2003 draft was even more international, featuring fourteen Europeans, one Chinese, and one African out of fifty-eight picks (Appendix 20). Furthermore, the United States men's basketball team, which was predominantly African-American and featured NBA notables such as Paul Pierce and Ben Wallace was eliminated by Yugoslavia in the quarterfinals and lost to Spain in the consolation game of the 2002 World Championships (Appendix 21). Worse is the fact that they were held in the United States! America finished seventh, and the only African nation in the competition finished in an abysmal eleventh place. These results do not indicate that Africans are dominating professional or international basketball. Instead we see that African Americans currently dominating the NBA and U.S. national team. However, this domination is only a transient phenomenon. With the NBA's global popularity, it will continue to recruit from all over the globe. Eventually, both the NBA and the U.S. national team will reflect the world's genetic diversity. Remember, African Americans, who currently dominate the game, are a genetically and culturally unique population that is not equivalent to any particular West African population, either in genes or in culture. In fact, it would make just as much sense to argue due to the current numerical advantage of European over West African players in the NBA, that it is the European genes in African Americans, or the fact that African Americans are mixed with genes from Europe and Asia, that allows them to excel in basketball! We really have no scientific way of separating the genetic from the environmental or cultural effects in determining athletic predisposition. So, all such claims of African genes providing superior athletic performance are at best speculation, at worst, racist ideology.

What About Track and Field?

The African-American athlete emerged as the symbol of American success in track and field, as well as the contradictions in American social structure at the 1968 Mexico City Olympics. After finishing first and second in the 200 meter dash, John Carlos and Tommy Smith donned black gloves and gave the black power salute during the national anthem. Needless to say, the U.S. Olympic Committee was incensed. Carlos and Smith were stripped of their medals and ushered out of the Olympic village. However, the 1968 Mexico City games were surrounded in controversy from the start. African-American athletes were planning to boycott the 1968 games in protest against the violation of black civil rights in America. At the last minute, the athletes decided to allow African-American participants to show their black pride in their own way at the games. Civil unrest was not limited to the United States. The Mexican army was called in to quell student demonstrations against the lack of democracy in Mexico before the games could even begin. There are estimates that the army arrested and killed thousands of students to allow the games to take place. Later on in those games, a Czechoslovakian gymnast who finished second to a Soviet gave a similar political demonstration on the medal podium as that of Carlos and Smith during the Russian national anthem. She was not stripped of her medal; instead, she was hailed as a hero by the Western press.

Over the next two decades, African Americans and Afro-Europeans dominated international sprinting. This rekindled the debate as to the genetic superiority of the African runner. However, just as with basketball, we cannot assume that the socially constructed blacks of the western hemisphere excel in sprinting because of their West African genes. For example, world-record sprinters are mainly from the United States, Canada, Great Britain, France, and the Caribbean.[10] To demonstrate this point, we can look at the results in the 100 meter dash from the 1988 Seoul Olympics. The three best times came from two Americans and one Englishman of West African descent; Carl Lewis, Linford Christie (UK), and Calvin Smith, winners of the gold, silver, and bronze medals, respectively. However, if we examine the best times of all of the West Africans, Caribbeans, Europeans, and East Asians we find some startling results. The average times for these regions were 10.74 seconds for West Africans, 10.67 for Caribbeans, 10.56 seconds for Europeans, and 10.62 seconds for East Asians! Even if we exclude Europeans with West African ancestry (like Linford Christie of the U.K.), Europeans still were faster, on average, than the West Africans at 10.56 seconds! So, if we examine all the results of the 100 meter dash, they show the exact opposite of the social stereotype: Europeans and East Asians were faster on average than runners from the Caribbean and West Africa.

At the Sydney Olympics in 2000, the men's 100 and 400 meter events were swept by individuals displaying some West African ancestry. However, an individual from Greece won the men's 200 meter event. In the high jump the winner was Russian and, in the long jump, the silver and bronze were taken by an Australian aboriginal and a Ukrainian respectively. (Remember, white men can't jump!) Finally, in the decathlon, an event that crowns the world's greatest athlete, the gold went to an Estonian, and the silver to a

Czech. In the women's competition, everyone knew that the United States's Marion Jones would win the 100 and 200 meters, however, she was followed closely by Ekaterini Thanou from Greece in the 100 meters, and a Sri Lankan woman, Susanthika Jayasinghe, took bronze in the 200 meters. The Australian Aboriginal symbol of the Sydney Games, Kathleen Freeman, dominated the 400 meters event over two Afro-British competitors (remember that Australian aborigines are the furthest away from sub-Saharan Africans in gene frequencies). Women from Britain, Russia, and Belarus won the medals in the heptathlon.[11] We see less of a pattern of West African or African-American dominance in the women's events, suggesting again that cultural values may be influencing individual genetic potential.

The results of the 2000 Sydney Olympics show that a variety of people won in the sprint and jumping events. No clear pattern of West African dominance emerged. In fact, if we examine the medal count from the West African nations where most supposedly black North Americans, African British and French, and African Caribbeans originated, their total medal count was only four (Appendix 22). An examination of the male sprint events from 1981, 1985, 1989, 1993, 1995 show no one from a West African country holding any of the world records.[12] Arguments that blacks are superior athletes to whites have relied heavily on track and field. It has been argued further that, since track and field events require the lowest expenditures, they are the only truly international sports, meaning these sports should be accessible to even the poorest nations. Once again, if we look at the entire picture of track and field, we don't see evidence that strongly suggests that having West African genes alone is sufficient to make any individual successful at the world class level.

In the early sixties, the track-and-field mantra was that blacks were fast, but couldn't run long distances. This held until the great East African distance runners emerged in the mid-1980s. Before the 2001 Boston Marathon, many were predicting that a runner of East African (Kenyan) descent would win. However, a

South Korean won the men's race with an Ecuadorean finishing in second place. East Africans (mostly Kenyans) did perform well in the race, finishing in places three, four, five, ten, twelve, fifteen, sixteen, and seventeen. On the other hand, the women's race gave no evidence of East African domination, with only one, four, and five going to East Africans. The rest of the top twenty were four Eastern Europeans, ten of Western European origin (mostly American) and three East Asians.[13] An explanation that relies solely on racial origin to account for athletic success is simply untenable here. No simple biological mechanism can account for the difference in results between the male and female competitions. Genetically, two X chromosomes are required to form women, and men result from an X and Y chromosome. During development, females inactivate one of their X chromosomes, so the gene complement of men and women is very similar. Significant secondary biological differences between men and women result from their different sex hormones. However, this process is uniform in all humans. Thus, there is no simple reason why naturally occurring sex hormones should make women of African descent less athletic than European women. Clearly, the answer lies in understanding the general social progress that women have made in various societies. In many African and Arab societies women are still systematically denied access to general human rights. The chador is worn, women must be subservient to their husbands, fathers, and brothers, and, in some countries, genital mutilation of females is still a common practice. We should not expect that such nations would provide athletic training for women, particularly at the early ages necessary to prepare athletes for international competition. On the other hand, in countries where women have made social and political progress, we see broader participation in sports. The 1996 book *Great Women in Sports* listed over 150 female athletes who excelled in over thirty-seven sports, and all were from Western nations. Countries that have wanted to make international political statements about equality, such as the former Soviet bloc nations, made extraordinary efforts to build their female sports program. The East German women's sports program of the 1970s and 1980s utilized a number of draconian measures to insure their success, including the widespread use of drugs. China's diving and gymnastics programs are also examples of state commitment to excellence in women's sports. Young children are screened in China for athletic ability. The large size of the Chinese population guarantees that if enough are screened, truly outstanding individuals will be found. Those deemed talented enough are given over by their parents to state-run training facilities. These young girls receive the best coaching, endure rigorous training regimes, and are separated from their families, to prepare them for future competition at the international level. The result, of course, is that China has made great strides in dominating international diving, and become a respected power in world gymnastics. However, does the Chinese government really care about the price these young women pay to achieve this state-directed goal?

Thus, cultural and social conditions always interact with individual genetic predispositions for athletic ability. This simple fact dismisses the idea that biological variation, let alone race, could be used as a sole predictor of athletic excellence. In fact, thirty-two out of forty African nations are actually below the world norm in their production of world-class male track and field athletes per capita.[14] This is hardly an argument for African superiority in athletic ability. It is more likely an argument that in countries of sufficient population size, social, economic, and cultural factors are more important in determining any individual's chances of becoming a world-class athlete. In fact, of the people who are socially defined as black in the world, only 8.3 percent are African Americans, compared to 86 percent who are West Africans. Yet the success of African Americans in international athletics is vastly greater than that of West Africans. If genetic differences between supposed races does not account for athletic performance, what does?

*   *   *

The first and second place finishers of the 2001 Boston Marathon (men's division) came from mountainous countries (South Korea and Ecuador). There are two ways that runners whose ancestry is from countries at high altitude are advantaged relative to those from lower altitudes. All organisms, including humans, are capable of nongenetic physiological adaptation, called *acclimation*. As the altitude increases, the air pressure decreases. For the body to maintain its ability to carry out cellular respiration (which requires oxygen), it must acclimatize to the smaller pressures at higher altitudes. These mechanisms include an increase in lung capacity, blood volume, red blood cell and hemoglobin content, enzyme activity that facilitates oxygen uploading in the tissues, and, finally, a reduction in plasma volume, which also helps to concentrate red blood cells and hemoglobin. In addition prolonged training at high altitude will cause changes to occur in the muscles. Training at high altitude will increase the percentage of slow twitch relative to fast-twitch muscle fibers.

We also know that all of the acclimation responses are under genetic control. Thus genetic predisposition exist for these traits, and we would expect to find these genes disproportionately represented in any population that has historically lived at high altitude (such as the Incans in the Andes, or South Koreans from the Táebaek-Sanmaek mountains, or Swiss from the Alps, or Sherpa from the Himalayas, or in Kenyans from the Kalenjin region). We know that people living in the Andes, for example, have more hemoglobin than do people who live at sea level. Natives of the Tibetan plateau, in contrast, have similar hemoglobin levels to their low-living counterparts, but a greater percentage of the protein binds to oxygen molecules in the blood. Neither of these mechanisms have been found in Ethiopians living at high altitudes. High-altitude adaptations do not map into the world's socially constructed races. Instead, we find high-altitude features in all populations that evolved at high altitude. Thus, if such adaptations increase the probability that an individual will become a world-class endurance runner (or other sports in which endurance is required, like cross country skiing), we would expect champions to come from a diversity of nations, all other factors being equal. We know of course, that cultural and social factors are not held constant, and play a large role in who gets to participate and achieve excellence in any given sport.

Once again, we see this when we examine the role of gender relations in long-distance running. For example, the women's division of the Boston Marathon showed no East African dominance. In fact, East African women have never dominated this sport. The winners of the women's divisions of the Boston, New York, and World Marathon Cup from 1990 to 1995 were eastern Europeans five times, western Europeans six times, Kenyans twice, Chinese once, Mexican once, and South African once. The Boston and New York Marathons were held every year and the World Marathon Cup was held every other year.[15] Also, the nations surrounding Kenya, Tanzania, and Uganda have not produced significant numbers of elite distance runners.[16] In fact, people from one region of Kenya, the Kalenjins, dominate their long-distance running. This region is at the altitude of 5,000 to 8,000 feet, and this population group comprises only 11 percent of Kenya's population. The Nandi district has produced 22.9 times more world-class long distance runners than would be expected for a population of that size, as opposed to 3.7 times more in the Rift Valley, 0.3 times less in the western region, 0.6 times less in Nyanza, 0.4 times less in the central, and 0.4 times less in the eastern district of Kenya. The northeastern and coastal portions of Kenya have not produced any world-class runners.[17] It seems that the simplest way to explain the recent Kalenjin success in long-distance running is to accept the idea that this group has some genetic predispositions that might help individuals succeed, but that there is also a cultural history of running and runners who were champions in this region. For example Kip Keino's (a member of the Nandi tribe) accomplishments in international distance running had a profound impact on the culture of this region.

Can We Really Make a Case for Racial Differentiation for Athletic Ability?

All of the pillars of racist thinking are buttressed by the idea that biological races can be unambiguously identified within the human species, and that these races have an innate essence that distinguishes them from other races. The case for racial differences in athletic ability does not differ in any way from the core racist argument. In general, the proponents of this idea have relied on poor and uninformed scientific reasoning. However, the public still believes that an individual's race determines their athletic ability. This is true, in part, because the critics of this idea have relied mainly on arguments that originate in the humanities and sociology. They have pointed out the role of racist ideology in the interpretation of the supposed scientific arguments; however, due to their own lack of clarity on the scientific issues they have not been able to mount a truly effective dismissal of this pseudointellectual racist program. However, without the biological reality of race, all racial origins of athletic ability arguments fall flat.

Another contributing factor supporting ideas of racial predisposition for sports is a result of these arguments focussing on the sports that have the greatest U.S. popularity, in particular, football and basketball. However, if we look at sports that are more popular internationally, such as soccer and volleyball, we see no evidence of racialized dominance in these sports. In addition, the composition of basketball has changed considerably over the twentieth century, and is rapidly changing now due to its international popularity. It is highly likely that the next generation of American basketball will be more diverse, deriving from America and international contributions to teams at the collegiate and professional levels. The European-American dominance in sports such as golf and tennis is rapidly being undermined, particularly as more historically oppressed groups enter the social status in which early athletic training for these sports becomes available. In fact, a measure of our society's progression toward social justice may be found in the degree that sports such as tennis, golf, and swimming begin to reflect our cultural diversity.

One final example will help illustrate the fallacy of racist thinking concerning athletic ability. Chess players, like professional athletes, require immense concentration and training. The Soviet Union dominated world chess from 1960 through the early 1990s. In 1961, they could boast one million rated chess players and twenty International Grand Masters. The world champion Mikhail Botvinnik was Russian. The world's second place nation was the United States, with only 10,000 rated chess players, but ten International Grand Masters. There was a large gap, however, between the Russians and Americans at the Grand-Master level. The only recent American world champion is Robert James Fischer, who won the title in 1972. Chess is a game that requires particular cognitive skills. Yet during the thirty year Soviet dominance of chess no one argued that this was a sign of the innate, racial superiority of eastern Europeans over Americans in intelligence. Indeed, the great Russian Grand Masters Kotov and Yudovich made no claims of the genetic superiority of the Russians in their analysis of Russian chess dominance. They pointed instead to the fact that chess was a part of Russian culture and to the superiority of their training techniques.[18]

Thus, the dominance of any particular population in a specific sport or cognitive activity is not evidence of innate racial superiority. The biological evidence now resoundingly rejects the existence of races in the human species. We have concluded that humans do not exhibit genetic variability sufficiently large to justify the use of the term *race*. It is clear however, that localized populations differ in gene frequencies and, therefore, in physical traits. Some physical traits may be sufficient to predispose populations to advantages in particular sports. However, populations do not participate in sports, individuals do. Biomechanical analyses of world-class athletes show that they have specific physical traits responsible for their superior performance relative to average people. Height may predispose one to be a great basketball player, but there are not many members of the Watusi tribe playing basketball in the NBA. Neither are all Africans tall; the Khoi-San and Pygmies are, on average, some of the shortest populations in the world. Some of these features may result from their genetic ancestry, or may be the result of training, and finally others may be due to intangible factors such as motivation. Neither is ethnic and cultural dominance in any given sport robust over time. Irish Americans dominated boxing in the early twentieth century. Europeans greatly resisted the emergence of East Africans in distance events. The present-day domination of sprinting by North Americans with detectable West African ancestry may be ephemeral. Biological factors are important in sports performance, but we should be clear that environment and culture always influence human biological variation. There is clearly a genetic contribution to any individual's ability to perform in sports. However, biological variation observed at the level of family and local populations does not imply the existence of race or racial predisposition to sports excellence.

Why We Must Deracialize Our Sports Ideology

In the late 1940s, the lure of basketball for African Americans was easy to understand. It required little equipment (basketball shoes and a ball), and public courts were near most residential areas in northern cities. In addition, little coaching was required to learn the basic offensive and defensive skills.

In those early days, as fans watched teams excel on the court, they had little idea that Bill Russell and the other African Americans were still struggling to be accepted on their merits inside the NBA. Russell was once quoted: "The practice is to put two black athletes in the basketball game at home, put three in on the road, and put five in when you get behind . . ."

Children especially don't see race as in issue in sports. Children don't see race as adults do, they still have the love of play and the love of the game, and for them it isn't about money. None of them care about the color of the kids on the team. They just care about playing and having fun. Unfortunately, so long as we believe that socially constructed race determines athletic potential we will destroy the love of sports for many of them. If you tell a Euro-American kid he can't play basketball because he cannot jump or an African-American kid that he can't swim because he can't float, you limit what they can become and further reinforce segregation. The message that genetically determined racial traits are responsible for athletic performance as opposed to desire, coaching, and culture, reinforces racism. The effect of this racist ideology is felt far beyond the world of sports. This is precisely why it must be resisted.

CHAPTER 7

On Whose Nature Nurture Never Could Stick: Race, Genetics, and Intelligence in the New Millennium

Sir Francis Galton, Charles Darwin's first cousin, was the founder of *psychometry,* or the measurement of human intelligence. Galton wrote his monumental *Hereditary Genius: An Inquiry Into Its Laws and Consequences* in 1869. Although Galton did not have a complete grasp of the rules of genetics, his work demonstrated that intelligence as he defined it was inheritable and showed the features of a complex genetic trait. However, psychometry from its onset was elitist and racist. In *Hereditary Genius*, Galton compared the intellect of the long dead Greeks (450 B.C.) with those of modern Englishmen, Negroes, Australians, and dogs. He thought the Greeks were one intelligence grade above the English, who were in turn two grades above the Negroes, who were one grade above the aboriginal Australians, who were eight grades above the most intelligent dogs. He even thought that there were grades of ancient Greeks, Englishmen, Negroes, and Australians that were not as intelligent as the most sapient canines! It was Galton who coined the term nature versus nurture from the line in Shakespeare's *The Tempest* where Prospero describes his wretched slave Caliban: "On whose nature-nurture never could stick."

Galton had been widely influenced by his travels in Africa concerning the intellectual inferiority of the Negro. He saw Negroes as inherently inferior, and he did not have a much higher opinion of the laboring masses of Europe or America either. Galton's disciplines would play a very important role in the founding of the international eugenics movement, which sought to use controlled breeding to better the genetic stock of the human, particularly "white," race. One of these was Madison Grant, an amateur zoologist and New York society man. Grant would serve as the treasurer of the second (1921) and third (1932) International Congresses of Eugenics, cofound the Galton Society, serve as president of the Eugenics Research Association, and cofound the American Eugenics Society. Grant was a vicious anti-Semite and in 1916 wrote one of the early twentieth century's most influential pieces of scientific racism, *The Passing of the Great Race*. Grant felt that the immigration of Irish, Italians, and Jews had pushed America to the brink of racial degeneration. He felt that all that was fine and good in the world was the result of the efforts of the Nordic race. The official organs of American science and the popular press hailed his work. In 1921, an admirer of Madison Grant, Vice President Calvin Coolidge wrote, in *Good Housekeeping* magazine: "biological laws tell us that certain divergent people will not mix or blend. The Nordics propagate themselves successfully. With other races the outcome shows deterioration on both sides. Quality of mind and body suggests that observance of ethnic law is as great a necessity to a nation as immigration law."

Coolidge's views were based on the prevailing science of the time. Unfortunately, the American public was being hoodwinked by the popularization of pseudoscientific intelligence testing carried out on both immigrants and U.S. Army recruits from 1917 to 1919. Soon after, William Stern, a German psychologist, had invented the intelligence quotient scale (IQ) in 1912. The scale was employed in mental tests designed to protect America from dysgenic immigration. Psychologist Henry Herbert Goddard started using the scale to categorize mental defectives at his Vineland, New Jersey, Training School for Feeble-minded Girls and Boys. That same year, Goddard began visiting Ellis Island in the New York Harbor to test Jewish, Italian, Hungarian, Polish, and Russian steerage passengers who were attempting to immigrate to the

United States. In a monumental paper published in the *Journal of Delinquency* in September 1917, Goddard concluded that average intelligence of the third-class immigrant is low, perhaps of moron grade (Appendix 23).

Results such as this led the chairman of Harvard's psychology department William McDougall to write *Is America Safe for Democracy?* in 1921. Two years prior to this, the U.S. Army had tested 1,726,966 adult recruits and, from the results, concluded that the average mental age of this group was about fourteen years old! McDougall and others argued that this fact was a danger to American social institutions. How could mental defectives be expected to vote and govern themselves? Indeed Goddard's data suggested that the situation was getting worse due to the immigration of non-Nordic, low-intelligence races from Europe.

Of course, the army intelligence tests showed that both Negroes and foreigners were of less intelligence than native-born whites. Native-born white officers scored higher than foreign-born enlisted men, who were higher than "colored" enlisted men born in the North, who were higher than colored enlisted men from the South. These results were not surprising given that the army mental tests really only tested the degree to which one was a member of white American society. Furthermore, the army tests showed that social factors, such as education, had powerful impacts on the results (Appendix 24).

This study shows that years of education had a strong influence on the average group scores. It also shows the sacred cow of intelligence testing, that is, in general the colored enlisted men performed more poorly than any of the white enlisted men at all levels of education (although northern colored enlisted men with high school and college education did as well as their peers of foreign birth).

The army intelligence tests were written by a committee headed by Robert Yerkes, the chairman of the Eugenics section of the American Breeders Association Committee on the Inheritance of Mental Traits. He was also the president of the American Psychological Association. Other leading eugenicists were also members of the committee, including Henry H. Goddard and Lewis Terman. Princeton psychologist Carl Brigham wrote the most influential book on the social significance of the army tests entitled: *A Study of American Intelligence* in 1923. Madison Grant heavily influenced Brigham's thinking on race. Brigham concluded that the army tests showed the intellectual superiority of the Nordic over the Alpine, Mediterranean, and "Negro" races. Brigham felt that the superior performance of northern Negroes in the army intelligence tests was the result of their greater admixture of white blood compared to the southern Negro, along with other social environmental factors such as better education, higher wages, better living conditions, and less complete social ostracism. He also felt that the amount of Nordic blood predicted the performance of the white races on the test. Without any physical anthropological evidence to support his claims, Brigham ranked the percentages of Nordic blood in the European races. The five highest were, in order: Sweden, Norway, Denmark, Netherlands, and Scotland (Appendix 25). Amazingly, Brigham thought that the Germans were only 40 percent Nordic and 60 percent Alpine. However, this may have resulted from the fact that Germany had been an adversary of the United States in World War I. In 1918, Henry Fairfield Osborn, a professor at the American Museum of Natural History, and a noted eugenicist, went so far as to claim he could prove that the German leaders were not Nordics, but Tartars. This he accomplished by the use of cranial angles. Brigham claimed that the lowest percentages of Nordic ancestry was found in the following races, in descending order: Portugeuse, Russian, Italians, Greeks, and Turks (Appendix 25).

Brigham ended his study of American intelligence with what became the clarion call of twentieth century psychometry and eugenics. He claimed that all available evidence suggested that American intelligence was declining and that it would proceed at an accelerating rate as racial admixture in America became more extensive. He predicted that the decline in American intelligence would be much faster than the decline in Europe, due mainly to the presence of the "Negro" in America. From this, he argued that American immigration policy needed to be favorable toward the Nordic countries. Harry Hamilton Laughlin, of the Eugenics Record Office (ERO) at Cold Spring Harbor, seized upon Brigham's work to influence the Committee on Immigration and Naturalization of the U.S. House of Representatives. The formation of the ERO had resulted from Galton's influence on American eugenicist Charles B. Davenport. Laughlin presented an expert report on the biological aspects of immigration to the U.S. Congress on April 16, 1920. His work aided materially in the Immigration Act of 1924 that biased entry to the United States toward the Nordic countries. The ERO would continue its work until 1940. It was also responsible for authoring model eugenical sterilization laws that helped to sterilize at least sixty-eight thousand Americans against their will by 1968, and were the template for similar laws adopted by Nazi Germany.

Galton's Legacy

Galton and his acolytes set all of the scientific and social issues of psychometry and eugenics by the beginning of World War II. The world saw the practical implications of their reasoning in the Holocaust. The Nazi regime sentenced people deemed intellectually inferior and genetically unworthy to extermination. Yet the ideology of psychometry survived the war unscathed. Several German race scientists, who faced trial at Nuremberg, actually claimed that they were simply following the established science of their discipline and were acquitted. Psychometry reared its ugly head again in America over the battles for school integration in the 1950s and 1960s. The champions of racial inferiority, William Shockley, Arthur Jensen, and others claimed that the Negro was genetically less educable than whites, while simultaneously reproducing faster than whites. They raised the specter of genetic enslavement for a substantial portion of the new America, due to untrammeled black reproduction.

By this time, the eugenicists had changed their tune concerning who or who was not white. The social changes wrought by the New Deal and World War II had redefined whiteness in America. Groups such as the Irish, Italians, Poles, and Russians that Brigham deemed intellectually inferior and no better than Negroes had been assimilated into whiteness. In his 1924 report on immigration to congress, Laughlin had actually ranked the intelligence of Northern American Negroes above Russians, Italians, and Poles. He ranked Negro officers third on the hierarchy of groups possessing superior intelligence, after white commissioned and noncommissioned officers. The intelligence ranking descended from there, following Brigham's scheme of the percentage of Nordic blood in each race. The coalitional allegiances in America had changed. We could no longer speak of an unchallenged Anglo-Saxon dominance of American social and economic life. Whiteness now referred to ancestry in any of the European countries as opposed to in Africa, the Middle East, or Asia. Consequently, modern psychometricists no longer broke down the white population into subraces when comparing them to Negroes or Hispanics.

In 1954, the psychometrists argued that school integration would hurt both Negroes and whites. The former would be unable to keep pace with their white classmates, which would create a great blow to their self-esteem, while the latter would feel resentment that they would have to be schooled with those genetically and socially inferior. They further feared that school integration would lead to miscegenation. Interracial marriage did not accelerate due to integration of the public schools and neither did school integration solve the difference in intelligence tests scores between whites and blacks. In 1964, the U.S. Congress, under Section 402 of the Civil Rights Act, ordered a study concerning the lack of availability of equal educational opportunities for individuals by reason or race, color, religion, or national origin in public institutions at all levels. The study was headed by a sociologist from John Hopkins named James Coleman, and its findings are known as the Coleman Report, published in 1966. The Coleman report stated that the "Negro" had failed in American schools, beyond statistical doubt, or sentimental apology, and that the failure was beyond explanation. Yet Coleman could not see the obvious explanations for the failures to achieve contained in his own report. For example, the report showed that the higher the socioeconomic class average of any school, the higher the test scores of all students within that school (regardless of so-called race). Conversely, the lower the socioeconomic average of the school, the lower the overall test scores. Six years later, G. W. Mayeske would show that a range of socioeconomic factors determined the average test scores of racial and ethnic groups from the Coleman Report, significantly adjusting ranks and scores of minorities for the better. The application of six socioeconomic variables not only changes the overall ranking of the racial and ethnic groups, but decreases the gap between the highest and lowest scoring groups considerably, (Appendix 26). Results like this can be interpreted two ways, the residual difference between groups resulted mainly from unaccounted for social factors influencing test scores, or it could still be used to claim that there are genetic differences between the groups.

The more we learned about genetic and environmental impacts on test performance, the weaker the scientific arguments for differences in intelligence due to racialized genetic differences became. Genetic explanations for racial differences stayed submerged throughout the late 1970s and 1980s but reemerged in the 1990s. Richard Herrnstein and Charles R. Murray's *The Bell Curve: Intelligence and Class Structure in American Life* reenergized the claim that genetic differences were responsible for the longstanding racial differences in IQ observed in the United States. They utilized IQ scores they derived from the Armed Forces Qualifying Test (AFQT.) They separated the scores into racial groups and showed that they could be described as normal curves. It has been long known that the frequency of IQ scores will produce a normal curve. Remember, many genes and environment affect a trait normal curve's result (Appendix 15). The normal curve is described by its average and standard deviation. The average is produced by adding up all the scores and dividing by the number of scores (a measure of central tendency) and the standard deviation is calculated by summing up the deviations from the average for each score, squaring it, and dividing that by the number of scores minus one. This quantity is called the *variance* and the standard deviation (SD) is the square root of the variance. The standard deviation is a measure of the spread of a normal curve. The statistical tests that allow one to determine if two groups have significantly different scores rely on the difference between the averages and the sizes of their standard deviations.

Herrnstein and Murray found a one-standard deviation difference between the mean of the black and white distribution of IQ scores. This difference is a very large one statistically. They also found that once they adjusted their data for the percentage of each so-called race in the American population, they concluded that the numbers of blacks in high IQ categories should be even smaller. They further claim that this 1-SD deviation difference was robust over the twentieth century. Given these facts, they claimed that the white dominance of American society was expected since IQ structures social life and the black and Hispanic races have lower IQs than the white and Asian races. In addition, they warned that the overreproduction of individuals genetically deficient in IQ within the population would lead to a serious decline in average American intelligence. In summary, the core claims of the *Bell Curve* were that:

- Generalized intelligence is a major determinant of social status.
- Generalized intelligence can accurately be measured by a variety of standardized tests such as IQ.

- Historically, IQ test scores have differed between racial groups; there is a one-standard deviation difference in IQ test scores between Whites/Asians and Blacks/Hispanics.
- The difference is historically stable (1918–1990).
- Therefore, this difference must be in part genetic (they claim 60 percent genetic to 40 percent environment).

The Bell Curve's curves arguments are plausible only if one assumes that biologically defined races exist within our species and that they correspond to the socially defined American races, that IQ really does determine the majority of the differential in social stature in societies, and that IQ tests reliably measure all pertinent aspects of cognitive function and are unbiased.

The arguments contained in *The Bell Curve* were shown to be fallacious in a number of ways. It relied on dubious statistical methods, cited studies that were strongly biased in favor of the authors' ideas, and utilized genetic reasoning that was deeply flawed. One of the biggest problems in the authors' genetic reasoning was that they provided no reason for why such genetic differences for intelligence should exist between human races. Instead, they relied heavily on the work of Canadian psychologist J. Phillipe Rushton. He is cited eleven times in the book's bibliography. Herrnstein and Murray wrote in Appendix 5:

> Rushton argues that the differences in the average intelligence test scores among East Asians, blacks, and whites are not only primarily genetic but part of a complex of racial differences that includes such variables as brain size, genital size, rate of sexual maturation, length of menstrual cycle, frequency of sexual intercourse, gamete production, sexual hormone levels, the tendency to produce dizygotic twins, marital stability, infant mortality, altruism, law abidingness, and mental health.—For each variable, Rushton has concluded, the three races—Mongoloids, Caucasoids, and Negroids—fall in a certain order . . . and so on.

Rushton had proposed an evolutionary theory that purportedly explains why and how genes related to intelligence and reproduction differ between races. He claimed that these differences result from natural selection for particular reproductive strategies in the various racial groups. This theory relies on the concept of r- and K-selection, first explicitly outlined by two ecologists, Robert MacArthur and Edward Wilson, in 1967.

However, there are insurmountable problems with the application of Rushton's theory of human biology, in particular his reliance on the concept of r- and K-selection. For example, professional biologists now consider r- and K-selection theory as virtually useless. Biologists began to expose the fallacies in this concept in the late 1970s. Since that time, multiple experiments have failed to corroborate the core premises of r- and K-selection theory. It would have been impossible for any serious scientist to have not noticed this event, as it would have been like an elephant taking up residence in one's living room. Sadly, some biologists and writers continue to rely upon it, perpetuating racist science and ideology.

What Do We Actually Know About the Genetics of Intelligence?

The most difficult thing about investigating the genetics of intelligence is that no one can seem to agree what actually makes up intelligence or whether standardized tests accurately measure it. In general, one can think of intelligence as the ability to reason, learn, remember, connect ideas, deduce, and create. Modern IQ tests are usually a short battery of exams that measure verbal fluency, mathematical reasoning, memory, and spatial visualization skills. Since most people tend to have correlated scores on these tests, some psychologists propose that a generalized intelligence exists, symbolized as small g. Modern brain-imaging techniques have found ambiguous evidence for the existence of g. A study utilizing positron emission tomography examined brain activity for mental tasks that supposedly utilize general intelligence (spatial, verbal, perceptuo motor tasks) versus those that did not. The results suggested that both the high and low g tasks utilized the same frontal areas of the brain. High g tasks would be those that rely more heavily on generalized intelligence, as determined by the correlation of various IQ test scores. However, analyses of this report criticized the researchers for not specifying how they actually measured which areas of the brain were being recruited for the specific tasks.[1]

The most controversial aspects of the genetics of intelligence have been measuring the degree to which IQ is inherited, whether there are other intelligences, such as practical or emotional intelligences (PQ and EQ), whether any aspect of intelligence determines one's social standing, and finally whether alleged races differ in average IQ, and to what degree those differences result from genetics. Accepting that any one of these premises is true does not automatically make the rest follow. We have overwhelming evidence that genes do influence intelligence, however defined, and that these influences act very early in life. However, many researchers make the mistake of assuming that because many severe mutations lower an individual's intelligence, such as Fragile-X syndrome, Down Syndrome, sickle-cell anemia, phenylketonuria (PKU), and sex chromosome trisomies (23 XXY, 23 XXX); that there must also be genes of major effect that are causing the differences in intelligence observed in society between individuals and socially defined groups. Similar mistakes were made in the study of another complex trait, longevity. Virtually every gene contributes to the lifespan of complex organisms. If you knock out the function of a gene, you clearly will lower the expected longevity of the individual. Again, this is very different from locating specific genes that are responsible for the observed differences in the lifespan in individuals not suffering from major mutations. Here, we are looking at the cumulative effect of many loci, all with small impacts on the final phenotype, that is how genetic controls of intelligence operate.

Estimates of the heritability, the amount of the genetic contribution, of intelligence have ranged from 40 to 80 percent over the last 100 years. These estimates have been rife with fraud and error. The most difficult problem in estimating heritability has come from the reliance on twin studies. The general method for estimating heritability using twins is to measure a trait in identical twins, who share 100 percent of their genetic material on average, and compare the correlation of identical twins to fraternal twins, who share only 50 percent of their genetic material on average. The difference between the correlations supposedly results from environmental effects. However, all twins share maternal environments in ways that nontwins do not, thus, estimates of heritability from twin studies are always overestimates. One study that examined 212 twin estimates of heritability showed that the maternal environment contribution was not negligible, as the researchers thought, and accounted for the striking similarity of the twins. The heritability of intelligence is not the real issue when addressing the race and intelligence question, however. All it states is that genes contribute to intelligence differences between families, but we have always known that. To make the racial hypothesis work, one needs to demonstrate which genes are responsible for high intelligence, and what are their frequencies in various human populations. Furthermore, to really make the case, one needs to explain why human beings should have drastically different frequencies of genes contributing to or detracting from intelligence. So far, no one has advanced a credible theory. Alternatively, someone wishing to make an argument for environmental causes for the differences in IQ we observe between racial groups needs to explain why and how such environmental differences should exist. The theory of social oppression explains exactly why and how such environmental differences were created and why and how they are being maintained in the United States.

*   *   *

Neurobiologists estimate that as much as 40 percent of the genes in the human genome contribute to cognitive function. This means that intelligence is an extremely complex trait. For example, studies of inbreeding show that children of outbred populations do better on intelligence tests and school performance than inbred groups in Brazil and Northern India. Inbreeding would depress overall intelligence precisely if there were many genes of small effect involved in producing the trait. Recent genome-level studies attempting to identify loci contributing to intelligence have just begun and have had little success. This is not unexpected, given how much of our genome contributes to this trait. For example, one study used 1,842 DNA markers to examine the DNA of a very high IQ group, with an IQ of 160 and an average IQ group, with an IQ of 102. The goal was to identify quantitative trait loci (QTLs) that were associated with high g. The study used a five-step design to eliminate false positives. They found 108, 6, 4, 2, and 0 QTL loci at each level of resolution. The most conservative interpretation of this study was that they did not identify any QTLs, and the most liberal says that they found 108. Even if we accept the liberal interpretation of the study, it implies that human intelligence is a very complex genetic trait; the more conservative ones suggest that they did not identify any genes. The authors suggested that for a locus to survive the five levels of inspection they would actually need 100,000 DNA markers applied to the human genome!

Other studies have examined candidate loci for human intelligence with various degrees of success. One study utilizing SNP found allelic variants in the neural adhesion molecule (N-CAM) locus that associated with high IQ. There was no significant association of genetic variation at the D2 dopamine receptor locus. D2 dopamine receptors are found on nerve cells and bind with the neurotransmitter dopamine. *Dopamine* is a neurotransmitter involved in the brain's perception of reward and punishment, and variation in dopamine receptors have been associated with a number of mood disorders. Variation at the apolipoprotein E locus has been examined for association with general intelligence. The Apo-E locus plays a role in memory function and decline predisposing patients to Alzheimer's disease in old age. Some studies have shown that the Apo-E4 allele is associated with greater educational attainment and others have found no association with ApoE genetic variants with intelligence in children.

We know very little about the identity of genetic variants that predispose people to high IQ and much more about genetic defects that lower IQ. There is no evidence at present that shows that the frequency of either of these genetic variants is racially distributed. However, we have a lot of evidence showing that toxic aspects of the environment, including heavy metals, malnutrition, and exposure to stress and violence *in utero* impact IQ. We also have a great deal of evidence that these environmental factors are distributed by socially defined race. Lead exposure is associated with socially constructed race and implicated in numerous diseases and behavioral problems. A recent study of Mexican schoolchildren found that there was an average of 8.4 mg/dl of blood and a range of 2.5–44.8 mg/dl of blood. Some of these children end up as immigrants to the United States. They and their parents will face additional neurotoxicity from organo-choloride pesticides while they pick fruits and work on lawns in America. Similar high lead levels have been found throughout the United States. The National Health and Nutrition survey showed that African-American and Mexican-American children exposed to silico-fluoride water had 2.6 and 1.8 times as much lead in their blood as European Americans. Silico-fluorides are added to water supplies to provide fluoridation, however, unlike sodium fluoride, they seem to transport lead into the human body. Poor and minority communities often have elementary schools located near hazardous-waste dumps.

The impact of environmental differences is complex. We have already seen that differential stress exposure plays a role in predisposing some African Americans to hypertension. Numerous studies show that lasting adult pathology can result from stress in the maternal environment. In a 2000 study of the impact of organochloride compounds with known neurotoxic effects on breast cancer risk in women from New York City, DDE levels were highest in African Americans and Hispanics, DDT highest amongst Hispanics, HPCB highest in African Americans, and trans-nonachlor highest in African Americans.

Even things as subtle as dietary differences influence IQ in children. Studies of malnutrition in rats showed that maternal effects on adult health extended over several generations. Micronutrient supplementation increases IQ test scores for children with low intakes of micronutrients in their diets. Alcoholism and drug use by parents impacts the IQ of children over the course of their lives. The offspring of alcoholic mothers show fluctuating asymmetry (FA) in their teeth, and FA is linked to lower IQ in college students. Fluctuating asymmetry is a complex genetic trait, measuring the degree to which anatomical structures are symmetrical. The more asymmetry, the more subtle and negative genetic effects are in play in the specific anatomical trait. Recent experiments with monkeys have shown that the monkey's social position determined its susceptibility to cocaine addiction. Monkeys housed alone or those socially dominant were less likely to self-administer cocaine than were socially subordinate monkeys. There is abundant evidence that socially subordinated humans are also more likely to use drugs and alcohol, although in American society drug and substance abuse is creeping into the socially dominant groups. Several studies have shown that the amount of early intervention significantly impacts cognitive growth. Parents or relatives who are at home with children are in a better position to bring out their IQ potential; neglected children do not receive this benefit. Finally, exposure to violence lowers scores on IQ tests. A 2002 study of 299 urban schoolchildren found that those who reported exposure to violence had significantly lower overall IQ and reading level scores. The researchers also showed that trauma-related distress also had an effect on reading levels. These results are consistent with brain-imaging studies that show that persons who have been exposed to or have been the victims of violence show changes in their brain structures. Sociologist Claude Steele has also shown that social stereotypes influence the ability of students to perform on standardized tests. Students told ahead of time that a test was biased to lefthanded students did not fare as well as lefthanded students who were also told this on the same test. The effect was entirely reversible. In another trial, lefthanded students did worse than righthanded students when both groups were informed that the test was biased to righthanders. Socially defined racial minorities in America live in an environment in which performance stereotypes are well known. Asian Americans are thought to be naturally smarter than every one else, while Hispanics and African Americans are not expected to perform well on cognitive tests.

Concluding Remarks: Mental Testing and the Sound Order

Mental testing since the time of Galton has been preoccupied with justifying racial and class stratification in modern society. In other words, the proponents of mental testing wanted to retain their social dominance. They argued that intelligence was linked to Darwinian fitness, that individuals with superior mental ability were best able to survive and pass on their intellect to succeeding generations. Yet, they were never able to answer the question that, if intelligence were so intimately linked to fitness, why did so much genetic variation for the trait still exist in anatomically modern humans? More so, why were the majority of people of such low intelligence, arguing in reality that natural selection had worked against improving the fitness of individuals? Actually, evolutionary theory suggests the exact opposite. Genes that are crucial to fitness rapidly spread through populations, so that after several generations all individuals possess those genes. It is much more likely that the genetic basis of the human intellect was fixed long before any emigrants left Africa sometime over seventy thousand years ago. Given that so much of the genome contributes to mental function and that we find very small differences between large populations of human beings, it is highly unlikely that any genetically based differences for intellectual ability exist between major groups of people (or races).

J. P. Rushton, Richard Herrnstein, Charles R. Murray, and their colleagues attempted to explain how genetic variation for human intelligence could still exist and have a racial basis. Their reasoning is based almost entirely on the thinking of Rushton. However, his view of human evolution suffers from the use of antiquated and simplistic theoretical models concerning life-history evolution. In addition, the sources of his data, methods of data analysis, and results call into question the legitimacy of his research. One can observe the use of Rushton's work to influence popular opinion by visiting *www.duke.org,* the website of the former Louisiana Klansman David Duke.

What we can say about the genetic basis of intelligence is very limited. We know that genes influence intelligence, but we think intelligence is a complex trait produced by very large numbers of genes, and is profoundly influenced by a variety of environmental sources. We can definitely say that IQ is heritable, that is, offspring's mental abilities generally resemble those of their parents, identical twins resemble each other, and close relatives have similar mental abilities. This is a long way from justifying genetic causes to racial differences in IQ. The socially constructed races in America differ slightly in overall gene frequencies. If they shared similar social and physical environments, we would expect to find the entire range of mental abilities in all groups. However, it is precisely in their exposure to toxic aspects of the physical and social environment that America's socially defined races are the most different. Furthermore, these toxic factors are known to influence cognitive ability. So long as social injustice exists, it will be impossible to scientifically test whether these populations have genetic differences in IQ. What purpose is served by embarking on such an investigation, anyway? If America had made a determined and conscientious effort to eliminate poverty, social bigotry, and environmental pollution, and, if after this task was accomplished, IQ deficits persisted between the races, there might be some utility to such research. In reality, the racialization of IQ stands in the way of addressing issues of social inequality. In 1994, Richard Herrnstein and Charles R. Murray said that we should not expect African Americans to be found at representative levels in high-IQ professions. This could not happen because there were not enough high intellect genes in the black population. The entire history of the intelligence research program has been to justify not making any effort to provide equal life opportunities for the groups it has targeted as inferior. This branch of psychology has always been associated with social oppression. If we studied the social dominance orientation of race and IQ among researchers, they would all score very high on the scale.

The evidence that IQ plays a causal role in the stratification of society is very weak. Standardized tests like the Scholastic Aptitude Test (SAT) or the Graduate Record Examination (GRE) predict what institution a student will attend, but they are very weak indicators of how students will fare once they enter college or graduate school. Other factors, such as practical or social intelligence, physical appearance, and parental social networks are more likely to influence how an individual fares in our society. Neither is there any strong evidence that overall intelligence is declining. IQ scores actually went up over the twentieth century (known as the *Flynn Effect*). The gains are much too fast to have resulted from changes in brain physiology, proving that these changes must be resulting from environmental sources. The fact that such rapid gains exist sheds very serious doubt that the IQ score difference between blacks and whites is of genetic origin.[2] Instead, the IQ score gap should be thought of in the same light as the health disparity. Both result from the action of social oppression throughout American history. We must challenge ourselves to see what we can gain in human potential by acting today to eliminate social injustice in America. How much faster will we move forward in solving our emerging economic, industrial, social and environmental problems if we harness more of our population's intellect, rather than polluting and criminalizing those minds by rearing them in poverty and neglect.

Herrnstein and Murray gave us an alarming vision of the future in the introduction to *The Bell Curve*. They suggested that American society was polarizing into the IQ haves and havenots. The haves would utilize the new electronic technology to build fortresses against the increasing lawlessness of the havenots, themselves sedated by that new technology in the forms of video games and television. Their vision of future society must also be racially polarized. They plainly state that lower IQ is associated with black genes. In reality, they are only stating what is already beginning to take shape, although not for the reasons they proposed. Genetic deficiency in IQ is not polarizing American society. The ongoing denial of economic, social, and environmental equality to nonwhites is responsible for bringing about their nightmarish vision.

Alternatively, we could begin to redress the mechanisms that maintain European-American social dominance. We could start providing adequate funding for daycare, increase expenditures on Head Start type programs, and increase funding for K through 12 schooling particularly in underserved areas. We could start compensating K through 12 teachers at levels that would attract more talented and dedicated people into education. We could redress discrimination in hiring, salaries, housing, and health care. Nothing prevents us as a society from doing these things. It is simply a choice. We are at a crossroads in which we shall as a society be forced to choose between two incompatible futures, the road of polarization or that of justice and unity.

CONCLUSION

Two Paths . . . Choosing up Sides or Joining Hands

The Turner Diaries, written by white supremacist William Pierce, under the pseudonym Andrew Macdonald, began with the bombing of a federal building and ends with the mass annihilation of Jews and African Americans. Some will feel that it would be impossible for anyone to take such a story seriously, but at least one person did: Timothy McVeigh, when he planned and executed the bombing of the Alfred P. Murrah Federal Building in Oklahoma City. Undoubtedly, many Germans ignored the warnings concerning Hitler. Since the Holocaust, historians have sought to uncover reasons for the insanity. They call Hitler a madman and say the Nazi party did not represent the German people. However, Hitler and the Nazi party could not have carried out the systematic extermination of more than six million people by themselves. The Holocaust could only occur because the socially dominant Germans saw the subordinated Jews, Gypsies, mentally ill, labor leaders, and socialists as worthy of destruction. For Hitler to take power, many good people must have stood by and watched. By the time they realized the danger it was too late.

The relations between America's socially constructed races are getting worse, not better. There have been cosmetic changes that indicate that European Americans have become more accepting of minority groups yet, contrary to all factual evidence, the majority of European Americans feel that institutionalized racism and discrimination no longer exist. Ten to 15 percent of the European-American population still practices overt, old-fashioned racism. Another study found that 56 percent of Americans do not believe that discrimination is holding "blacks" down. Worse of all is that physical disparities, particularly between "whites" and "blacks," have increased over the last thirty years. We are told that no one is to blame for these inequities, that we are witnessing the action of nature, not nurture. Some races are better equipped in the struggle for existence to live longer than others.

Anatomically modern humans do not have biological races. We are a relatively young species that has not gone through a lot of genetic change. Isolation by distance best describes human genetic diversity. In our species, indigenous groups living closest together share a higher proportion of their genes than groups that live farther apart. Human migration has tended to spread genes among localized groups, both in ancient and modern times. For this reason, while geographic variation in gene frequencies and physical traits are real, we cannot develop schemes to unambiguously define racial groups.

In America, the average person on the street thinks of the socially defined white, yellow, and black, as if they correspond to the anthropologist's conception of the Caucasian, Mongoloid, and Negroid, but they do not. The nineteenth century anthropological categories were created based on the idea that variation was imperfection and the ideal type represented reality. Modern genetics has reversed this logical syllogism, embraced our variation, and recognized that there is genetic continuity between all populations of anatomically modern humans.

Our genes are ultimately responsible for all aspects of our health, reproduction, and behavior. However, all genetic systems operate in response to the environment, and gene-by-environment interactions are very complex. When we carefully scrutinize human genetic variation, we see that the idea biological races exist and differ in sexual behavior, health, athletic ability, and intellect is false. At the same time, socially constructed races do differ in sexual behavior, health, athletic participation, and intellectual performance. For example, the American College Test (ACT) and SAT score gaps between black and white students have increased between 1998 and 2002. Referring to national averages, the ACT and SAT gaps grew from 4.5 to 5.0 and 190 to 200 points, respectively. The largest gaps appeared in the southern states, the region that has always maintained the largest disparities between black and white education.[1] We have seen that disparities, such as these, result from past and ongoing social conflict. The more salient question is: How did these social conflicts come about and how may we end them?

The power of evolutionary theory is that it alone can explain the features we see in biological organisms. For years, however, psychologists and social scientists have resisted the application of evolutionary theory to human behavior and social organization. New results in these fields are rapidly ending this failure in reasoning. We understand that natural, kin, and sexual selection has driven genetic evolution in primates, including the human species. Primates share many aspects of their behavior, including social hierarchy, outgroup hostility, and territorial defense. Males in all four closely related primate species (humans, chimpanzees, bonobos, and apes) initiate and maintain them. Kin and sexual selection may have played a greater role in the evolution of social dominance systems than individual selection. Natural, kin, and sexual selection also drive cultural evolution; however, group selection plays a greater role here. In addition, the mechanisms that transmit culture allow nonrelated groups to adopt or reject specific cultural elements. The rapid movement of agriculture into Europe was an example of a highly useful component of culture adopted by groups not closely related to the original farmers of the Fertile Crescent. So, cultural is much faster than genetic evolution. The rate of cultural evolution accelerated after the widespread adoption of agriculture and even more with the origin of permanent settlements, industry, and technology. This means that our hunter-gatherer minds, having evolved well over 150,000 years ago, are now attempting to cope with postindustrial society. As such, we have retained behaviors that may have worked a long time ago, but are poorly adapted to the modern world; craving sweets in an era of food abundance contributes to obesity, just as maintaining ingroup/outgroup prejudice produces social injustice and can lead to global Armageddon.

Human racial conflict is a relatively new phenomenon, but human ingroup/outgroup conflict most likely goes back to our hunter-gatherer days. War and colonialism in the ancient world were not based on race, nor did ancient philosophers develop a concept of race as we know it. The Greeks fought the Trojans over trade routes in the Aegean, the Romans fought the Carthaginians over trade in the Mediterranean, the Christians and Muslims fought over the Holy Land, and, throughout the Crusades, race did not play a role in military alliances. The voyages of discovery ushered in racially based warfare. The European edge in shipbuilding and warfare technology allowed them to sail great distances and overwhelm populations that had no such technology. However, not all the initial contacts were violent: The Wampanoag helped the Pilgrims survive in what later became Massachusetts, until the latter made war upon them.

At America's beginning, an individual's social allegiance was clearly identifiable by their genetic origin. The founding fathers did not envision Africans or American Indians ever being citizens of the United States. But the more these groups came into contact, the more clear it became that they all shared fundamental aspects of the human condition in common, most notably the desire to re-sist social domination, the desire to be free. Crispus Attucks, an African-American freedman, was one of the first to die for the principal of independence. American colonists fought a war to end taxation without representation, offered freedom to African

Americans who fought for the colonial cause, then reneged on that promise when the war ended. The Afro-Canadian population has it roots in former slaves who left America with the British after the Revolutionary War. The slaves were set free because the British kept their promise. Ironically, those same patriots who would not bow to English tyranny could not see to offer that same freedom to their own slaves. This is not ironic if we understand that the European-descended colonists did not see African-descended Americans as part of their social coalition. The southern slaveholders actively feared what might happen if African Americans were allowed freedom, education, and the right to bear arms. One example of their fear come to light was how American Indians of the Seminole Nation and African slaves united in Florida to resist slavery and colonialism. They raided and destroyed plantations and freed the slaves that they found there. Future president Andrew Jackson led an expeditionary force against them, and finally defeated the Negro Fort in Florida when a fortuitous shell found a powder magazine.

Eventually, the issue of human slavery created new social coalitions. Abolitionists, men and women like the Lane Theological rebels, who fled Cincinnati with a lynch mob on their heels, moved north and founded Oberlin College in 1833. Organized on the principle of "learning and labor," Oberlin was America's first coeducational college and it voted to admit "Negroes" in 1835. Oberlin students were active in the underground railway and at least one of them died with John Brown. With the election of Abraham Lincoln in 1860, two great social coalitions went to war and shed their blood in rivers for another five years. Even within each coalition there was discord. The North's inept military operations were in part the result of Copperheads (Northerners with pro-Southern sympathy) in its officer corp. Draft riots broke out in New York, led primarily by Irish immigrants incensed at the draft and the provisions that allowed rich people to buy out of the draft for three hundred dollars. They turned their rage on African Americans, burned down an orphanage, and killed hundreds of innocent African Americans. On the other hand, plantation-owning African Americans in Louisiana raised a regiment to serve in the Confederate Army. They fought to preserve the institution of chattel slavery because they themselves benefited from it. Examples such as this show that socially constructed race is in reality playing second fiddle to the interests of individuals and their immediate kin.

The social coalitions kept shifting in American social life and politics, especially with the arrival of more ethnic groups from Europe, the Middle East, and Asia, with the concept of race always explicitly or implicitly playing a role. Japanese immigrants were denied citizenship because they were thought to be an inassimilable race. Congress biased immigration policies toward Nordic countries because of their supposed superior intelligence. Neighborhoods and cities sprang up as the country of origin defined where you lived and what your social affiliation would be. In 1919, fear of black competition for jobs led to white race rioting and hundreds were killed or injured in Chicago and St. Louis.

Nothing better illustrates our present-day racial conundrum than the 2000 presidential race between then Texas Governor George W. Bush, Jr. and Vice President Al Gore. The Republican primaries dealt with two particularly sensitive racial issues, the Confederate Flag and interracial dating. In the middle of the South Carolina primary, a local Bush supporter labeled National Association for the Advancement of Colored People (NAACP) as the National Association for the Advancement of Retarded People"! Worse, was that he "apologized" a day later for insulting retarded people by associating them with the NAACP. Bush called the remarks unfortunate but did not call the NAACP to apologize for several days after the remarks were made, clearly not wanting to alienate his white supremacist base of support in South Carolina. He also refused to take a stand on the Confederate flag issue, calling it an issue the people of South Carolina should decide. Republican candidate John McCain was similarly spineless over the issue, at first calling the Confederate flag a symbol of "racism and slavery," but reversing himself the next day to echo Bush's states' rights position. Bush's visit to Bob Jones University in South Carolina made it very clear where he stood on American racial issues. Bob Jones was founded by white supremacists who believed in segregation and that Catholicism and Mormonism were evil. Although Bob Jones had recently admitted blacks, it still maintained that interracial dating was against God's will. The McCain campaign fared no better, having hired Richard Quinn, editor of *Southern Partisan,* a magazine that held that the South should have won the Civil War and that slavery had not been that bad for blacks. McCain even used the word "gooks" to refer to his Vietnamese captors during the war.[2]

With a minority of the popular vote, George W. Bush, Jr. won the 2000 election. He received only 5 percent, 7 percent, and 8 percent of the African-American vote in Texas, Florida, and nationally, respectively. There is solid evidence to show that African Americans were systematically denied voting access in Florida. African Americans were more likely to vote at precincts with error-prone voting machines, and were aggressively struck from the rolls the year before the election. Florida had hired an outside vendor with Republican ties to remove felons from the rolls, and at least eight thousand disproportionately minority names were illegally deleted. The Reverends Jesse Jackson and Al Sharpton, and the NAACP's Kweisi Mfume called for a federal investigation. However, after a Republican-dominated court halted the election, George W. Bush, Jr. was declared the winner. The GOP has not failed with all minorities; they increased their vote among Asian Americans and captured 31 percent of the Hispanic vote.[3]

Genetic differences between groups of human beings did not explain their voting patterns or the ongoing injustice in America. Substandard African or superior European and Asian genes for IQ are not the reason for the wage and wealth, health, and other disparities between African Americans, Afro-Caribbeans, and Hispanics compared to European and some Asian Americans. Rather, the legacy of American social oppression by the European American majority against the non-Europeans is the cause of the disparities. George W. Bush, Jr. was able to win the presidential election because of the history of voter-denial mechanisms utilized in the white supremacist South. Florida was the focus of the voter irregularities but undoubtedly they existed in other, particularly the southern, states. Many voting district lines are still gerrymandered to prevent African Americans and other minorities from ever having majorities. Some districts are so contorted that one has to have an advanced degree in geometry and topography to make any sort of sense of them, other than the obvious explanation that they exist to maintain white social domination. The largest failure of the Democratic Party in the 2000 election was its failure to call the entire racially and class-biased electoral process into question. They did not do that because, in actuality, the Democrats serve the same social coalition as the Republicans (American whites) and did not want to invalidate the same tactics they use to win elections in northern cities such as Boston, Chicago, New York, and Philadelphia. Some say that dead people still vote in Chicago, some more than they ever did when they were alive.

The 2004 Philadelphia mayoral election illustrates the problem the Democrats face. The incumbent Democratic mayor, John F. Street, was elected in 1999 by a margin of fewer than ten thousand votes. Democrats outnumber Republican voters in Philadelphia by a margin of four to one but, in the coming election, 70 percent of African Americans favor Street and 72 percent of European Americans favor his opponent, Sam Katz.[4] Clearly, based on the larger amount of registered Democrats in Philadelphia, many European-Americans voters are crossing party affiliation to vote for the challenger. The Republicans realized this problem in 1960 and, since then, have abandoned any civil-rights issues as part of their party platform because they know that they can win most elections without black support, and may lose more white support by trying to acquire it. In that sense, Republicans have defined their social coalition to the exclusion of African Americans, except when they can use them in visible public positions to blunt the overtly white-interested character of their party. The Democrats are not much better, while expecting the allegiance of African Americans and other minorities, their program is still biased toward the interests of white, upper-class America.

We are still a nation divided around the interests of its socially constructed races. For that reason, realization of the nonexistence of biological races is only the beginning, not the end of our dilemma. By eliminating the refuge that racists have in biology, we reveal their true program, which is, and has always been, a social one. Racists design and utilize their ideology to help maintain their privilege against other social groups. They invented American racial categories to identify who was a member of the in- versus the outgroup. Even today, the prevailing bigotry of individual Americans and the operation of institutionalized racism force individuals into membership of one of America's social coalitions, whether that person wants to be or not. Consider the case of Tiger Woods, or actors Vin Diesel and Halle Berry.

Americans who truly believe in our nation's creed must look these facts squarely in the face. We must take on our racialized social life. How is it that Sunday morning is still the most segregated time of our week? How can we have black and white Baptist churches within blocks of each other, believing in the same God, believing in the same religious principles, but whose memberships are completely racially segregated?

Whither Affirmative Action?

To destroy racialized society we must examine the mechanisms that perpetuate it. European Americans still have privileged access to the education and training required to acquire the best jobs, found businesses, and acquire personal fortunes. The European-American elite has carried over greater wealth from past generations, much of it derived from the exploitation of American Indians, Chinese laborers, European immigrants, and African slaves. European Americans are still more likely to live in communities that are least likely to suffer from industrial pollutants, more likely to have the best health care and medical insurance. If these things had happened due to the superior drive and ability of people of European descent, then there would be no ethical or moral reason to call for redress, but that is not how it happened. Affirmative action was one proposal designed to eliminate these injustices.

Despite its good intentions, affirmative action is still part of the program to maintain European-American social dominance. President John F. Kennedy coined the term "affirmative action." He felt that years of discrimination, particularly against African Americans, could not be reversed unless the federal government took an active, affirmative role in redressing ongoing injustice. Kennedy did not live long enough to pursue this idea. Federal affirmative action programs designed to redress racial discrimination began in earnest with President Lyndon Johnson's executive order 11246, and were later significantly expanded by President Richard Nixon and his secretary of labor George Schultz. Affirmative action by the federal government did not begin with Kennedy.

Most European Americans have been receiving federal or state affirmative action since the beginning of our nation; it just was not called by that name. Governor DeWitt Clinton was elected based on his support for state funds to construct the Erie Canal, which began in July 1817. This canal allowed settlers who were predominantly European American to move from the Atlantic states to the Great Lakes. The homestead law enacted by Congress in 1862 also favored European Americans. It provided that anyone who was either the head of a family, twenty-one years old, or a veteran of fourteen days of active service in the U.S. armed forces, and who was a citizen or had filed a declaration of intent to become a citizen, could acquire a tract of land in the public domain not exceeding sixty-five hectares (160 acres, equal to a quarter section). In 1862, most people who fell into the category of citizen, or intent to be a citizen, were of European descent. The land had all originally been in the domain of American Indians, but either purchased with federal monies, or seized by warfare against them. To acquire title to the land, the homesteader was obliged to settle on or cultivate the homestead for five years. The federal homestead laws provided an incentive, in the form of easily obtainable land, for the settlement of the West. Since there were hostile Indian tribes and bandits in the West, the federal and state governments also had to spend money on troops and marshals to defend the settlers. America's Buffalo soldiers, cavalrymen of African-American descent, fought hostile Indian tribes and bandits to open the migration of European Americans to large parts to the Southwest. Then there is the eighty-six years of legalized segregation and second-class citizenship forced on nonwhites by the *Plessy v. Ferguson* decision of 1896. This meant that in addition to the greater than 260 years of forced labor expropriated from slaves of African descent, freed African Americans were paid lower wages and in return had fewer tax dollars spent in their interest. This is still true; African Americans of similar education and years of experience are paid less in the same professions than European Americans. During Jim Crow, southern states spent higher amounts on education for whites and denied access to certain professions on the basis of race. Discrimination in housing loans redefined American life in the 1950s and further contributed to the wealth differential between white and black Americans. The ongoing social dominance of European Americans is easy to gauge. Every American president, the vast majority of senators and congressmen, governors, mayors, academicians, and CEOs of major corporations are always white men. This is not because of their innate superiority over all the rest of us; it is the legacy of European-American social domination. At first, the power of law openly supported European-American social dominance. In the Dred Scott Decision of 1857, Chief Justice Taney said that Scott had: ". . . no rights that a white man is bound to respect." After decades of struggle, culminating in the civil-rights struggles of the 1960s, European-American dominance went underground, became clandestine, but is just as effective.

Forty years of affirmative action programs have not come close to equalizing social opportunities in the United States for American Indians, African Americans, and Hispanics. To be sure, affirmative action has helped minorities enter professions where they had been barred and underrepresented, but the largest beneficiaries of affirmative action programs to date have been European-American women. Due to affirmative action, women increased from 1.2 percent of the top earning corporate officers in 1995 to 5.2 percent in 2002. These women usually end up marrying European-American men. So, affirmative action has probably improved white America's standard of living as much as any other group. The small amount of increases of minorities in the professions alone shows that affirmative action is not discriminating against white men.

In some arenas, such as academe, the numbers of underrepresented minorities has actually not changed or declined slightly over the forty years of affirmative action. This is crucial, since higher education plays an essential role in our society, educating doctors, lawyers, teachers, and other professionals. An unintentional impact of affirmative action has been to disperse African-American students and professors. Prior to desegregation, the majority of African-American students went to historically black colleges (HBCUs), which also boasted a large percentage of the top African-American scholars in the country. With affirmative action in place, top tier universities now attract both students and professors of African-American descent away from the HBCUs. In theory, this should have been socially progressive. However, European-American backlash against affirmative action at these universities has created a hostile environment that has particularly negative impacts on both minority faculty and students. Many universities maintain a revolving door, routinely deny tenure to minority faculty, or their hostility toward nonwhites simply drives them out the door. Promotion and tenure for nonwhites often boils down not to academic achievements but to how palatable or how controllable they are deemed by those who maintain white social domination within that university. The recent assault on the scholarship of the highly esteemed and visible Professor Cornel West while he was at Harvard is a case in point, although there are many more people who have suffered in silence. For example, all over the country, ethnic studies programs are under retrenchment and their rationale for existence under assault. Students evaluate their courses more poorly precisely because they bring to light white America's racism and the student's own social privileges.[5]

The Supreme Court's ruling of June 23, 2003, in upholding the University of Michigan's use of affirmative action in admissions illustrates the problems inherent in attempting to bring about social justice. Upperclass European-American individuals live in a society that provides them with every conceivable benefit to ensure their success. University admissions criteria operate to evaluate differences in the records of this type of student. The criteria evaluate high-school grade point averages, standardized test scores, letters of recommendation, and extracurricular activities. The number of spots at America's finest undergraduate schools is far lower than the number of students who are qualified to attend these universities. The public has been hoodwinked into thinking that admission to these universities, based on these criteria, is fair and objective. However, at many of these schools, if we replaced the admitted students with those who were rejected we would not notice any difference in the accomplishments of the student body. Neither is there any real difference in the quality of educational experience the undergraduate student experiences at any of the best colleges and universities. Anyone truly knowledgeable about academe takes the annual *U.S. News and World Report* rankings of universities and colleges with several grains of salt.

What happens when you add to the equation students who were not given every conceivable resource to pursue their educations? What if we know that such students are routinely discriminated against in education due to the color of their skin? What if we know that such students add more or different social values to the institution itself, and to society in general compared to students of the former group? Do you admit the European-American student with a 4.0 grade-point-average (GPA) 1400 SATs, strong letters of recommendation, and excellent extracurricular activities, or the African-American student with the 4.0 GPA, 1200 SATs, strong letters of recommendation, and excellent extracurricular activities? The opponents of affirmative action would say admitting the student with the lower SATs would be reverse discrimination based on race. The proponents of affirmative action would say admitting the African-American student would be fostering social justice. Again, we know that such rankings are themselves biased, and more biased further up the social structure. Experiments have shown that white evaluations of black and white candidates for low-, mid-, and high-level positions are systematically biased in favor of the white candidate, even when the candidates have identical records. Worse is that the bias is stronger for the high-level positions. Furthermore, white evaluators more frequently include negative nonsubjective material when they evaluate blacks and other minorities for high-level positions.[6]

The high court ruled 6-3 that Michigan's policy was narrowly tailored to further a compelling interest in "obtaining educational benefits that flow from a diverse student body." The court did not favor Michigan's point system that awarded twenty bonus points on its 150-point scale to black, Hispanic, and American-Indian applicants. Twenty points in the Michigan system was significant, in that a student with a 4.0 grade-point average received twenty points more than a student with a 3.0 grade-point average, and was also the same advantage that varsity athletes receive compared to nonathletes (but no one was complaining about the use of the point system to admit college athletes)!

The gist behind the assault on affirmative action was that more qualified students of European-American and Asian descent were being denied admission while lesser-qualified African-American, American-Indian, and Hispanic students were admitted. For those who opposed affirmative action in admissions their definition of *qualified* revolved around scores on standardized tests such as the SAT, Law School Aptitude Test (LSAT), or GRE, and high-school grade-point averages. The opponents of affirmative action in particular argue that the scores on standardized exams are linked to the concept of generalized intelligence (g), and the idea that (g) should determine who should be given admittance to higher education in a *meritocracy* (where individual merits are rewarded). Furthermore, they argue that since races are genetically different in IQ, college admissions should naturally reflect that difference.

The problem with that reasoning is that standardized test scores are very poor indicators of success in college and the interpretation of the scores are biased against minority applicants (i.e., underpredict their success in college). In addition, scores on the SAT are correlated with several social variables, including parental income. The score on the math section of the SAT is strongly correlated with the number of math courses taken in high school. Clearly, districts that have better math curricula can be expected to better prepare their students. These districts happen to be wealthy, disproportionately white, suburban districts, not inner city or poor rural ones. Students who can afford to pay for SAT preparatory courses, such as the Kaplan course, often increase their scores by hundreds of points. These are evidence alone to show that the score on the SAT is not an indicator of intrinsic merit, but more an indicator of one's social position. Thus, in actuality, what the opponents of affirmative action in college admissions are arguing is the right to allow the benefits of their past and present social dominance to operate unfettered by the action of the state and federal governments. The fact that these groups never argued against other preferential university admissions policies such as for the children of alumni or student athletes make their motivations clearer. They want to keep America's elite universities the bastion of white social privilege with just enough black athletes to keep them competitive against their rival schools.

The problem is somewhat thornier when we consider the position of Asian Americans. The term itself is misleading, since Asia is a very large continent, with diverse cultures, all of whose ethnic groups have different stories in relation to their immigration to America. Chinese and Japanese immigrants began coming to America in large numbers in the latter portion of the nineteenth century. Large-scale immigration of groups such as the Koreans, Vietnamese, Thai, Mong, and others began after the Korean War. There have also been recent immigrations from India, Pakistan, and other western Asian countries. For the most part, Asian immigrants to the United States arrived in a country where the racial hierarchies had already been established and hence are not responsible for the creation of the racialized social dominance system here. Individual stories varied from professionals immigrating to secure better financial opportunities to poor refugees fleeing political repression in their home nations. Yet the American social system has discriminated against all of these groups, but they have been systematically denied inclusion in affirmative-action programs.

Simply put, Asian Americans have excelled without these programs. The success of some Asian Americans, despite active discrimination against them, has been used by psychometricists as evidence of their innate intellectual superiority. But neither explanation is satisfactory, since not all Asian-American individuals have excelled in America. There is evidence that the groups who immigrated to America first, such as Chinese and Japanese Americans, utilized strong social networks to help them overcome racist oppression. If racist oppression is the rationale for inclusion in affirmative action programs, then there are many Americans of Asian descent who should qualify.

The problem is that affirmative action was never designed to redress social inequity, neither was its implementation ever controlled by those groups whom it was meant to benefit. It has always been a palliative whose purpose was to placate social unrest. The most socially dominant class of European Americans had no difficulty with allowing some entry of non-European Americans into the professional classes, so long as the system of power and privilege remained unchanged. We need to take this system to task. What if we created open access to all public universities by an open admission system? There would be no reason to be concerned with affirmative action anymore. This would solve a number of other problems. It would expand the workforce at public universities, since the larger enrollments would require more faculty and staff. At the same time, states could create better alternatives to college education, such as expanded vocational training opportunities in high school. There is evidence that such programs are desperately needed. High school dropout rates may be as high as 30 percent, much higher than the 10 percent reported by the Department of Education. The reports also indicate that minority youth are more likely to drop out compared to majority youth.[7] In the short term, bridge programs could be created to help students who came from poorer school districts prepare for the rigors of the university. Some will ask where will the money come from to afford this expanded system?

There are a number of ways these revenues could be generated, not the least of which would be closing tax loopholes that allow corporations and wealthy individuals to pay disproportionately lower taxes than poorer Americans. Other ways of generating the money would include putting more people to work. We should be insisting on full employment for all Americans. How might this be accomplished? One immediate way would be to shorten the work week for those already employed, particularly at large corporations, without a loss of paid hours or benefits. This would allow more people to be hired to make up for the percentage loss of person hours on the job. While this may seem an extreme measure, it is actually a win–win scenario for those institutions that can afford to do it. First, people who are employed consume more commodities than those who are not. Therefore, this would stimulate the economy. People who work less have more time to see their families, relax and reduce stress, and contribute to their communities. This could mean lower expenditures for health and behavioral health problems. People with jobs also pay taxes. Stockholders, who might think this will lead to losses in profits, should realize that such a measure could quickly recover their investment, both financially and indirectly by benefits to the society in which we all live.

We could also decriminalize victimless offenses, such as illegal drug use. This does not mean that we should encourage or support drug use; rather, we should see it for what it is, signs of depression and other forms of mental illness, especially since mental illness is linked for many to their social oppression. Rather than imprisoning people, destroying families, encouraging violence, paying for more prisons and larger police forces, we should be treating addicts, paying for education and vocational training, and thereby eliminating the market for drug use.

We can also divert federal monies to the purposes of expanding educational opportunities, not the least of which could be funds from our expanding military budget. As I write, Congress is considering an eighty-seven-billion-dollar request from President Bush to be spent on the wars in Iraq and Afghanistan. This is at a time when the federal deficit is now approaching five hundred billion dollars. We should ask ourselves if this is really how we want to spend this money. Not appropriating this money for war would require the United States taking on a different foreign policy, one that seeks peaceful means of protecting American interests, as opposed to creating an atmosphere in which more and more of the world's population has reasons to hate and seek vengeance against America.

Why We Should Mend Our Fences and Join Hands

We have seen that in primate species, males seek power and status because it leads to greater reproductive success. This was true for ancient humans as it is also true in modern humans. European males were the chief agents of the colonization of the New World and the enslavement of Africans. Anglo-Saxon males were also the chief agents in the ongoing subordination of other Europeans, particularly Irish, Italians, Jews, and others they deemed not worthy of assimilation. They did this so that they could increase their social status and, as a consequence, have greater choices of women with whom to reproduce. However, males do not ever willingly accept social subordination. The consequence of English domination over Northern Ireland has been hundreds of years of war and civil unrest. The southern slaveholder's mastery of the plantation meant sleeping with one eye open, a gun under the pillow, and fear while eating his dinner, lest it be poisoned. America's domination of the post World War II world has meant civil unrest at home and fighting wars in Korea, Vietnam, Cambodia, El Salvador, Guatemala, Iran, Afghanistan, and Iraq.

Modern social domination has health consequences for those subordinated. Stanford biologist Robert Sapolsky recently told *Newsweek*: "Low socioeconomic status carries with it an enormously increased risk of a broad range of diseases . . . and this gradient cannot be explained by factors such as health care access."[8] If social dominance benefits those in power and is detrimental to those who are not, why should those in power ever concede to give it up? The answer is that power concedes nothing without demand. The world we live in is becoming more and more dangerous. Maintaining social dominance may be a formula for the collapse of our civilization. President Harry S. Truman realized this in 1948, when he ordered the integration of the armed forces before the Korean War. It would not have been possible to carry out a war against communist ideology if the American military remained segregated. American democracy had to seem superior to revolutionary communist ideals. Neither can we afford to ignore things that are happening in the poorest nations of the world. The HIV/AIDS epidemic may have started in central Africa, but it quickly made its way to Europe and North America. The drug epidemic may have originally been contained to the poor, but rapidly found its way into the middle class. Neither can we be sure who has access to nuclear weapons. Disgruntled enemies may soon decide that airliners crashing into to skyscrapers are not enough, and decide to destroy an entire American city. Whether we want to or not, we must realize that our world is smaller, and what happens to our neighbor must be our concern.

Working for a world with social justice means working against evolved brain mechanisms in males that make them want to be socially dominant over other males. There's good news: Social dominance is not the only behavior encoded in our brains. We also seek fair exchanges. Evidence of this comes from brain-imaging experiments conducted while individuals played the economic bargaining *ultimatum* game. This game is played by offering two players a sum of money to be divided between them. One player offers the split, the other player can respond. The players only get to keep the money if the responder agrees to the split. A selfish player might think that any split will be acceptable to the respondent, since they will not get any money if they refuse. However, the most common solution of this game is a fifty-fifty offer. This occurs because players refuse unfair splits. The brain-imaging experiment showed that unfair offers activated areas in the brain related to emotion and cognition. This means that we get angry when we are treated unfairly. Other studies have shown that anger plays an important role in economic human cooperation.[9]

Fortunately, half our species is not saddled with the problem of needing to socially dominate others, and males do respond to what women want. Women have always been important activists for justice and peace, and men need to start listening to them more. We are no longer living in subsistence hunter-gatherer bands. Our technology has the potential to eliminate hunger and reduce major disease mortality throughout the world, but these realistic goals will never happen with different social coalitions warring with each other over world dominance. International trade can be made to benefit all parties.

Our children are not born as racists, but they are born predisposed to learning the social rules and to obeying legitimate authority figures. Our brain has regions designed to understand and detect those who cheat at the established social rules. Our behavior indicates that we avoid poor social-exchange partners, and that we stigmatize and exclude them.[10] So, when we teach children some groups of people are to be avoided, our children are predisposed to accept those ideas at face value. If we teach them tolerance, expose them to positive role models from other ethnic groups, and discuss with them the concept of social justice, they will be more likely to act on those ideals. These lessons require our active participation by example. When you stand up and show your children that racial intolerance is wrong by the way you live, you teach them a more valuable lesson than reading to them about the Civil Rights movement.

The early mate preferences of human females has shaped other features of our brain, in particular intellect and morality. For the human male, the evil that we can do involves the desire to dominate others, whereas our morality is what guides our sense of justice. In any individual, the social dominance or social justice orientation may coopt the intellect. Ironically, men may even use their social-dominance traits to achieve altruistic goals or may use their social-justice capacities to enslave others to their will. Neither are women silent partners in our social drama. Throughout human history, women have struggled to achieve better situations for themselves and their children. What women have wanted in many ways has directed the social activities of their male partners.

Our sense of justice has allowed us to conceive of social utopias, to stand against kings and despots, and to understand that every human being needs to feel respected and validated. While we conceive of it, we do not live it. We cannot expect people to willingly reject the ideology of *whiteness* and the practice of social domination, so long as being defined as white in America means that you receive so many social benefits. The present situation cannot last, and how it ends will depend on what we do now. All people participate in society for what they can get out of it. Our behavior tends to support our offspring and close relatives, but also allows for reciprocal altruism with people who are not our close relatives. We already live in a society where many people have blended kin networks that touch all of the socially constructed races. The more this phenomenon increases, the faster we will erode racial prejudice.

The task is to design social systems that maximize winner–winner scenarios, as opposed to winner–loser scenarios between our social coalitions. If we all win, then we are likely to cooperate. We have already seen where winner–loser games lead us. Campaigns for full employment, better housing, affordable daycare, affordable health care, and controlling industrial pollution are win–win scenarios. Redistributing resources to bring about equal educational opportunity in the K–12 system and creating open admission policies for higher education are win–win scenarios. Aligning U.S. foreign policy interests against the reign of despotic governments and with the empowerment of the downtrodden can only improve support for our nation in the world. We must cease to support landed oligarchies that allow American multinational corporations to further promulgate social dominance around the world. Diplomatic power must be used to force land reform and real economic opportunities for the world's poor.

I wrote this book to convince you that race was not a biological fact. Despite what we have been taught, despite what we seem to see, race isn't like gravity. It is a social construct, a myth in the service of social dominance. We have seen that the myth's impact is wide ranging, infiltrating our beliefs throughout our history and into the modern day. I have also outlined what disasters await us if this myth continues unchallenged.

This book is also a call to action. The choice of what sort of world you want to live in is yours. There are numerous ways to challenge the myth in your everyday life. There are numerous ways to reject social dominance and to work for justice and equality. I am not utopian. I do not expect everyone to read the facts I have summarized here and fall down like Paul on the road to Damascus. However, history tells us that great change can be brought about by even small groups with a vision. I have outlined a vision of what our world can look like without racism. I fervently hope that these words have convinced some of you that the myth can be defeated and that we are better off without it.

Appendix 1: Comparison Illustrating Strong Subdivision in Sewall Wright's population statistic, F_{st}

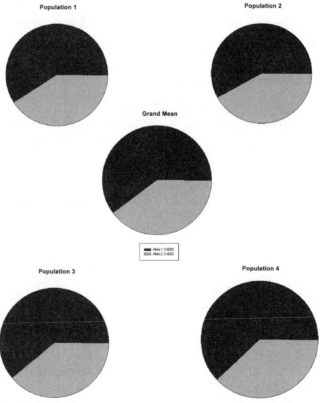

The circle at the center represents the grand average of all populations. Each subpopulation is not greatly different in distribution from the circle representing the grand total population. This shows weak subdivision.

Appendix 2: Comparison Illustrating the Principle of Sewall Wright's Population Subdivision Statistic, F_{st}

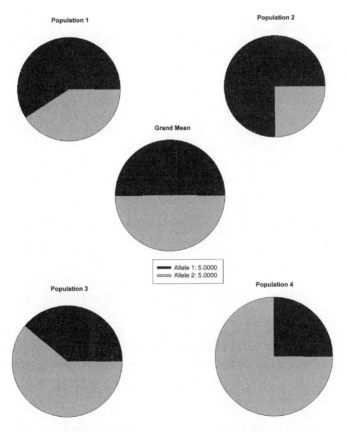

The circle at the center represents the grand average of all populations. The circles above show that each individual population is greatly different in color distribution from each other and from the grand total. This represents strong subdivision.

Appendix 3. Comparison of Some Features of Genetic and Cultural Evolution

Feature	Genetic	Cultural
Mechanism of Inheritance	DNA, fidelity high, enzymes that check and repair errors in copies of DNA, intergenerational	Memes, fidelity low, intra- and intergenerational, individuals can acquire cultural elements from peers and strangers
Selection	Individual predominates, sexual, kin, and reciprocal altruism Group selection rare	Individual, sexual, kin, and reciprocal altruism Group selection common, conditions require competition among small groups, with internal cohesion required for survival
Fitness Consequences	Deleterious genes at low frequency, extinction or new species can result	Deleterious behaviors discouraged by punishment and rewards system, extinction, or new culture can result

Appendix 3 is by no means an exhaustive description of the complexity of genetic and cultural evolution. It illustrates the major differences among the mechanisms controlling each process. Genetic evolution occurs because organisms replicate their genetic code DNA each generation and pass it on to off-spring. However, it is impossible for physical mechanisms to copy DNA without making mistakes. The code is resistant to change because most genetic change *(mutation)* is bad. Mutation allows the accumulation of genetic variation and natural selection chooses the variants that are suitable for any specific environment.

Cultural evolution differs in that the basic unit of cultural transmission, the *meme,* is less resistant to change and can be passed on within a generation to nonrelatives. Group selection is also more prominent in models of cultural change. Therefore, cultural evolution proceeds at a much faster pace than genetic evolution.

Appendix 4: Adaptive Problems for Females in Long-Term Mating and Hypothesized Problems

Adaptive Problem	Evolved Mate Preference
Selecting a mate who is able to invest	Good financial prospects Social status Older age Ambition/industriousness Size, strength, athletic ability, and health
Selecting a mate who is willing to invest	Dependability and stability Love and commitment cues Positive interactions with children
Selecting a mate who is able to physically protect self and children	Size (height) Strength Bravery Athletic ability Kin networks Social Status
Selecting a mate who will show good parenting skills	Dependability Emotional stability Kindness Positive interaction with children
Selecting a mate who is compatible	Similar values Similar ages Similar personalities

After D. Buss, *Evolutionary Psychology: The New Science of the Mind*, Boston: Allyn and Bacon, 2000, pg. 105.

Appendix 5: Adaptive Problems for Males in Long-Term Mating and Hypothesized Problems

Adaptive Problem	Evolved Mate Preference
Selecting a mate who is fertile	Youth Physical beauty and health Symmetry Body fat and waist–hip ratio Signs of ovulation
Paternity uncertainty	Dependability and stability Chastity or virginity Love and commitment cues
Selecting a mate who will show good parenting skills	Dependability Emotional stability Kindness Intelligence Positive interactions with children Kin network
Selecting a mate who is compatible	Similar values Similar ages Similar personalities

After D. Buss, *Evolutionary Psychology: The New Science of the Mind*, Boston: Allyn and Bacon, 2000, pg. 105.

Appendix 6: Sex Ratio Differences between Blacks and Whites from 1830 to 2000

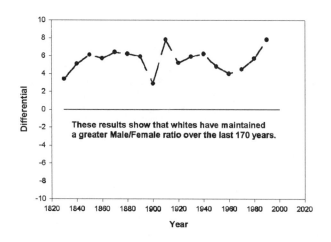

Sex Ratio Differential Between Blacks and Whites
1830 - 2000

These results show that whites have maintained a greater Male/Female ratio over the last 170 years.

Although more males are born, females have a better chance of survival. For this reason, human sex ratios are slightly biased toward females across all age groups. The figure above shows the difference in percentage points between black and white male–female sex ratios in America. The zero line represents no difference between black and white sex ratios. This figure shows that whites have always maintained between 3 to 8 percent more males in their population than blacks. This trend has seemed to increase in the last seventy years.

Appendix 7: The Odds Ratio

Odds ratio
Odds Ratio = [#black–black marriages)/(#white–black marriages)]
/ [#white–white marriages)/(#white–black marriages)]

This formula compares the odds that blacks or whites will marry members of the other group.

Appendix 8. Ratios of the Age-adjusted Death Rates for the Top Ten Causes of Death for Nonwhites–Whites*

Cause of Death	Hisp.	As./Pac.	Am. Ind.	Af. Am.
Heart disease	0.68	0.55	0.78	1.5
Malignant neoplasms	0.62	0.61	0.68	1.3
Cerebrovascular diseases	0.80	0.98	0.86	1.8
Pulmonary diseases	0.41	0.40	0.59	0.8
Accidents and adverse effects	0.97	0.54	1.93	1.2
Motor vehicle accidents	0.94	0.54	2.02	1.0
All other accidents and adverse effects	1.7	0.65	0.58	1.5
Pneumonia and influenza	0.80	0.81	1.15	1.5
Diabetes mellitus	1.57	0.73	2.32	2.4
HIV/AIDS	2.26	0.31	0.58	5.8
Suicide	0.58	0.52	1.12	0.6
Chronic liver disease and cirrhosis	1.73	0.36	2.84	1.3
Homicide and legal intervention	3.09	1.15	3.09	6.2

*Homicide and Legal Intervention ranks as cause number 14.

Appendix 9: Wright's Population Subdivision Statistic (F_{st}) for Different Categories of DNA from World Populations

Category	No.	Avg. F_{st} +/-SE
Coding	238	0.107 +/-0.008
Intronic (noncoding)	5,455	0.118 +/-0.002
Noncoding	13,615	0.123 +/-0.001

Coding DNA is responsible for producing the proteins that run our cells. Intronic DNA is found interspersed within our coding regions, but normally does not produce messages that contribute to our proteins. Finally, noncoding DNA, or "junk" DNA, makes up the vast majority of DNA in our cells. DNA was active in our evolutionary past. Composed of self-replicating DNA, it does not code for our proteins and is in really a form of genomic parasite. Wright's F_{st} statistic can range from 0.00 to 1.00, with a value of 0.00 indicating that there is no subdivision and 1.00 indicating strong subdivision. Typically, population geneticists begin to identify the existence of races with F_{st} values 0.250. None of the gene categories in this study approach this critical value.

Appendix 10: Genotypes at the Cytochrome Locus CYP1A1 Msp1 by Population:

Locus	Caucasian	Asian	African
Number of individuals	4,453	638	461
Homozygous (+)	82.4%	42%	58.1%
Heterozygous	16.4%	44%	36%
Homozygous (variant)	1.2%	14%	5.9%

If we assume no dominance for this genetic system, this data means that there are about eight out of ten, four out of ten, and six out of ten in Caucasians, Asians, and Africans, respectively, of normal metabolizers for any drug affected by this locus (conversely there would be two out of ten, six out of ten, four out of ten affected metabolizers in these groups.)

Appendix 11: Results of Genotyping Using 16 Chromosome-1 and 23 X-Chromosome Genetic Markers

	A	B	C	D
CYP1A2	0.66	0.69	0.60	0.59
GSTM1	0.47	0.53	0.31	0.45
CYP2C19	0.09	0.37	0.27	0.25
DIA4	0.22	0.11	0.19	0.53
NAT2	0.74	0.17	0.46	0.33
CYP2D6	0.53	0.39	0.70	0.42

The table shows the frequency of the variant allele for each genetic locus in each cluster. Individuals were assigned to groups using the program STRUCTURE, and found that four clusters (labeled A, B, C, D) best fit their data. More revealing is the within population distribution in the genetically defined clusters. This variation is shown in Appendix 12.

Appendix 12: Within Population Distribution in the Genetically Defined Clusters of Wilson et al. 2001

Population	A	B	C	D
Bantu	4%	2%	**93%**	2%
Ashkenazi	96%	1%	1%	2%
Ethiopian	62%	8%	24%	6%
Norwegian	**96%**	2%	1%	1%
Armenian	90%	4%	2%	5%
Chinese	9%	5%	1%	**84%**
Papuan, New Guinea	2%	**95%**	1%	2%
Afro-Caribbean	21%	3%	73%	3%

Appendix 13: The Percentages for the Three Possible Hemoglobin Phenotypes in High Malaria Transmission Zones for Nigeria and India

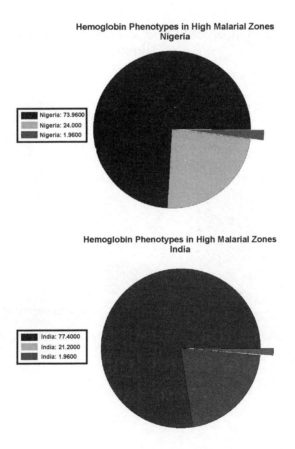

Hemoglobin Phenotypes in High Malarial Zones
Nigeria

Nigeria: 73.9600
Nigeria: 24.000
Nigeria: 1.9600

Hemoglobin Phenotypes in High Malarial Zones
India

India: 77.4000
India: 21.2000
India: 1.9600

Nigerians are sub-Saharan Africans. East Indians have been included as non-European Caucasoids or Asians, depending upon the analysis.

Appendix 14: Ratios of Hemoglobin Phenotypes in High Malarial Zones from Nigeria

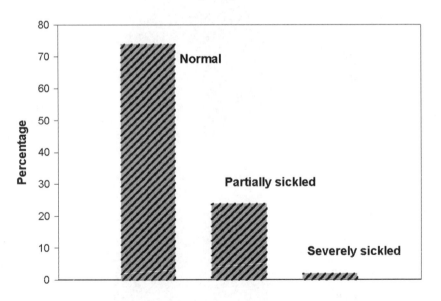

Ratios of Hemoglobin Phenotypes in High Malarial Zones Nigeria

Appendix 15: Relative Frequencies for Phenotypes Generated from Five Loci

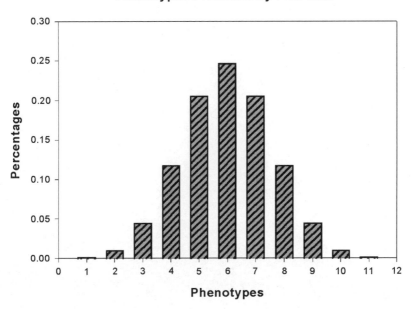

Phenotypes Produced by Five Loci

The figure shows very clearly that distribution of phenotypes is beginning to approach that expected of a normal or bell-curve distribution. This is precisely what happens once more genes are added or if the environment influences the expression of the genes. For the vast majority of traits, environmental effects are a factor.

If this were a graph of male adult height it would say that phenotype class six is the most common and the intermediate height around six feet. People in phenotype class 11 would be seven footers and people in phenotype class 1 would be shorter than four-and-a-half feet. The genetics of complex traits requires the use of descriptive statistics, such as measures of central tendency (the mean or average, median, and mode) and measures of spread (range, variance, and standard deviation).

Appendix 16: Genetic Variants and Hypertension

The study of hypertension has included the following physiological/genetic systems: angiotensin converting enzyme (ACE), angiotensinogen I and II, α and β –adrenergic receptors, plasma kallikrein, and G protein-β-3. The AGT genetic system—codes for *angiotensinogen,* a protein made by the liver and that circulates in excess. At the AGT locus the 235T mutant has the amino acid tyrosine switched for methionine in position 235 of the protein chain. In Euro-Americans, 235T is associated with an increased risk of hypertension; the 235T allele occurs at a frequency of 85 percent in African Americans. Immediately, some researchers supposed that this must be a candidate gene for hypertension and that the differential in hypertension rates easily explained by the difference in gene frequency between the groups. However, 235T is not associated with increased hypertension risk in Nigerians. The following are the percentages of 235T and hypertension percentages in Nigerians, Afro-Caribbeans, and African and European Americans.

Population	235T	Hypertension
Nigerians	0.90	8%
African Americans	0.85	30%
Jamaicans	0.82	25%
European Americans	0.40	23%

Data from R. S. Cooper, C. N. Rotimi, and R. Ward "The puzzle of hypertension in African Americans," *Scientific American* February 1999, 56–62.

Nigerians have the highest percentage of the 235T allele, yet the lowest amount of hypertension. Conversely, African Americans and Jamaicans have much higher percentages of 235T, yet only a slightly higher percentage of hypertension compared to European Americans. Some studies find no association at all between the 235T mutation and hypertension in African Americans or East Asians.

The case for African-American genetic predisposition at the ACE locus is not any better. This locus produces angiotensin-converting enzyme. Here, a common Alu insertion polymorphism affects the activity of this enzyme. *Alus* are transposable genetic elements that code for their own replication inside of host's genome. They are genetic parasites. Usually, these genetic elements copy themselves inside noncoding regions and, therefore, do not affect the host's genetic fitness. However, they can sometimes find their way into coding sequences and, there, they and their kin are responsible for causing a variety of genetic diseases, such as Huntington's chorea and mytonic dystrophy. In humans, the (D) or deletion allele at the ACE locus is characterized by an absence of these Alu insertions. Those without the insertions have higher enzymatic activity. The (I) or insertion allele contains various numbers of the Alu insertions. The available evidence shows that the enzymatic activity of II, ID, and DD genotypes are similar in Nigerians, Jamaicans, and in the United States (all populations). In the United States, the (D) allele was found associated with elevated blood pressure in European but not African Americans, and not hypertension in either group. Contradictory results have also been found in different geographical regions of the United States. One study found that there was no association with hypertension for the (D) allele in African Americans in the South, but a positive association for European Americans in Massachusetts. However, controlling for body mass index, triglycerides in blood, and history of coronary disease, a positive association for the (D) allele and hypertension resulted for African Americans. Another study found the (D) allele associated with greater risk for myocardial infarction in African-American males, but not females. In Jamaica, higher ACE enzyme activity resulted from the (D) allele, but not hypertension. A study in the United Kingdom found that the (D) allele was associated with impaired glucose metabolism in native English, people of Western African ancestry, and Southern Asians. These contradictory results show that the effect of the deletion genotype is not simple or clearly understood.

The results of the β2-adrenergic polymorphisms are not any clearer. This locus has a polymorphism in the protein at amino acid residue 16 that contains either arginine or glycine (arg16 gly.) The gly16 variant has been associated with hypertension in Afro-Caribbeans and Norwegians, but not African or European Americans. The frequency of the arggly16 variant was slightly higher in European Americans; it was not significantly different between the normals and hypertensives in either group.

ArgGly16 genetic variant	African American frequency	European American frequency
Normal study 1	0.50	0.47
Normal study 2	0.180	0.352
Average frequency	0.34	0.411
Hypertensives study 1	0.51	0.40
Hypertensives study 2	0.184	0.358
Average frequency	0.347	0.379

Finally, the frequency of the arggly16 allele was found to be different in European versus Asian Americans (0.543 versus 0.413). However, the frequency difference was not associated with differences in hypertension levels. The story of G-protein β3 and the other thirty-three genetic systems examined with regard to hypertension predisposition is no clearer. This tells us that the genetics of hypertension are still complex and it vitiates assumptions that the basis of the hypertension differential we currently observe in America can be explained solely by differences in gene frequencies between populations.

Appendix 17: Environmental Risks by Race and Ethnicity, Income, and Home Ownership

Source: www.scorecard.org Income = high versus low Ownership = owners and nonowners	Ratio by race	Ratio by Income	Ratio by ownership
Releases of toxic chemicals	1.43	1.54	1.56
Cancer risk from hazardous air pollutants	1.50	1.31	1.47
Facilities emitting criteria air pollutants	3.68	2.38	5.00
Superfund sites per sq. mile	3.04	2.03	3.57

This data shows that, in three of the four categories, the race and/or ethnicity disparity was greater than the high versus low income disparity. However, home ownership was an even greater indicator of toxic exposure in New Jersey. Minorities do not own homes at the rate that European Americans do, an indicator of social oppression.

Appendix 18: Muscle Fiber Distribution in Inactive College-age Men and College Football Players by "Race"

Population	type I	type IIa	type IIb
blacks, college	39.5 +/-11.5	40.0 +/-8.4	22.8 +/-9.8
whites, college	44.9 +/-8.5	36.6 +/-6.9	18.3 +/-9.6
	% fat	FFM	
blacks, football	18.8 +/-4.6	89.9 +/-15.6	
whites, football	17.2 +/-5.6	89.1 +/-10.4	

%fat = percentage of fat in muscle, FFM = fat-free muscle mass. No significant differences in muscle fiber proportions and muscle architecture are shown by so-called race.

Appendix 19: Bone Mass Density of Black and White Boys

	Hip	Trochanter	Femoral neck	Total body	Forearm	Lumbar spine
black	0.755*	0.617*	0.710*	0.768ns	0.405ns	0.612ns
	+/-.02	+/-.01	+/-0.018	+/-0.01	+/-0.01	+/-0.013
white	0.663*	0.552*	0.638*	0.741ns	0.380	0.609ns
	+/-0.02	+/-.01	+/-0.02	+/-0.01	+/-0.008	+/-0.021

Units are in grams/cm of bone.
* = statistically significant difference at <0.01
ns = not statistically different
Data from Wright, N. M., Papadea N., Veldhuis J. D., and Bell, N. H. "Growth hormone secretion and bone mineral density in prepubertal black and white boys," *Calcified Tissue International,* 70 (3): 146-52, 2002.

Appendix 20: Selected International Players in the 2003 NBA Draft

Player	Country	Team	Draft
Darko Milicic	Yugoslavia	Detroit	2
Mickael Pietrus	France	Golden State	11
Zarko Cabarkapa	Yugoslavia	Phoenix	17
Aleksandar Pavlovic	Serbia and Montenegro	Utah	19
Boris Diaw-Riffiod	France	Atlanta	21
Zoron Planinic	Croatia	New Jersey	22
Carlos Delfino	Italy	Detroit	25
Maciej Lampe	Spain	New York	30
Sofolkis Schortsanitis	Greece	Los Angeles Clippers	34
Szymon Szewczyk	Poland	Milwaukee	35
Slavko Vranes	Serbia and Montenegro	New York	39
Malick Badiane	Senegal	Houston	44
Remon Van de Hare	Spain	Toronto	52
Nedzad Smanovic	Bosnia	Portland	54
Xue YuYang	China	Dallas	57
Andreas Glyniadakis	Greece	Detroit	58

Appendix 21: Final Standings of 2002 Men's World Basketball Championships

	Final Standings
1	Yugoslavia (7-2)
2	Argentina (8-1)
3	Germany (6-3)
4	New Zealand (4-5)
5	Spain (7-2)
6	USA (7-2)
7	Puerto Rico (6-3)
8	Brazil (4-5)
9	Turkey (4-4)
10	Russia (3-5)
11	Angola (2-6)
12	China (1-7)
13	Canada (2-3)

Appendix 22: Medal Count from 2000 Summer Olympics for Selected West African Nations

Country	Total Medals	Country	Medals
Senegal	0	Ghana	0
The Gambia	0	Togo	0
Guinea-Bissau	0	Benin	0
Guinea	0	Nigeria	3
Sierra Leone	0	Cameroon	1
Côte d'Ivoire	0	Gabon	0
Republic of the Congo	0		

Appendix 23: H. H. Goddard's Intelligence Ranking of European Immigrants, 1917

Race	%Normal	%Borderline	%Feebleminded	%Moron	%Imbecile
Jews, N = 55	5.4	3.6	45.4	41.8	3.6
Hungarians, N = 36	0.0	11.2	44.4	44.4	0.0
Italians, N = 86	3.5	8.1	44.2	44.2	0.0
Russians, N = 82	0.0	4.9	47.6	45.1	2.4

Figures recalculated from Goddard, *Journal of Delinquency,* 2(5), 1917.

Appendix 24: Army Mental Test Scores and School Grades Completed

Army Mental Tests and School Grades Completed

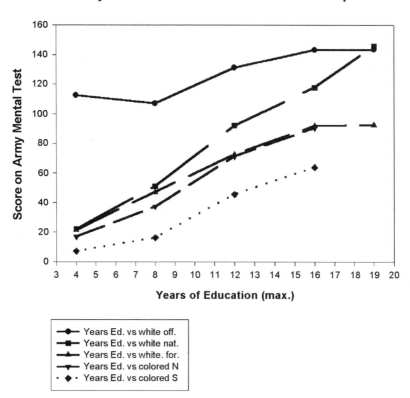

Data extracted from O. Klineberg, *Racial Differences,* 1935.
The average army test score is plotted against the maximum years of education for the group of army recruits, white officers, white native-born enlisted men, white foreign born enlisted men, Northern colored enlisted men, and southern colored enlisted men.

Appendix 25: Brigham's Ranking of the Percentage of Nordic Blood in European Races

Highest Nordic Ancestry

Race	%Nordic	%Alpine	%Mediterranean
Sweden	100	0	0
Norway	90	10	0
Denmark	85	15	0
Netherlands	85	15	0
Scotland	85	0	15

Lowest Nordic Ancestry

Race	%Nordic	%Alpine	%Mediterranean
Turkey	0	20	80
Greece	0	15	85
Italy	0	25	70
Russia (w. Poland)	5	95	0
Portugal	5	0	95

Appendix 26: Socioeconomic Variables and Test Scores

Group	Nonadjusted Rank and Score	Adjusted Rank and Score
White	(1) 53.0	(2) 50.4
Oriental	(2) 49.2	(1) 51.2
Indian	(3) 44.0	(4) 48.9
Negro	(4) 42.4	(3) 49.5
Mexican	(5) 42.0	(5) 47.4
Puerto Rican	(6) 38.2	(6) 47.0

The variables in this study were socioeconomic status; home background, including family structure, family attitudes toward education; family background, including educational status, family background, and area, including rural versus urban; and quality achievement and type of school attended. G. W. Mayeske's table shows the intelligence test score and ranks if no variables are accounted for and, alternatively, if six different socioeconomic variables are examined.

Notes

Chapter 1

1. Fox, Maggie. "First Look at Human Genome Shows How Little There Is." Washington (Reuters), February 11, 2001.

2. Crow, James, F. "Unequal by Nature: A Geneticist's Perspective on Human Differences." *Daedalus,* Winter 2002: 85.

3. Templeton, A. R. "The Genetic and Evolutionary Significance of Human Races." In J. Fish, editor, *Race and Intelligence: Separating Science From Myth:* 37. Mahwah, NJ: Lawrence Erlbaum, 2002.

4. Relethford, J. H. "Human Skin Color Diversity Is Highest in Sub-Saharan African Populations." *Human Biology* 2000 October 72 (5): 773-80.

Chapter 2

1. Kurzban, R., J. Tooby, and Cosmides, L. "Can Race Be Erased? Coalitional Computation and Social Categorization." *Proceedings of the National Academy of Sciences,* vol. 98, no. 6: 15387–92. December 18, 2001.

2. Petition of Kentucky Negroes to Congress, March 25, 1871, reprinted in Aptheker, H. *A Documentary History of the Negro People in the United States: From Reconstruction Years to the*

Founding of the N.A.A.C.P. in 1910. Seacaucus, NJ: The Citadel Press, 1972.

Chapter 3

1. Buss, D. M. and D. P. Schmitt. "Sexual Strategies Theory: An Evolutionary Perspective on Human Mating." *Psychological Review* 100 (1993): 204–32.

2. The following discuss race theory in Japan: Siddle, Richard. *Race Resistance and the Ainu of Japan,* London and New York: Routledge, 1996. Yoshino, Kosaku. *Cultural Nationalism in Contemporary Japan: A Sociological Enquiry.* London and New York: Routledge, 1992. Japanese atrocities in biological warfare during WWII are described in: Williams, P. and Wallace, D., *Unit 731: The Japanese Army's Secret of Secrets,* London: Hodder and Stoughton, 1989. Finally, the true story of the bridge on the river Kwai is recounted in La Forte, R. S. and Marcello, R. E. eds., *Building The Death Railway: The Ordeal of American POWs in Burma, 1942–1945.* Wilmington, DE: Scholarly Resources, 1993.

3. W. Wetherall. "Nakasone Promotes Pride and Prejudice." *Far Eastern Economic Review*, (February 19, 1987): 86–87.

Chapter Four

1. LaFree, G. D. *Rape and Criminal Justice: The Social Construction of Sexual Assault.* Belmont, CA: Wadsworth, 1989. Spohn, C. "Crime and the Social Control of Blacks: Offender-Victim Race and the Sentencing of Violent Offenders." *Inequality, Crime, and Social Control* edited by G.S. Bridges and M. A. Myers. Boulder, CO: Westview 1994: 249–68. Walsh, A. "The Sexual Stratification Hypothesis and Sexual Assault in Light of the Changing Conceptions of Race." *Criminology* 25 (1987): 153–73.

2. From J. Sidanius, S. Levin, and F. Pratto. "Hierarchical Group Relations, Institutional Terror, and the Dynamics of the Criminal Justice System," in *Confronting Racism: The Problem*

and the Response, edited by Eberhardt and Fiske. Thousand Oaks, CA: Sage Publishers, 1998.

Chapter Five

1. Recent scientific evidence further supports this view. Researchers in Ethiopia just announced that they have found the earliest fossils of modern humans, dated at around 160,000 years ago. Monastersky, R. "Scientists Say They Have Found Remains of Humanity's Closest Ancestors." *Chronicle of Higher Education,* June 12, 2003.

2. King, M. C. and A. G. Motulsky. "Mapping Human History." *Science,* vol. 298 (December 20, 2002): 2342–43.

3. Studies showing social impacts on hypertension rates. Neser, W. B. et al., "Obesity and Hypertension in a Longitudinal Study of Black Physicians: The Meharry Cohort Study," *Journal of Chronic Diseases* 39 (1986): 105–13; Broman, C. L., "Social Mobility and Hypertension Among Blacks," *Journal of Behavioral Medicine* 12 no. 2 (1989): 123; D. Calhoun, "Hypertension in Blacks: Socioeconomic Stress and Sympathetic Nervous System Activity," *American Journal of Medical Sciences* 304, no. 5 (1992): 306; K. Light, "Job Status and High-Effort Coping Influence Work Blood Pressure in Women and Blacks," *Hypertension* 25, no. 4 (1995): 1; Tull, S. E. et al., "Relationship of Internalized Racism to Abdominal Obesity and Blood Pressure in Afro-Caribbean Women," *Journal of the National Medical Association* 91(8): 447–52, 1999; Webb, M. S. & Beckstead, J. W., "Stress-related Influences on Blood Pressure in African American Women," *Research in Nursing and Health* 25(5): 382–93, 2002; Appel, S., Harrell, D. S., & Deng, S., "Racial and Socioeconomic Differences in Risk Factors for Cardiovascular Disease among Rural Southern Women," *Nursing Research* 51(3): 140–7, 2002.

4. Wallace et al. "Tobacco, Alcohol, and Illicit Drug Use: Racial and Ethnic Differences Among U.S. High School Seniors, 1976–2000." *Public Health Reports* (2002); vol. 117 (supplement 1).

Chapter Six

1. Rushton, J. P. *Race, Evolution, and Behavior: A Life History Perspective.* New Brunswick, NJ: Transaction Publishers, 1995.

2. Anderson, J. L., P. Schjerling, and B. Saltin, "Muscle, Genes, and Athletic Performance." *Scientific American* (September 2000): 48–55.

3. Ama, P. F. M. et al. "Skeletal Muscle Characteristics in Sedentary Black and Caucasian Males." *Journal of Applied Physiology,* 61:5 (1986): 1758–61.

4. More recent studies showing no difference between muscle fiber types and muscle architecture were Duey, W. J. et al. "Skeletal Muscle Fiber Type and Capillary Density in College-aged Blacks and Whites." Annals of Human Biology (Jul.–Aug. 1997) 24(4): 323–31. Brown, A. T. and W. F. Brechue, "Architectural Characteristics of Muscle in Black and White College Football Players. *Medical Science and Sports Exercise,* (Oct. 1999): 31(10): 448–52.

5. Anderson, J. L., P. Schjerling, and B. Saltin, "Muscle, Genes, and Athletic Performance." *Scientific American* (September 2000) 48–55.

6. Ellis, L. and H. Nyborg. "Racial/Ethnic Variations in Male Testosterone Levels: A Probable Contributor to Group Differences in Health." *Steroids,* 57 (1992): 72–75.

7. Jones, R. *Human Reproductive Biology.* San Diego and New York: Academic Press, 1991.

8. F. H. Bronson "Seasonal Variation in Human Reproduction: Environmental Factors," *Quarterly Review of Biology, 70(2)* (1995): 141–64; Kreuz, L. E., R. M. Rose, and J. R. Jennings, "Suppression of Plasma Testosterone Levels and Psychological Stress," *Archives of General Psychiatry* 26 (1972): 479–82; Mazur, A. and T. A. Lamb, "Testosterone, Status, and Mood in Human Males," *Hormonal Behavior 18,* (1980): 249–55; Morberg, G. P., ed. *Animal Stress,* Bethesda, MD: American Psychological Society, (1985); Nelson, R. J. *An Introduction to Behavioral Endocrinology,* Sunderland, MA: Sinauer 1985.

9. Gapstur, S.M. et al., "Serum Androgen Concentration in Young Men: A Longitudinal Analysis of Associations with Age, Obesity, and Race. The Cardia Male Hormone Study." *Cancer Epidemiological Biomarkers and Prevention* October; 11 (10 Pt. 1): 1041–7, 2002. Ukkola, O. et al., "A Genome Wide Scan for Steroids and SHBG Levels in Black and White Families: the HERITAGE Family Study." *Journal of Clinical Endocrinology and Metabolism,* August 87(8): 3708–20, 2002.

10. Entine, J. *Taboo: Why Black Athletes Dominate Sports and Why We Are Afraid to Talk About It, 35.* New York: Public Affairs, 2000.

11. *Encyclopedia Britannica* 1992 and 1996 yearbooks, Sports records.

12. *The World Almanac and Book of Facts 2001,* 895–96. New York: World Almanac Books.

13. Associated Press, Monday April 16th, 2001: "Bong-ju Ends Kenya's 10-year Stranglehold." at ESPN.com Sports.

14. Entine, J. *Taboo,* figure 4.1, 32.

15. Encyclopedia Britannica 1996 *Yearbook,* Sports Records, 346.

16. Entine, J. *Taboo,* 41.

17. Ibid, 32.

18. Kotov, A. and M. Yudovich. *The Soviet School of Chess,* 79–81. New York: Dover Publications.

Chapter 7

1. Duncan, J., et al. "A Neural Basis for General Intelligence," *Science* vol. 289, No. 5478 (July 21, 2000): 457–460, also, response to Sternberg, R. J., "Cognition, the Holy Grail of General Intelligence.

2. Flynn, J. R. "IQ Gains, WISC Subtests and Fluid g: g Theory and the Relevance of Spearman's Hypothesis to Race," *Novartis Foundation Symposium,* 233 (2000):202–16.

Conclusion

1. Hamiliton, K. "Testing's Pains and Gains." *Black Issues in Higher Education,* vol. 20(8) (June 5, 2003):26–27.

2. Mayer, J. M. *Running on Race: Racial Politics in Presidential Campaigns, 1960–2000,* 277–78. New York: Random House, 2002.

3. Ibid, 288–90.

4. Caruso, D. "Racial Split in Mayoral Campaign in Philadelphia." Associated Press, Sunday June 29, 2003.

5. An excellent account of these struggles can be seen in B. Tu-Smith and M. T. Reddy, *Race in the College Class Room: Pedagogy and Politics.* New Brunswick, NJ: Rutgers University Press, 2002.

6. These studies are recounted in J. F. Dovidio and S. Gaertner, "On the Nature of Contemporary Prejudice: The Causes, Consequences, and Challenges of Adversive Racism," in *Confronting Racism: The Problem and the Response,* edited by J. Eberhardt and S. T. Fiske, 17–20.

7. "New Study Uncovers Hidden Drop Out Crisis, Black Issues in Higher Education," Vol. 20(8) (June 5, 2003): 10. A copy of the Business Round Table report on high school dropout rates can be found at their website: *www.brt.org.*

8. From G. Cowley, "Why We Strive for Status." *Newsweek* (June 16, 2003): 68–9.

9. Ananthaswamy, A. "Anger Plays a Role in Human Cooperation. *New Scientist,* January 9, 2002. A. G. Sanfrey et. al., "The Neural Basis of Economic Decisionmaking in the Ultimatum Game." *Science* vol. 300, no. 5626 (June 13, 2003): 1755–8.

10. Stone, V. E. et al. "Selective Impairment of Reasoning about Social Exchange in a Patient with Bilateral Limbic System Damage." *Proceedings of the National Academy of Sciences vol. 99(17)* (2002): 11531–6. R. Kurzban and M. Leary. "Evolutionary Origins of Social Exclusion: The Functions of Social Exclusion." *Psychological Bulletin* vol. 127(2): 187–208.

References

Chapter 1

Books

Cavalli-Sfroza, L. L., P. Menozzi, and A. Piazza, *The History and Geography of Human Genes,* Princeton, NJ: Princeton University Press, 1994; Graves, J. L., *The Emperor's New Clothes: Biological Theories of Race at the Millennium,* New Brunswick, NJ: Rutgers University Press 2001.

Primary Reports

Brace, C.L., "Region Does Not Mean Race: Reality versus Convention in Forensic Anthropology," *Journal of Forensic Sciences* 40(2) (1995): 29–33; Brown, W. M., "Polymorphism in Mitochondrial DNA of Humans as Revealed by Restriction Endonuclease Analysis," *Proceedings of the National Academy of Sciences USA* 77(6) (1980): 3605–9; Cann, R., M. Stoneking, and A. C. Wilson, "Mitochondrial DNA and Human Evolution," Nature" (Lond.) 325 (1987): 31–6; Jorde, L. B. et al, "Microsatellite Diversity and the Demographic History of Modern Humans," *Proceedings of the National Academy of Sciences USA* 94 (1997): 3100–3; Kaessmann H. et al., "DNA Sequence Variation in a Non-Coding Region of Low Recombination on the Human X Chromosome," *Nature Genetics* 22(1) (1999): 78–81; Long, J. C.

and R. A. Kittles, "Human Genetic Diversity and the Nonexistence of Biological Races," *Human Biology,* in press, 2003; Nei, M. and G. Livshits, "The Genetic Relationship of Europeans, Asians, and Africans and the Origin of Modern Homo sapiens," *Human Heredity* 39 (1989): 276–81; Owens, K. and M. C. King, "Genomic Views of Human History," *Science* 286 (1999): 451–3; Shriver, M. D. et al., "Skin Pigmentation, Biogeographical Ancestry, and Admixture Mapping," *Human Genetics* 112 (2003): 387–99.

Chapters 2 & 3

Books

Bloom, R. and N. Dess, *Evolutionary Psychology of Violence: A Primer for Policy Makers and Public Policy Advocates.* Westport, CT: Praeger, 2003; Dunbar, R., C. Knight, and C. Power, eds., *The Evolution of Culture,* New Brunswick, NJ: Rutgers University Press, 1999; Miller, G., *The Mating Mind: How Sexual Choice Shaped the Evolution of Human Behavior,* New York: Anchor Books, 2000; Ridley, M., *The Origins of Virtue: Human Instincts and the Evolution of Cooperation,* New York: Penguin Books, 1996; Sober, E. and D. S. Wilson, *Unto Others: The Evolution and Psychology of Unselfish Behavior,* Cambridge, MA: Harvard University Press, 1998; Williams, G. C., *Sex and Evolution,* Princeton, NJ: Princeton Univ. Press, 1975. Randolph Nesse and George C. Williams, *Why We Get Sick: The New Science of Darwinian Medicine,* New York: Vintage Books, 1994, pp. 9–10, 91–92, 103–4.

Primary Reports

Betzig, L. and S. Weber, "Polygyny in American Politics," *Politics and the Life Sciences* 12(1) (1993): 45–52; Golby, A. et al., "Differential Responses in the Fusiform Region to Same-Race and Other-Race Faces," *Nature Neuroscience* 4(8) (2001): 845–50; Gravlee, C. C., H. R. Bernard, and W. R.

Leonard, "Heredity, Environment, and Cranial Form: A Re-analysis of Boas's Immigrant Data," *American Anthropologist* 105(1) (2003): 125–38; Heinrich, J. and F. Gil-White, "The Evolution of Prestige Freely Conferred Deference as a Mechanism for Enhancing the Benefits of Cultural Transmission," *Evolution and Human Behavior* 22 (2002): 165–96; Kurzban, R., J. Tooby, and L. Cosmides, "Can Race Be Erased? Coalitional Computation and Social Categorization," *Proceedings of the National Academy of Sciences* 98(26) (2001): 15387–92, 2001; Urdy, J. and B. Eckland, "Benefits of Being Attractive: Differential Payoffs for Men and Women," *Psychological Reports* 54 (1984): 47–56.

Chapter 4

Books

Betzig, L., *Despotism and Differential Reproduction: A Darwinian View of History*, New York: Aldine, 1986; Betzig, L., M. B. Mulder, and P. Turke, *Human Reproductive Behavior*, New York: Cambridge University Press, 1988; Buss, D., *Evolutionary Psychology: The New Science of the Mind*, Needham Heights, MA: Allyn & Bacon, 1999; Buss, D. and N. M. Malamuth, eds., *Sex, Power, and Conflict: Evolutionary and Feminist Perspectives*, New York: Oxford University Press, 1996; Dray, P., *At the Hands of Persons Unknown: The Lynching of Black America*, New York: Random House, 2002; Eberhardt, J. and S. Fiske, *Confronting Racism: The Problem and the Response*, Thousand Oaks, CA: Sage Publishers, 1998; Espiritu, Y. L., *Asian American Panethnicity: Bridging Institutions and Identities*, Philadelphia: Temple University Press, 1992; Friedman, D. M., *A Mind of Its Own: A Cultural History of the Penis*, New York: The Free Press, 2001; Hernton, C. C., *Sex and Racism in America*, New York: Grove Press, 1965; Hodes, M., ed., *Sex, Love, and Race: Crossing Boundaries in North American History*, New York: New York University Press,

1999; Johnson, R. A., *Religious Assortative Marriage in the United States,* New York: Academic Press, 1980; Jordan, W., *White Over Black: American Attitudes Toward the Negro, 1550–1812,* Kingsport, TN: University of North Carolina Press, 1968; Kelly, G. F., *Sexuality Today: The Human Perspective, 7th ed.,* Boston: McGraw Hill, 2004; Klassen, A., C. J. Williams, and E. E. Levitt, *Sex and Morality in the U.S.: An Empirical Enquiry under the Auspices of The Kinsey Institute,* Wesleyan, CT: Wesleyan University Press, 1989; Madison, J. H., *A Lynching in the Heartland: Race and Memory in America,* New York: Palgrave, 2001; Miller, J., *The Mating Mind: How Sexual Choice Shaped the Evolution of Human Nature,* New York: Anchor Books, 2000; Omi, M. and H. Winant, *Racial Formation in the United States: From the 1960s to the 1990s. 2nd ed.,* New York: Routledge, 1994; Rushton, J. P., *Race, Evolution and Behavior: A Life History Perspective,* New Brunswick, NJ: Transaction Publishers, 1995; Schiller, L. and J. Willwerth, *American Tragedy: The Uncensored Story of the Simpson Defense,* New York: Random House, 1996; Shaefer, R. T., *Racial and Ethnic Groups, 7th ed.,* New York: Longman, 1997; Stember, C. H., *Sexual Racism: The Emotional Barrier to an Integrated Society,* New York: Harper & Row, 1976; M. B. Tucker, and C. Mitchell-Kernan, *The Decline in Marriage Among African Americans: Causes, Consequences, and Policy Implications,* New York: Russell Sage Foundation.

Primary Reports

Blau, P. M., T. C. Blum, and J. E. Schwartz, "Heterogeneity and Intermarriage," *American Sociological Review* 47 (1982): 45–62; Davis, K., "Intermarriage in Caste Societies," *American Anthropologist* 43 (1941): 376–95; Fang, C. Y., J. Sidanius, and F. Pratto, "Romance Across the Social Status Continuum: Interracial Marriage and the Ideological Asymmetry Effect," *Journal of Cross-Cultural Psychology* 29(2) (1998): 290–305; Fu, V. K., "Racial Intermarriage Pairings," *Demography* 38(2) (2001):

147–59; Gardyn, R., "Love Is Colorblind—or Is It?," *American Demographics* Vol. 22(6) (2000): 11–12, 14; Gilbertson, G., J. Fitzpatrick, and L. Yang, "Hispanic Intermarriage in New York City: New Evidence From 1991," *International Migration Review* 30 (1996): 445–59; Glaser, J., "Studying Hate Crimes with the Internet: What Makes Racists Advocate Racial Violence?" *The Journal of Social Issues* 58(1) (2002): 177–93; Glenn, N., "Interreligious Marriage in the United States: Patterns and Recent Trends," *Journal of Marriage and the Family* 44 (1982): 555–66; Goldstein, J. R., "Kinship Networks that Cross Racial Lines: The Exception or the Rule?," *Demography* Vol. 36(3) (1999): 399–407; Gurak, D. T. and J. P. Fitzpatrick, "Intermarriage among Hispanic Ethnic Groups in New York City," *American Journal of Sociology* 87 (1982): 921–33; Hall, R. E., "Eurogamy among Asian-Americans: A Note on Western Assimilation," *The Social Science Journal* 34(3) (1997): 403–8; Heer, D., "The Prevalence of Black-White Marriage in the United States, 1960 and 1970," *Journal of Marriage and the Family* 36 (1974): 246–58; Hwang, S., R. Saenz, and B. Aguirre, "The SES Selectivity of Interracially Married Asians," *International Migration Review* 29 (1995): 469–91; Jones, F. L., "Convergence and Divergence in Ethnic Divorce Patterns: A Research Note," *Journal of Marriage and the Family* 58 (1996): 213–18; Kalmijn, M., "Trends in Black/White Intermarriage," *Social Forces* 72 (1993): 119–46; Kalmijn, M., "Intermarriage and Homogamy: Causes, Patterns and Trends," *Annual Review of Sociology* 24 (1998): 395–421, edited by K.S. Cook and J. Hagan. Palo Alto: Annual Reviews Inc; Kalmijn, M., "Status Homogamy in the United States," *American Journal of Sociology* 97 (1991): 496–523; Kaplan, S., "Historical Efforts to Encourage White Indian Intermarriage in the United States and Canada," *International Social Science Review,* 65(3) (1990): 126–132; Kitano, H. H. L., W. Yeung, L. Chai, and H. Hatanaka, "Asian-American Interracial Marriage," *Journal of Marriage and the Family* 46 (1984): 179–90; Maddox, K. and S. Gray, "Re-exploring the Role of Skin

Tone," *Personality and Social Psychology Bulletin,* (2003): 250–9; Manning, W. D. and P. J. Smock, "Why Marry? Race and the Transition to Marriage among Cohabitors," *Demography* 32 (1995): 509–19; Merton, R. "Intermarriage and Social Structure: Fact and Theory," *Psychiatry* 4 (1941): 361–74; Model, S. and G, Fisher, "Black–White Unions: West Indians and African Americans Compared," *Demography* Vol. 38(2) (2001): 177–85; Pagnini, D. L. and S. P. Morgan, "Intermarriage and Social Distance among U.S. Immigrants at the Turn of the Century," *American Journal of Sociology* 96 (1990): 405–32; Root, M., "The Color of Love," *American Prospect* Vol. 13(7) (2002): 54–5; Qian, Z., "Breaking the Racial Barriers: Variations in Interracial Marriage Between 1980 and 1990," *Demography* 34 (1997): 263–76; Sandefur, G. and T. McKinnell, "American Indian Intermarriage," *Social Science Research* 15 (1986): 347–71; Schoen, R., "The Widening Gap Between Black and White Marriage Rates: Context and Implications," in *The Decline in Marriage among African Americans,* edited by M. B. Tucker and C. Mitchell-Kernan. New York: Russell Sage Foundation, 1995, 103–16; Schulman, G., "Race, Sex, and Violence: A Laboratory Test of the Sexual Threat of the Black Male Hypothesis," *American Journal of Sociology* 79(5) (1974): 1260–77; Seielstad, M. T., E. Minch, and L. L. Cavalli-Sfroza, "Genetic Evidence for a Higher Female Migration Rate in Humans, *Nature Genetics* 20(3) (1998): 278–80; Shinagawa, L. and G. Pang, "Marriage Patterns of Asian Americans in California, 1980," in *Income and Status Differences Between White and Minority Americans: A Persistent Inequality,* edited by S. Chan, Lewiston, NY: Mellen Press, 1980, 225–82; U.S. Bureau of the Census, *Statistical Abstract of the United States: 1995,* 115th ed. Washington, DC: U.S. Bureau of the Census.

Chapter 5

Primary Reports

Akey, J. M. et al., "Interrogating a High Density SNP Map for Signatures of Natural Selection," *Genome Research* 12 (2002): 1805–14; Appel, S., D. S. Harrell, and S. Deng, "Racial and Socioeconomic Differences in Risk Factors for Cardiovascular Disease among Rural Southern Women," *Nursing Research* 51(3) (2002): 140–7; Baker, E. H. et al., "Association of Hypertension with T594M Mutation in Beta Subunit of Epithelial Sodium Channels in Black People Resident in London," *Lancet* 351(9113) (1998): 1388–92; Baker, E. H. et al., "Amiloride, a Specific Drug for Hypertension in Black People with T594M Variant?, *Hypertension* 40(1) (2002): 13–7; Barbeau, P. et al., "Association between Angiotensin II Type I Receptor Polymorphism and Resting Hemodynamics in Black and White Youth, *Ethnic Disparities* 12(1) (2002): S1–68–71; Barbujani, G. et al., "An Apportionment of Human DNA Diversity," *Proceedings of the National Academy of Sciences USA* 94 (1997): 4516–19; Barley, J. et al., "Angiotensin Converting Enzyme Gene I/D Polymorphism, Blood Pressure and the Rennin-Angiotensin System in Caucasian and Afro-Caribbean Peoples, *Journal of Human Hypertension* 10(1) (1996): 31–5; Borecki I. B., "Associations of Candidate Loci Angiotensinogen and Angiotensin-Converting Enzyme with Severe Hypertension: The NHLBI Family Heart Study," *Annals of Epidemiology* 7(1) (1997): 13–21; Burchard, E. G. et al., "The Importance of Race and Ethnic Background in Biomedical Research and Clinical Practice, *New England Journal of Medicine* 348(12) (2003): 1170–5; Busher, R. et al., "Variability in Phenylephrine Response and Essential Hypertension: A Search for Human Alpha(1B)-Adrenergic Receptor Polymorphisms," *Pharmacology and Experimental Therapy* 291(2) (1999): 793–8; Candy, G. et al., "Association Analysis of Beta2 Adrenoreceptor Polymorphisms with Hypertension in a Black African Population, *Journal of Hypertension* 18(2) (2000):

67–72; Chen, W. et al., "Combined Effects of Endothelial Nitric Oxide Synthase Gene Polymorphism (G894T) and Insulin Resistance Status on Blood Pressure and Familial Risk of Hypertension in Young Adults: the Bogalusa Heart Study, *American Journal of Hypertension* 14(10) (2001): 1046–52; Chow, J. C.-C., K. Jaffee, and L. Snowden, "Racial-Ethnic Disparities in the Use of Mental Health Services in Poverty Areas, *American Journal of Public Health* 93(5) (2003): 792–8; Collet, C. et al., "Prevalence of the Missense Mutation Gly574Ser in the Hepatocyte Nuclear Factor-1alpha in Africans with Diabetes," *Diabetes Metabolism* 28(1) (2002): 39–44; Coon, H. et al., "Genome-wide Linkage Analysis of Lipids in the Hypertension Genetic Epidemiology Network (HyperGen) Blood Pressure Study," *Arteriosclerosis, Thrombosis, and Vascular Biology* 21(12) (2001): 1969–76; Cooper R. S. et. al., "Hypertension Prevalence in Seven Populations of West African Origin," *American Journal of Public Health* 87 (1997): 160–8; Cooper, R. S. et al., "Genome Scan among Nigerians Linking Blood Pressure to Chromosomes 2,3, and 19, *Hypertension* 40(5) (2003): 629–33; Cooper, R. S., J. S. Kaufman, and R. Ward, "Race and Genomics," *New England Journal of Medicine* 348(12) (2003): 1166–70; Diley, A. et al., "Mutations in the Genes Regulating Methylene Tetrahydrofolate Reductase (MTHFR C→T677) and Cystathione Beta-synthase (CBS G→ A919, CBS T→ c833) Are Not Associated with Myocardial Infarction in African Americans," *Thrombosis Research* 103(2) (2001): 109–15; Destro-Bisol, G. et al., "Estimating European Admixture in African Americans by Using Microsatellites and a Microsatellite Haplootype (CD4/Alu)," *Human Genetics* 104(2) (1999): 149–57; Dong, Y. B. et al., "T594M and G442V Polymorphisms of the Sodium Channel Beta Subunit and Hypertension in the Black Population," *Journal of Human Hypertension* 15(6) (2001): 425–30; Dong, Y. B. et al., "T594M Mutation of the Beta-subunit of the Epithelial Sodium Channel in Ghanaian Populations from Kumasi and London and a Possible Association between Hypertension," *Genetic Testing* 6(1) (2002): 63–5;

Dries, D. et al., "Efficacy of Angiotensin-Converting Enzyme Inhibition in Reducing Progression from Asymptomatic Left Ventricular Dysfunction to Symptomatic Heart Failure in Black and White Patients," *Journal of the American College of Cardiology* 40(2) (2002): 311–7; Eicher, J. E. et al., Angiotensin-Converting Enzyme Gene Polymorphism in a Cohort of Coronary Angiography Patients," *Atherosclerosis* 154(3) 2001: 673–9; Forrester, T. et al., "The Angiotensin Converting Enzyme and Blood Pressure in Jamaicans," *American Journal of Hypertension* 10(5 pt 1) (1997): 519–24; Freedman, B. I. et al., "Linkage Heterogeneity of End-Stage Renal Disease on Human Chromosome 10," *Kidney Internist* 62(3) (2002): 770–4; Fuller, K. and J. M. Casperian, "Vitamin D: Balancing Cutaneous and Systemic Considerations, *Southern Medical Association* 94(1) (2001): 58–64; Fuller, K., "Health Disparities: Reframing the Problem," *Medical Science Monitor* 9(3) (2003): SR9-15; Gainer, J. V. et al., "Angiotensin II Type I Receptor Polymorphism in African Americans Lower Frequency of the C1166 Variant," *Biochemistry and Molecular Biology* 43(1) (1997): 227–31; Gainer, J. V. et al., "Altered Frequency of a Promoter Polymorphism of the kinin B2 Receptor Gene in Hypertensive African Americans," *American Journal of Hypertension* 13(12) (2000): 1268–73; Garte, S. et al., "Metabolic Gene Polymorphism Frequencies in Control Populations," *Cancer Epidemiology, Biomarkers, and Prevention* 10 (2001): 1239–48; Garte, S., "The Racial Genetics Paradox in Biomedical Research and Public Health," *Public Health Reports* 117 (2002): 421–5; Goodwin, R. et al., "Association between Childhood Physical Abuse and Gastrointestinal Disorders and Migraine in Adulthood," *American Journal of Public Health* 93(7) (2003): 1065–7; Hansson J. H. et al., "A De Novo Missense Mutation of the Beta Subunit of the Epithelial Sodium Channel Causes Hypertension and Liddle Syndrome, Identifying a Proline-Rich Segment Critical for Regulation of Channel Activity," *Proceedings of the National Academy of Sciences* 92(25) (1995): 11495–9; Harshfield, G. A. et al., "Impaired Stress-Induced Pressure Natriuresis Is Related to Left Ventricle Structure in Blacks," *Hypertension* 39(4) (2002): 844–7; Heckbert, S. R. et al., "Beta2-adrenergic Receptor Polymorphism and the Risk of Incident Cardiovascular Events in the Elderly," *Circulation* 107(15) (2003): 2021–4; Herrmann, V. et al., "Beta2-adrenergic Receptor Polymorphisms at Codon 16, Cardiovascular Phenotypes and Essential Hypertension in Whites and African Americans," *American Journal of Hypertension* 13(9) (2000): 1021–6; Hooper W. C. et al., "Relationship of Venous Thromboembolism and Myocardial Infarction with the Rennin-Angiotensin System in African Americans," *American Journal of Hematology* 70(1) (2002): 1–8; Jain, S. et al., "Angiotensinogen Gene Polymorphism at –217 Affects Basal Promoter Activity and Is Associated with Hypertension in African Americans," *Journal of Biological Chemistry* 277(39) (2002): 36889–96; Jarvis, J. K. and G.D. Miller, "Overcoming the Barrier of Lactose Intolerance to Reduce Health Disparities," *Journal of the National Medical Association* 94(2) (2002): 55–66; Jorde, L. B. et al., "Microsatellite Diversity and the Demographic History of Modern Humans," *Proceedings of the National Academy of Sciences USA* 94(7) (1997): 3100–3; Kaufman, J. S. and S.A. Hall, "The Slavery Hypertension Hypothesis: Dissemination and Appeal of Modern Race Theory," *Epidemiology* 14(1) (2003): 111–26; Kittles, R. et al., "Extent of Linkage Disequilibrium between the Androgen Receptor Gene CAG and GGC Repeats in Human Populations: Implications for Prostate Cancer Risk," *Human Genetics* 109(3) (2003): 253–61; Kittles, R. and K. Weiss, "Race, Ancestry, and Genes: Implications for Defining Disease Risk," *Annual Reviews of Genomics and Human Genetics*, Vol. 4 (2003): pp. 33–67 September 2003; Kotchen T. A. et al., "Identification of Hypertension-related QTL's in African American Sib Pairs," *Hypertension* 40(5) (2002): 634–9; Larson, M., R. Hutchinson, and F. Boerwinkle, "Lack of Association of 3 Functional Gene Variants with Hypertension in African Americans," *Hypertension* 35(6) (2000): 1297–3000; Marth, G. et al., "Sequence Variation in the Public

Human Genome Data Reflect a Bottlenecked Population History, *Proceedings of the National Academy of Sciences* 100(1) (2002): 376–81; Morrison, A. C. et al., "G-protein Beta3 Subunit and Alpha-Adducin Polymorphisms and Risk of Subclinical and Clinical Stroke," *Stroke* 32(4) (2001): 822–9; Moskowitz, D. W., "From Pharmacogenomics to Improved Patient Outcomes: Angiotensin I-converting Enzyme as an Example," *Diabetes Technology & Therapy* 4(4) (2002): 519–32; Nakajima, T. et al., "Nucleotide Diversity and Haplotype Structure of the Human Angiotensinogen Gene in Two Populations," *American Journal of Human Genetics* 71(2) (2002): 443–4; Nelson, T. L. et al., "Obesity and Associated Coronary Heart Disease Risk Factors in a Population of Low-income African-American and White Women: The North Carolina WISEWOMAN Project," *Preventive Medicine* 35(1) (2002): 1–6; Nkeh, B. et al., "Association between an Atrial Natriuretic Peptide Gene Polymorphism and Normal Blood Pressure in Subjects of African Ancestry," *Cardiovascular Journal of South Africa* 13(3) (2002): 93–5; Onipinla, A. K. et al., "Relationship between the M235T and G(-6)A Polymorphisms of the Angiotensinogen Gene, *Journal of Human Hypertension* 13(12) (1999): 865–6; Province, M. A. et al., "Lack of Association of the Angiotensin-6 Polymorphism with Blood Pressure Levels in the Comprehensive NHLBI Family Blood Pressure Program, National Heart, Lung, and Blood Institute," *Journal of Hypertension* 18(7) (2001): 86776; Rankinen, T. et al.," G Protein Beta 3 Polymorphism and Hemodynamic and Body Composition Phenotypes in the HERITAGE Family Study," *Physiological Genomics* 8(2) (2002): 151–7; Risch, N. et al., "Categorization of Humans in Biomedical Research: Genes, Race, and Disease, *Genome Biology* 3(7) (2002): 1–12; Rosenberg, N. A. et al., "Genetic Structure of Human Populations," *Science* 298 (2002): 2381–5; Rosskopf, D., I. Manthey, and W. Siffert, "Identification and Ethnic Distribution of Major Haplotypes in the Gene GNB3 Encoding the G-protein Beta3 Subunit," *Pharmocogenetics* 12(3) (2002): 209–20; Rutkowski, M. P. et al.,

"Genetic Markers at the Leptin (OB) Locus Are Not Significantly Linked to Hypertension in African Americans, *Hypertension* 31(6) (1998): 1230–4; Rutledge, D. R., Y. Sun, and E.A. Ross, "Polymorphisms within the Atrial Natriuretic Peptide Gene in Essential Hypertension," *Journal of Hypertension* 13(9) (1995): 953–5; Sagnella, G. A et al., "A Population Study of Ethnic Variations in the Angiotensin-converting Enzyme I/D Polymorphism: Relationships with Gender, Hypertension and Impaired Glucose Metabolism," *Journal of Hypertension* 17(5): 657–64, 199; Sankar, P. and M. Cho, "Toward a New Vocabulary of Human Genetic Variation," *Science* 298 (2002): 1337–8; Schork, N.J., et al., "Lack of Association between a Biallelic Polymorphism in the Adducing Gene and Blood Pressure in Whites and African Americans," *American Journal of Hypertension*, 13(6 pt 1) (2000): 693–8; Siffert, W. et al., "Worldwide Ethnic Distribution of the G Protein beta3 Subunit 825T Allele and Its Association with Obesity in Caucasian, Chinese, and Black African Individuals," *Journal of American Society of Nephrology* 10(9) (1999): 1921–30; Song, Q., J. Chao, and L. Chao, "DNA Polymorphisms in the 5, Flanking Region of the Human Tissue Kallikrein Gene," *Human Genetics* 99(6) (1997): 727–34; Staessen, J. A. et al., "M235T Angiotensinogen Gene Polymorphism and Cardiovascular Renal Risk," *Journal of Hypertension* 17(1) (1999): 9–17; Stringer, C., "Human Evolution: Out of Ethiopia," *Nature* 423 (2003): 692–95; Stumpf, M. and B. Goldstein, "Genetic Evaluation of Variable Drug Response, *Encyclopedia of the Human Genome* (2003): 1–5; Suminski, R. R., C. O. Mattern, and S. T. Devor, "Influence of Racial Origin and Skeletal Muscle Properties on Disease Prevalence and Physical Performance," *Sports Medicine* 32(11) (2002): 667–73; Svetsky, L. P. et al, "Association of Hypertension with Beta2- and Alpha2c10-Adrenergic Receptor Genotype, *Hypertension* 27(6) (1996): 1210–5; Svetsky, L. P. et al., "Preliminary Evidence of Linkage of Salt Sensitivity in Black Americans at the Beta 2-Adrenergic Receptor Locus, *Hypertension* 29(4) (1997): 918–22; Tang, W. et al., "Linkage of Left Ventricular Early Diastolic Peak Filling Velocity to Chromosome 5 in Hypertensive African Americans: The HyperGen Echocardiography Study," *American Journal of Hypertension* 5(7 pt 1) (2002): 621–7; Tanus-Santos, J. E., M. Desai, and D. A. Flockhart, "Effects of Ethnicity on the Distribution of Clinically Relevant Endothelial Nitric Oxide Variants," *Pharmocogenetics* 11(8) (2001): 719–25; Tamura, T. et al., "Effect of Angiotensin-converting Enzyme Gene Polymorphism on Pregnancy Outcome, Enzyme Activity, and Zinc Concentration," *Obstetrics and Gynecology* 88(4 pt 1) (1996): 497–502; Tishkoff, S. and S. M. Williams, "Genetic Analysis of African Populations: Human Evolution and Complex Disease," *Nature Reviews Genetics* 3(8) (2002): 611–21; Treadwell, H. M. and M. Ro, "Poverty, Race, and the Invisible Men," *American Journal of Public Health* 93(5) (2003): 705–6; Tull, S. E. et al., "Relationship of Internalized Racism to Abdominal Obesity and Blood Pressure in Afro-Caribbean Women," *Journal of the National Medical Association* 91(8) (1999): 447–52; Vupputuri, S. et al., "Blood Lead Level Is Associated with Elevated Blood Pressure in Blacks," *Hypertension* 41(3) (2003): 463–8; Wade, N., "Race Is Seen as a Real Guide to Track Roots of Disease," *The New York Times,* July 30, 2002; Wade, N., "Gene Study Identifies 5 Main Populations, Linking Them to Geography," *The New York Times,* December 20, 2002; Webb, M. S. and J. W. Beckstead, "Stress-Related Influences on Blood Pressure in African-American Women," *Research in Nursing and Health* 25(5) (2002): 382–93; White, P. C. et al., "Possible Association but No Linkage of the HSD11B2 Gene Encoding the Kidney Isozyme of 11beta-hydroxysteroid Dehydrogenase to Hypertension in Black People," *Clinical Endocrinology* 55(2) (2001): 249–52; Wilk, J. B. et al., "Evidence for a Gene Influencing Heart Rate on Chromosome 4 Among Hypertensives," *Human Genetics* 111(2) (2002): 207–13; Wilson, J. F., et al., "Population Genetic Structure of Variable Drug Response," *Nature Genetics* 29 (2001): 265–9; Wong, M. D. et al., "Contribution of Major Diseases to Disparities in Mortality,"

New England Journal of Medicine 347(20) (2002): 1585–92; Wood, A., "Racial Profiling in Medical Research," *New England Journal of Medicine* 344(18) (2001): 1392–5; Xie, H. G. et al., "Alpha1A-adrenergic Receptor Polymorphism: Association with Ethnicity but Not Essential Hypertension," *Pharmocogenetics* 9(5) (1999): 651–6; Xie, H. G. et al., "Frequency of Functionally Important Beta2-adrenoreceptor Polymorphisms Varies Markedly among African Americans, Caucasians, and Chinese Individuals," *Pharmacogenetics* 9(4) (1999): 511–6; Xie, H. G. et al., "Human Beta2-Adrenergic Receptor Polymorphisms: No Association with Essential Hypertension in Black and White Americans," *Clinical Pharmacology and Therapy* 67(6) (2000): 670–5; Yu, H. et al., "Identification of Human Plasma Kallikrein Gene Polymorphism and Evaluation of Their Role in End-stage Renal Disease," *Hypertension* 31(4) (1998): 906–11; Yu, H. et al., "Human Na+/H+ Exchanger Genes: Identification of Polymorphisms by Radiation Hybrid Mapping and Analysis in End-stage Renal Disease," *Hypertension* 35(1 pt 1) (2000): 135–43; Yu, H. et al., "Genomic Structure of the Human Plasma Prekallikrein Gene, Identification of Allelic Variants, and Analysis of End Stage Renal Disease," *Genomics* 69(2) (2000): 225–34; Yu, N. et al., "Larger Genetic Differences within Africans Than between Africans and Eurasians," *Genetics* 161(1) (2002): 269–74; Zhu X. et al., "Associations between Hypertension and Genes in the Rennin-Angiotensin System," *Hypertension* 41(5) (2003): 1027–34; Zietkiewicz, E. et al., "Nuclear DNA Diversity in Worldwide Distributed Human Populations," *Genetics* 205(1–2) (1997): 161–71.

Chapter 6

Books

Entine, Jon, *Taboo: Why Black Athletes Dominate Sports and Why We Are Afraid to Talk About It,* New York: Public Affairs, 2000; Hugman, B., *The Olympic Games: Complete Track and Field Results, 1896–1988,* New York: Facts on File, 1988.

Primary Reports
Abe, T., J. B. Brown, and W. F. Brechue, "Architectural Characteristics of Muscle in Black and White College Football Players," *Medicine and Sports Exercise* 10 (1999): 1448–52; Ama, P. F. et al., "Skeletal Muscle Characteristics in Sedentary Black and Caucasian Males," *Journal of Applied Physiology* 61(5) (1986): 1758–61; Duey W. J. et al., "Skeletal Muscle Fibre Type and Capillary Density in College-Aged Blacks and Whites," *Annals of Human Biology*, 24(4) (1997): 323–31; Fukashiro, S. et al., "Comparison of Viscoelastic Characteristics in Triceps Surae between Black and White Athletes," *Acta Physiologica Scandinavia* 175(3) (2002): 183–7; Hall, R. E., "Clowns, Buffoons and Gladiators: Media Portrayals of African-American Men," *The Journal of Men's Studies*, 1(3) (1993): 239–51; Wenner, L., "The Good, The Bad and the Ugly: Race, Sport and the Public Eye," *Journal of Sport and Social Issues* 19(3) (1995): 227–31.

Chapter 7

Books and Reports
Agarwala, S. N., *India's Population Problems, 2nd ed*, New Delhi: Tata McGraw Hill, 1977; Barash, D. P., *Sociobiology and Behavior*, 2nd ed, New York: Elsevier, 1982; Bonner, J. T., *Size and Cycle*, Princeton, NJ: Princeton University Press, 1965; Bryant, B. and P. Mohai, eds; *Race and the Incidence of Environmental Hazards: A Time for Discourse*, Boulder, CO: Westview Press, 1992; Cavalli-Sfroza, L., *The Genetics of Human Races*, Burlington, NC: Carolina, 1983; Cavalli-Sfroza, L., P. Menozzi, and A. Piazza, *The History and Geography of Human Genes*, Princeton, NJ: Princeton University Press, 1994; Chase, A., *The Legacy of Malthus: The Social Costs of the New Scientific Racism*, New York: Alfred A. Knopf, 1977; China Financial and Economic Publishing House, *New China's Population*, New York: Macmillan Co., 1988; Cipolla, C. M., *Economic History of World Population*, 7th ed., Sussex: Harvestor, 1978; Coleman,

J. et al., Equality of Educational Opportunity, (Washington DC: U.S. Government Printing Office), 1966; Darwin, C., *On The Origin of Species by Means of Natural Selection or the Preservation of Favoured Races in the Struggle for Life*, Great Books, London: Encyclopedia Britannica, 1859; Darwin, C., *The Descent of Man* and *Selection in Relation to Sex*, Princeton, NJ: Princeton University Press, 1981, originally published 1871; Falconer, D. S. and MacKay, T., *Introduction to Quantitative Genetics*, 4th ed., London: Longman, 1996; Francis Galton, *Hereditary Genius: An Inquiry into Its Laws and Consequences*, London and New York: Macmillan, 1892; Graves, J. L., *The Emperor's New Clothes: Biological Theories of Race at the Millennium*, New Brunswick: Rutgers University Press, 2001; Huntington, E., *The Character of Races: As Influenced by Physical Environment, Natural Selection and Historical Development*. New York and London: Charles Scribner's Sons, 1925; Ellis, L., *Theories of Rape*, New York: Hemisphere, 1989; Havery, P. H. and M. D. Pagel, *The Comparative Method in Evolutionary Biology*, Oxford: Oxford University Press, 1991; MacArthur, R. H., and E. O. Wilson, *The Theory of Island Biogeography*, Princeton, NJ: Princeton University Press, 1967; Maynard-Smith, J., *Evolutionary Genetics*, Oxford: Oxford University Press, 1989; Moffet, D., S. Moffet, and C. Schauf, *Human Physiology: Foundations and Frontiers*, St. Louis: Mosby Press, 1993; Montagu, A., *Man's Most Dangerous Myth: The Fallacy of Race*, Oxford: Oxford University Press, 1974; Murdoch, W. W., *The Poverty of Nations: The Political Economy of Hunger and Population*, Baltimore: John Hopkins University Press, 1980; Poirer, F. E. and J. K. McGee, *Understanding Human Evolution 4th ed.*, Upper Saddle River, NJ: Prentice Hall, 1999; Rice, M. F. and W. Jones, Jr., *Black American Health: An Annotated Bibliography*, New York: Greenwood Press, 1987; Roff, D., *The Evolution of Life Histories: Theory and Analysis*, London: Routledge, Chapman and Hall, 1992; Rotberg, R. and T. K. Robb, eds., *Population and History: From the Traditional to the Modern World*, Cambridge: Cambridge University Press, 1986; Rushton, J. P., *Race, Evolution and Behavior: A Life History Perspective,* New Brunswick, NJ: Transaction Publishers, 1995; Rushton, J. P., *Race, Evolution and Behavior: A Life History Perspective,* special abridged edition, New Brunswick, NJ: Transaction Publishers, 1999; Stearns, S. C., *The Evolution of Life Histories,* Oxford: Oxford University Press, 1992; United Nations *Fertility Behavior in the Context of Development: Evidence from the World Fertility Study,* New York: United Nations Dept. of International Economic Studies, 1987; Vinovskis, M. A., *Demographic History and the World Population Crisis.* Worcester, MA: Clark University Press, 1976; Williams, V. J., *Rethinking Race: Franz Boas and His Contemporaries,* Lexington, KY: The University Press of Kentucky, 1996.

Primary Reports
Badaruddoza, A. M., "Inbreeding, Depression and Intelligence Quotient among North Indian Children," *Behavioral Genetics* 23(4) (1993): 343–7; Barclay, H. J. and P. T. Gregory, "An Experimental Test of Models Predicting Life History Characteristics," *American Naturalist* 117 (1981): 944–61; Bierbaum, T. J., L. D. Mueller, and F. J. Ayala, "Density-dependent Evolution of Life History Traits in *Drosophila melanogaster,*" *Evolution* 43(2) (1988): 382–92; Boas, F., "Human Faculty as Determined by Race," in *A Franz Boas Reader,* George Stocking, Jr. ed., Chicago: University of Chicago Press, 1974; Cody, M. L. "A General Theory of Clutch Size," *Evolution* 20 (1966): 174–84; Diamond, J. "Races without Color," *Discover* 15(11) (1994): 82–91; Deary, I. J. and P. G. Caryl, "Neuroscience and Human Intelligence Differences," *Trends in Neurosciences* 20(8) (1997): 365–70; Devlin, B., M. Daniels, and K. Roeder, "The Heritability of IQ," *Nature* 388(6641) (1997): 468–71; Dobzhansky, T. and A. Montagu, "Natural Selection and the Mental Capacities of Mankind," *Science,* 105 (1947): 587–90, Dobzahnsky, T., "Evolution in the Tropics, *American Scientist* 38 (1950):

209–31; Ellen J. M. et al. "Socioeconomic Differences in Sexually Transmitted Disease Rates among Black and White Adolescents, San Francisco, 1990 to 1992," *American Journal of Public Health* 85(11) (1995): 1546–8; Ellis, L., "Criminal Behavior and r- and K-Selection: An Extension of Gene-Based Evolutionary Theory," *Deviant Behavior* 8 (1987):149–76; Erwin, D., J. W. Valentine, and J. J. Sepkokski "A Comparative Study of Diversification Events: The Paleozoic versus the Mesozoic," *Evolution* 41 (1987): 1177–86; Gadgill, M. and W. H. Bossart, "Life Historical Consequences of Natural Selection," *American Naturalist* 104 (1977): 1–24; Garland, T. and P. Carter, "Evolutionary Physiology," *Annual Review of Physiology* 56 (1994): 579–621; Graves, J. L., "Evolutionary Biology and Human Variation: Biological Determinism and the Mythology of Race," *Race Relations Abstracts* 18(3) (1993): 4–34; Graves, J. L., "The Costs of Reproduction and Dietary Restriction: Parallels Between Insects and Mammals," *Growth, Development, and Aging* 57 (1993): 233–49; Graves, J. L. and M. R. Rose, "Population Genetics of Senescence in *Drosophila*," *Life Science Advances: Fundamental Genetics* 8 (1989): 45–55; Graves, J. L. et al., "Desiccation Resistance, Flight Duration, Glycogen, and Postponed Senescence in *Drosophila melanogaster*," *Physiological Zoology* 65(2) (1992): 268–86; Graves, J. L. and L. D. Mueller "Population Density Effects on Longevity," *Genetica* 91 (1993): 99–109; Graves, J. L. and L. D. Mueller, "Population Density Effects on Longevity Revisited: A Note in Response to 'Density and Age-specific Mortality' by J. W. Curtsinger," *Genetica* 96(3) (1994): 183–6; Graves, J. L. and T. Place "Race and IQ Revisited: Figures Never Lie, but Often Liars Figure," *Sage Race Relations Abstracts* 20(2) (1995): 4–50; Graves, J. L. and A. Johnson, "The Pseudoscience of Psychometry and the *Bell Curve*, Special Issue: Myth and Realities: African Americans and the Measurement of Human Difference," *The Journal of Negro Education* 64(3) (1995): 277–94; Graves, J. L., "The Misuse of Life History Theory: J. P. Rushton and the Pseudoscience of Racial Hierarchy, in *Race and Intelligence: Separating Myth from Science,* Jefferson Fish, ed., Mahwah, NJ: Lawrence Erlbaum Associates, 2002; Guo, P., L. D. Mueller, and F. J. Ayala, "Evolution of Behavior by Density Dependent Natural Selection," *Proceedings of the National Academy of Science USA* 88 (1991): 10905–6; Harvey, P. H., A. F. Read, and D. E. L. Promislow, "Life History Variation in Placental Mammals: Unifying the Data with the Theory," *Oxford Surveys Evolutionary in Biology* 6 (1989): 13–31; Harvey, P. H. and T. H. Clutton-Brock, "Life History Variation in Primates," *Evolution* 39 (1985): 559–81; Hegmann, J. P. and H. Dingle, "Phenotypic and Genetic Covariance Structure in Milkweed Bug Life History Traits," in *Evolution and Genetics of Life Histories,* Hegmann, J. P. and H. Dingle, eds. New York: Springer-Verlag, 1982; Henneberg, M., "Evolution of the Human Brain: Is Bigger Better?," *Clinical and Experimental Pharmacology and Physiology* 25(9) (1998): 745–9; Higuchi, S. et al., "Alpha sub(2)–Macroglobulin Gene Polymorphisms Show Racial Diversity and Are Not Associated with Alzheimer's Disease," *Neuroreports* 11(6) (2000): 1167–71; Hollocher, H. and A. R. Templeton, "The Molecular through Ecological Genetics of Abnormal Abdomen in *Drosophila mercatorum.* The Nonneutrality of the Y-chromosome rDNA Polymorphism," *Genetics* 136(4) (1994): 1373–84; Horowitz, I. L., "The Rushton File," in *The Bell Curve Debate: History, Documents, Opinions,* edited by R. Jacoby and N. Glauberman, New York: Time Books, Random House, 1995; Hrdlicka, A., "Human Races" in *Human Biology and Racial Welfare,* edited by E. Cowdry, New York: Paul B. Hoeber Inc., 1930 179–80; Hubacek, J. A. et al., "A Possible Role of Alipoprotein E Polymorphism in Predisposition to Higher Education," *Neuropsychobiology* 43(3) (2001): 200–3; Jablonski, D. and D. J. Bottjer, "The Ecology of Evolutionary Innovations: The Fossil Record," in *Evolutionary Innovations,* edited by M. H. Nitecki Chicago: University of Chicago Press, 1990; Joshi, A. and L. D. Mueller, "Evolution of Higher Feeding Rate in *Drosophila* Due to

Density-Dependent Natural Selection," *Evolution* 42 (1989): 1090–93; Joshi, A. and L. D. Mueller, "Directional and Stabilizing Density-dependent Natural Selection for Pupation Height in *Drosophila melanogaster, Evolution* 47(1) (1993): 176–84; Joshi, J. V. et al., "The Prevalence of *Chlamydia trachomatis* in Young Women," *National Medical Journal of India* 7(2) (1994): 57–59; Jung, R. E. et al., "Biochemical Markers of Human Intelligence: A Proton MR Spectroscopy Study of the Normal Human Brain," *Proceedings of the Royal Society of London, Series B: Biological Sciences* 266(1426) (1999): 1375–9; Kerfoot, W. C., "Competition in Cladoceran Communities: The Cost of Evolving Defenses against Copepod Predation," *Ecology* 58 (1977): 303–13; Ladd, J., "Philosophical Reflections on Race and Racism," *American Behavioral Scientist* 41(2) (1997): 212–22; Lauder, G. V., A. M. Leroi, and M. R. Rose, "Adaptation and the Comparative Method," *Trends in Ecology and Evolution* 8(8) (1993): 294; Law, R., A. D. Bradshaw, and P. D. Putwain, "Life History Variation in Poa Annua," *Evolution* 31 (1977): 233–46; Leroi, A. M., A. Chippendale, and M. R. Rose, "Long-term Laboratory Evolution of Genetic Life-History Trade-off in *Drosophila melanogaster*. 1. The Role of Genotype-by-Environment Interaction," *Evolution* 48(4) (1994): 1244–57; Leroi, A. M., M. R. Rose, and G. V. Lauder, "What Does the Comparative Method Reveal about Adaptation?" *American Naturalist* 143(3) (1994): 381–402; Luckinbill, L. S., "Selection of the r/K Continuum in Experimental Populations of Protozoa," *American Naturalist* 113 (1979): 427–37; Luckinbill, L. S., "An Experimental Analysis of Life History Theory," *Ecology* 65 (1984): 1170–84; MacArthur, R. H., and E. O. Wilson, "Some Generalized Theorems of Natural Selection," *Proceedings of the National Academy of Sciences USA* 48 (1962): 1893–7; Mertz, K. J. et al., "A Pilot Study of the Prevalence of Chlamydial Infection in a National Household Survey," *Sexually Transmitted Diseases* 25(5) (1998): 225–8; Moises, H. W. et al., "No Association between Dopamine D2 Receptor Gene (DRD2) and Human Intelligence," *Journal of Neural Transmission* 108(1) (2001): 115–21; Moore, H. D. M., M. Martin, and T. R. Birkhead, "No Evidence for Killer Sperm or Other Selective Interactions between Human Spermatozoa in Ejaculates of Different Males in Vitro," *Proceedings of the Royal Society London Series B* 266 (1436) (1999): 2343–50; Mueller, L. D., "Evolution of Competitive Ability in *Drosophila* by Density Dependent Natural Selection," *Proceedings of the National Academy of Science USA* 84 (1988): 1974–7; Mueller, L. D., "Ecological Determinants of Life History Evolution," *Philosophical Transactions of the Royal Society London B* 332 (1988): 25–30; Mueller, L. D. and F. J. Ayala, "Trade-off between r-Selection and K-Selection in *Drosophila* Populations," *Proceedings of the National Academy of Sciences, USA* 78 (1981): 1303–5; Mueller, L. D. and V. F. Sweet, "Density Dependent Natural Selection in *Drosophila*: Evolution of Pupation Height, *Evolution* 40 (1986): 1354–56; Mueller, L. D., P. Guo, and F. J. Ayala, "Density-dependent Natural Selection and Trade-offs in Life History Traits," *Science* Vol. 253 (1991): 433–5; Mueller, L. D., J. L. Graves, and M. R. Rose, "Interactions between Density-dependent and Age-specific Selection in *Drosophila melanogaster*," *Functional Ecology* 7 (1993): 469–79; "Inbreeding Studies in Brazilian Schoolchildren," *American Journal of Medical Genetics,* 16(3) (1983): 331–55; Orzack, S. H., and E. Sober, "Optimality Models and the Test of Adaptationism," *American Naturalist* 143(3) (1994): 361–80; Pagel, M. and P. H. Harvey, "Recent Developments in the Analysis of Comparative Data," *Quarterly Review of Biology* 63 (1988): 413–40; Parry, G. D., "The meanings of r- and K-selection," *Oecologia* 48 (1981): 260–81; McNaughton, S. J., "r- and K-selection in Typha," *American Naturalist* 109 (1975): 251–61; Pearl, R. and L. J. Reed, "On the Rate of Growth of the Population of the United States since 1790 and Its Mathematical Representation," *Proceedings of the National Academy of Sciences Washington,* 6 (1920): 275–88; Petrill, S. A. et al., "No Association between

General Cognitive Ability and the A1 Allele of the D2 Dopamine Receptor Gene," *Behavior Genetics* 27(1) (1997): 29-32; Pianka, E. R., "On "r" and "K" selection," *American Naturalist* 104 (1970): 592-7; Plomin, R. et al., "A Genome-wide Scan of 1842 DNA Markers for Allelic Associations with General Cognitive Ability: A Five Stage Design Using DNA Pooling and Extreme Selected Groups," *Behavior Genetics* 31(6) (2001): 497–509; Promislow, D. E. L. and P. H. Harvey, "Living Fast and Dying Young: A Comparative Analysis of Life History Variation among Mammals," *Journal of the Zoology London* 220 (1990):417–37; Ranaa, B. K. et al., "High Polymorphism at the Human Melanocortin 1 Receptor Locus," *Genetics* 151 (1999): 1547–57; Read, A. F. and P. H. Harvey, "Life History Differences amongst the Eutherian Radiations," *Journal Zoology, London* 219 (1989): 329–53; Reznick, D., "Cost of Reproduction: An Evaluation of the Empirical Evidence, *Oikos* 44 (1985): 257–67; Ricklefs, R. E., "On the Evolution of Reproductive Strategies in Birds: Reproductive Effort," *American Naturalist* 111 (1977): 453–78; Rose, M. R., "Genetic Covariation in *Drosophila* Life History: Untangling the Data," *American Naturalist* 123 (1984): 565–9; Rose, M. R., J. L. Graves, and E. W. Hutchinson, "The Use of Selection to Probe Patterns of Pleiotropy in Fitness Characters," In *Genetics, Evolution, and Coordination of Insect Life Cycles,* edited by Francis Gilbert, Berlin: Springer-Verlag, 1990; Rushton, J. P., "The New Enemies of Evolutionary Science," *Liberty,* March, Vol. II, No. 4 (1998), 31–35; Rushton, J. P. and C. D. Ankney, "The Evolutionary Selection of Human Races: A Response to Miller," *Personality and Individual Differences* 15 (1993), 677–80; Schioth H. B. et al., "Loss of Function Mutations of the Human Melanocortin 1 Receptor Are Common and Are Associated with Red Hair," *Biochemical Biophysical Research Communications* 260(2) (1999): 488–91; Service, P. T., E. W. Hutchinson, and M. R. Rose, "Multiple Genetic Mechanisms for the Evolution of Senescence in *Drosophila," Evolution* 42 (1988): 708–16; Skutch, A. F., "Do

Tropical Birds Rear as Many Young as They Can Nourish?" *Ibis* 91 (1949): 430–55; Snell, T. W. and C. E. King, "Lifespan and Fecundity Patterns in Rotifers: The Costs of Reproduction," *Evolution* 31 (1977): 882–90; Smith, B. H., "Dental Development as a Measure of Life-History in Primates," *Evolution* 43 (1989): 683–8; Solbrig, O. T. and B. B. Simpson, "Components of Regulation in a Population of Dandelions in Michigan," *Journal of Ecology* 63 (1974): 473–86; Stearns, S. C., "The Evolution of Life History Traits: A Critique of the Theory and a Review of the Data," *Annual Review of Ecology and Systematics* 8 (1977): 145–71; Stearns, S. C., "A New View of Life History Traits," *Oikos* 35 (1980): 266–81; Tattersall, I., "Once We Were Not Alone," *Scientific American* 282 (2000): 56–62; Taylor, C. E. and C. Condra, "r- and K-selection in *Drosophilia pseudoobscura*," *Evolution* 34 (1980): 1183–93; Templeton, A. R., "The Evolution of Life Histories under Pleiotropic Constraints and K-selection," in *Population Biology*, edited by H. I. Freedman and C. Strobeck, Berlin: Springer-Verlag, 1983; Templeton, A. R. and J. S. Johnson, "Life History Evolution under Pleiotropy and K-selection in a Natural Population of *Drosophila mercatorum*, in *Ecological Genetics and Evolution: The Cactus-Yeast-Drosophila System,* edited by J. S. F. Barker and W. T. Starmer, Sydney: Academic Press, 1982, 225–39; Templeton, A. R., H. Hollocher, and J. S. Johnson, "The Molecular through Ecological Genetics of Abnormal Abdomen in *Drosophila mercatorum*: V. Female Phenotypic Expression on Natural Genetic Backgrounds and in Natural Environments," *Genetics* 134 (1993): 475–85; Turic, D. et al., "No Association between Apolipoprotein E Polymorphisms and General Cognitive Ability in Children," *Neuroscience Letters* 299(1-2) (2001): 97–100; Tyler, R. et al., "The Effect of Superoxide Dismutase on Aging in *Drosophila*," *Genetica* vol. 91 (1993): 143–6; Vizitiu, O., and D. Badescu, "Incidence of *Chlamydia trachomatis* Genital Infections in Bucharest (1988–1996)," *Roumanian Archives Microbiology and Immunology* 55(4) (1996): 313–21;

Wagner, A., "Does Evolutionary Plasticity Evolve?" *Evolution* 50(3) (1996): 1008–23.

Conclusion

Books
Alba, R., *Ethnic Identity: The Transformation of White America.* New Haven: Yale University Press, 1990; Hacker, A., *Two Nations: Black and White, Separate and Unequal,* New York: Scribner's 1992; Takaki, R., *Strangers From a Different Shore: A History of Asian Americans,* Boston: Little, Brown, 1989.

Primary Reports
Beauvais, F. and E. R. Oetting, "Variances in the Etiology of Drug Use among Ethnic Groups of Adolescents," *Public Health Reports* 117 (Supplement 1) (2002): s8–s15; Cheng, L. and P. Q. Yang, "Asians: The 'Model Minority' Deconstructed," in *Ethnic Los Angeles,* edited by R. Waldinger and M. Bozorgmehr, New York: Russell Sage Foundation, 1996, 305–44; A. J. Hart et al., "Differential Response in the Human Amygdala to Racial Outgroup vs. Ingroup Face Stimuli," *Neuroreports* 11(11) (2002) (2000): 2352–5; Hout, M. and J. Goldstein, "How 4.5 Million Irish Immigrants Became 40 Million Irish Americans: Demographic and Subjective Aspects of Ethnic Composition of White Americans," *American Sociological Review* 59 (1994): 64–82; Kuhar, M. J., "Social Rank and Vulnerability to Drug Use," *Nature Neuroscience* 5(2) (2002): 88–90; Kurban, R. and M. R. Leary, "Evolutionary Origins of Stigmatization: The Functions of Social Exclusion," *Psychological Bulletin* 127(2) (2001): 187–208; Massey, D. S., "The Age of Extremes: Concentrated Affluence and Poverty in the Twenty-First Century," *Demography* 33 (1996): 395–428; Morgan, D. et al., "Social Dominance in Monkeys: Dopamine D2 Receptors and Cocaine Self-administration," *Nature Neuroscience* 5(2) (2002): 169–74; Sanfrey, A. et al., "The Neural Basis of Economic Decision-

Making in the Ultimatum Game," *Science* 300 (2003): 1755–58; Sewell, W., "Some Observations and Reflections on the Role of Women and Minorities in the Democratization of the American Sociological Association 1905–1990," *American Sociologist* 23(1) (1992): 56–62.

Acknowledgments

We cannot expect all Americans to reject racism and social oppression because they understand it to be morally wrong. I do, because my faith in my God and my savior Jesus Christ require me to. Surely, many people of various faiths agree with the need to fight for social justice as part of their creed. If we can agree on this point of theology, then we will make a powerful army for justice. Unfortunately, many Christians engage in their racist behavior in the guise of serving God. They must reexamine their faith, and they must ask if segregation and oppression is really what God wants. Jesus of Nazareth was born a carpenter's son. He lived in Judea, which was under the heel of the Roman Empire, the most powerful empire the world knew. Jesus walked amongst the poor and downtrodden, preached a message of peace, love for all, and love for God. For this message, the Romans crucified him and persecuted Christianity for over three hundred years. No one could claim that Jesus was in favor of social domination, oppression, or war.

Belief in God is not a necessary prerequisite for understanding that the world will be a better place without racism and other forms of social oppression. Some critics may even attempt to invalidate the science behind this book, precisely because my faith motivates my allegiance to social justice. The two are not mutually exclusive.

I would like to thank my wife, Suekyung, and sons, Joey and Xavier, for their support during the trying times that led to this book. In addition, a number of academic colleagues commented on various ideas in the manuscript or gave support: Drs. Jane Maienschein, Neal Lester, Leanor Boulin-Johnson, Shari Collins-Chobanian, and Harvey Pough at Arizona State University; along with Drs. Georgia Dunston, Rick Kittles, Charmaine Royal, Charles Rotimi, and George Bonney from the National Human Genome Center at Howard University. Beth Vesel gave invaluable guidance in the formulation of the project.

Index